MAKING
DOLLS' HOUSES
IN ¹⁄₁₂ SCALE

MAKING
DOLLS' HOUSES
IN 1/12 SCALE

BRIAN NICKOLLS

Photographs by Jonathon Bosley

A DAVID & CHARLES CRAFT BOOK

FRONTISPIECE *Builders at work in the Tudor House*

Photographs by Jonathon Bosley

British Library Cataloguing-in-Publication Data

Nickolls, Brian
    Making dolls' houses.
    I. Title
    745.592

    ISBN 0-7153-9848-2

745.592
NIC

Text and illustrations © Brian Nickolls 1991
Photographs © Jonathon Bosley 1991

The right of Brian Nickolls to be identified as author of this
work has been asserted by him in accordance with the
Copyright, Designs and Patents Act 1988.

Printed in Singapore by Saik Wah Press Pte Ltd
For David & Charles plc
Brunel House Newton Abbot Devon

CONTENTS

INTRODUCTION

Over the last few years public awareness and interest in making dolls' houses and miniatures has increased enormously. Many newcomers would like to make their own dolls' house, and are more than capable of completing the project, given a little guidance and encouragement. Some years ago when I first got hooked on miniatures there were relatively few books dealing with their construction; I had to develop my own ideas by trial and error — rather a lot of the latter! I have therefore tried to produce the kind of book that I myself would have welcomed at the outset. In order to provide instruction for varying levels of skill, the houses increase in complexity as the book progresses. The basic methods and equipment are covered in Chapter 1 and additional tools and techniques are discussed as the need arises. A scale of one-twelfth (1 inch=1 foot) is used throughout, this being the accepted standard amongst collectors. The furniture and accessories featured range from high-quality individually crafted pieces to cheaper mass-produced ones. In many cases these can happily co-exist in the same setting.

I hope that this book will not only give you detailed information on specific projects but will also inspire you to go on and develop ideas of your own.

NOTE The houses shown in this book were conceived and made in feet and inches, but metric equivalents (in brackets), rounded up or down to the nearest millimetre, are also given. Measurements of less than ⅛in (3mm) are not rounded up or down, for the sake of accuracy. Measurements referring to a plywood thickness are the manufactured size, eg, 1⁄16in = 1.5mm.

1
IN THE
WORKSHOP

Assuming that you already have a basic woodworking toolkit, attention in this chapter has been concentrated on more specialised tools and equipment that the DIY carpenter may not have.

SAFETY

Although they may appear obvious, it is worth repeating a few simple rules:

Never wear loose clothing that may get caught in a revolving machine.

Wear safety glasses.

Always use properly adjusted machine guards where these are fitted.

With sharp hand tools always keep both hands behind the cutting edge.

Always unplug power tools before making any adjustments, as in changing saw-blades or router cutters.

Ensure that all plugs are fitted with the correct fuse, and check periodically that all the connections inside the plug are tight. Use a circuit breaker between the outlet socket and the machine plug.

Use push sticks wherever possible, particularly when machining small parts, to keep your fingers out of range of the cutting edge.

Do not use power tools in poor light or low temperatures — your concentration should be on the task in hand, *not* distracted by shivering.

Keep the workshop floor clear of obstacles and trailing leads.

POWER TOOLS

Many well-known firms now produce small power tools with the do-it-yourselfer in mind and the outlay will be well repaid both in terms of projects in this book and for many other jobs around the home. If you do not have the power tools, the project can still be completed using just hand tools, but will obviously take a lot longer.

Circular-Saw-bench This should have a depth of cut around 2in (50mm) with a ripfence, cross-cutting guide (preferably adjustable for cutting mitres), rise and fall, and tilt adjustment to 45°. The Kity model 511 used in these projects is regrettably no longer available, but the Makita 2708 appears to be a suitable alternative.

A desirable addition is the Scheppach model TK, which has a depth of cut a little over 3½in (90mm). This saw-bench can be fitted with a folding panel-cutting table, and is particularly useful when handling large sheets of plywood. The extra depth of cut allows conversion of large-dimension timber to your own requirements.

Router Bosch make an excellent plunge router (model POF 500A). When fitted with the template guide which is supplied with the tool as part of a good range of accessories, it can be used to cut out door and window openings, particularly where several cutouts of identical size are needed. When (with the base removed) it is fitted to the drill stand with table and fence, it will cut the carcase joints in the plywood panels with ease. This machine is superb for cutting joints and rebates in small parts such as window bars, and door frames. A range of straight cutters ⅟₁₆in (1·5mm), ⅛in (3mm), ¼in (6mm) and ⅜in (9mm) will be needed; profile cutters are discussed in the section on mouldings (page 13).

Jigsaw Very useful, but not essential if you have a hand fretsaw. The model used in these projects was made by Bosch and is over twenty years old, and still working well.

Orbital Sander Again this is not essential, but it will make a better job when used with a simple jig for cleaning off, and thicknessing window assemblies. A block plane can be used here, but there is more risk of breaking or splitting small components.

12V Minicraft Drill and Transformer The Topi is the smallest drill in the Minicraft range, and can be helpful in tight corners. A wide range of accessories is available, particularly sanding discs, and the Dremel sanding drum can be used with it.

Although standard-size self-adhesive abrasive discs are readily available, in some applications better results can be achieved when the abrasive disc is a little larger than the backing pad, allowing greater flexibility inside curves. The Olfa compass cutter (available from Hobby's) will enable you to cut several small discs of whatever size you choose from one large disc of around 8in (200mm) in diameter. This method will also provide a wider range of grit sizes than those supplied as standard.

Soldering Iron A small soldering iron of about 25 watts will be needed for electrical connections.

Hot-melt Glue Gun This has proved to be the best method of applying wooden tiles or shingles to the roofs. Glue sticks are available with differing 'open' times. You will need those of around 60 to 90 seconds. This tool has no other application in the projects as the glue sets too quickly for adequate pressure to be applied to joints.

NOTE The glue in plywood laminates soon destroys the edge of high-speed steel saw-blades

Fig 1 *Basic carcase joints*

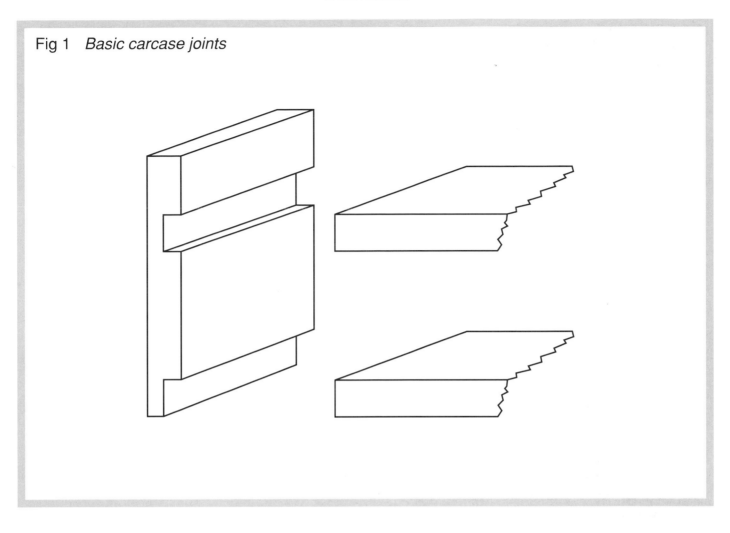

and router cutters. It is well worth the extra expense to fit blades and cutters with tungsten-carbide tips.

HAND TOOLS

The following will be needed over the whole range of projects; others with limited application will be introduced as the need arises.

Squares A 4ft (1·25m) T-square is best for marking out large plywood panels. This job can be done with the smaller 9in (225mm) square used for carcase assembly, and a straight edge, but is not so convenient.

A very small engineer's square — around 2½in (64mm) — will be needed for small assemblies such as windows.

Planes A jack plane around 14in (350mm) long (Stanley no 5) can be helpful on long straight edges, but with care a normal smoothing plane will suffice.

Apart from its more obvious use, a rabbet plane (Stanley no 78 or similar) will be needed in several situations where the inset blade of a normal plane will not cover the whole surface of the work to be trimmed, as in the angle between a wall and an overhanging roof.

A block plane 5–6in (150mm) long is used for fine cuts on smaller parts, and for end grain.

Fretsaw Small, shaped components are more easily cut with a fretsaw and it will also cut door and window openings if you do not have a router or jigsaw. It should have a 12in (305mm) throat.

Cramps G-cramps — you will need at least two of each of the following sizes: 2in (50mm), 3in (75mm) and 4in (100mm). Always use a small piece of waste wood between the cramp and the workpiece, to avoid denting the surface.

Chisels You should have at least four chisels, preferably of the bevel-edged type: ¼in (6mm), ⅜in (9mm), ½in (12mm) and ¾in (19mm). Additionally, very small chisels ¹⁄₁₆in (1·5mm) and ⅛in (3mm) can be made from broken needle files.

Scraper A small Skarsten scraper handle, used with both 1½in (38mm) and 3in (76mm) blades, will smooth small parts where a very fine cut is required, and also remove stray paint splashes or glue — particularly in awkward corners.

Sandplates Sandvik have a range of self-adhesive hardened-steel sanding plates in a variety of grades. When mounted on a backing of ¼in (6mm) plywood, they are ideal for cleaning up the inside edges of door and window openings. The smaller sanding plates can be used without a backing and being only a few thousandths of an inch thick, work well in cleaning out the slots for hinges in the door jambs.

Pliers Long-nosed pliers are useful for holding small panel or veneer pins while these are being hammered. This especially applies to work inside a carcase where a hand obscures visibility.

Hammer A small pin hammer, around 4oz (100g) will be needed.

Bevel and Protractor An adjustable bevel and a protractor are used to mark out and check roof angles, and also to set the mitre guide and tilt on the circular-saw-bench, which are normally graduated but can often be inaccurate.

SMALL TOOLS
The following small tools should also be included. For electrical work, a very small screwdriver and end or side cutters; and for small trimming cuts on wood, a razor saw and X-acto knife. A Swann-Morton knife (no 3 handle and no 10A blades) will also be needed, primarily for very light cuts, and for trimming wallpaper. The blades fitted to this knife are not as robust as the X-acto blades and are therefore not suitable for deep cuts in wood. Where very small holes are to be drilled, a hand-held pin chuck is required.

MATERIALS
The timber and plywood needed for each project is listed at the beginning of that chapter, classified for ease of reference, in groups with a common thickness. Lengths and areas are approximate and for guidance only.

Plywood All the houses are built from birch plywood (apart from the Victorian Shop, for which mahogany marine ply is preferable), mostly ⅜in (9mm), ¼in (6mm) and to a lesser degree ⅛in (3mm) thick. Doors and some other fittings require a small quantity of ¹⁄₁₆in (1·5mm) ply.

Always buy the best quality you can find and make sure that it is flat. Many inferior grades have a set in them caused by uneven drying of the various laminates, and although not noticeable when cut into smaller pieces, it will cause a major problem when making a large hinged panel, as in the Georgian House.

Mahogany Mahogany is used extensively in the Victorian Shop, largely because it gives a nice contrast to the lighter colour of birch and lime.

To avoid further depletion of rain forests, supplies can be obtained from old broken furniture — you may even be lucky enough to get some old Cuban or Honduras mahogany. Some woods can be stained to look like mahogany but it is preferable to avoid staining wherever possible as it is never truly convincing and can cause problems, such as inhibiting the drying of some surface coatings.

Elm Elm features strongly in the cottages. Always look for wood with a fine, straight grain and dark brown in colour. Avoid timber with a wild grain pattern, which will not cut or plane easily and is much more likely to warp.

Oak English oak is a fair substitute for elm if you can obtain it with a fine grain. Usually it is not dark enough without further treatment.

Lime (basswood) Very good for small components such as windows, edge veneers and mouldings. The colour when varnished matches well with birch plywood. It finishes well and is very stable, the only disadvantage being that it is rather soft and marks easily.

Beech An alternative to lime but not very good when cut to very small dimensions.

Teak Veneer Used only for the roof of the Thatched Cottage.

Microwood A range of plain or self-adhesive veneers is readily available at DIY stores or from Hobby's. Some of the lighter coloured varieties are very good for flooring when cut into strips and laid on top of plain plywood. It is *not suitable* for the roof of the Thatched Cottage.

Glues Evostik white PVA is best for carcase and window construction. Be careful when gluing parts that will later be varnished as it is very difficult to remove all traces from surfaces adjacent to the joint. If possible a sealing coat of varnish should be applied first (*not on the surfaces to be glued*) to

Router, saws and small tools

stop penetration where it is not wanted.

Evostik contact adhesive is used on some components where an immediate hold is required and pressure can easily be applied (preferably with a vice), and for edge veneering carcases and applying thatch. *Do not varnish* over contact adhesives for at least twenty four hours as polyurethanes act as a solvent. Even then, apply the first coat sparingly so that it does not penetrate through to the glued surface.

Quick-setting epoxy resin is used for door hinges.

Carcases All the carcases are constructed using lap or housed joints, glued and pinned or screwed (Fig 1). These joints are most easily cut with the router. Intermediate floors on some models are not glued or pinned so that they can be removed for decorating.

Windows Windows are cross-halved using a router in the following way:

Cut lime a little over ⅛in (3mm) thick × 2–3in (50–75mm) wide, in lengths according to the height and width of the finished window. (As a general rule a 2in (50mm) width will produce about ten bars ⅛in (3mm) wide, allowing for loss in the saw-cuts.)

Mark these lengths where the joints are to be cut and rout across the full width using a ⅛in (3mm) cutter set to a depth of ¹⁄₁₆in (1·5mm).

With the circular saw, slice the bars off the block a fraction over ⅛in (3mm) wide (Fig 2). A *push stick is essential*. One or two passes on each cut face with a fine block plane will prepare the bars for gluing. When you have sufficient vertical and horizontal bars for the window, glue them together and clamp the corners with a spring paperclip. As the basic timber was cut a little over ⅛in (3mm) thick you will find after gluing that the outer faces are not level. Prepare a simple jig from ⅛in (3mm) hardboard or ply as follows: cut a square approximately 6 × 6in (150 × 150mm) with a cutout in the middle just larger than the window. Nail this square to a scrap of plywood and clamp to the benchtop. The window is placed in the centre of the recess and surfaced on one side with the orbital sander, then reversed and sanded down to the ⅛in (3mm) thickness of the hardboard or plywood jig. Lightly plane the edges to fit inside the window linings. A sandplate can be helpful here as there is less risk of splitting out the corners.

Doors All the doors are made and hung in the same way, although some are panelled, and some are planked and braced. Start with a ¹⁄₁₆in (1·5mm) core, cut to the finished dimensions of the door. Lay the hinges on the door and mark round them with a sharp knife, allowing for half the barrel in addition

to the flap. Remove the surface veneer within these marks with a small chisel (Fig 3). The door is then planked or panelled on both sides using wood strip ¹⁄₃₂in (1mm) thick (¹⁄₁₆in/1·5mm in the case of the Victorian Shop, which needs a thicker door to accommodate the glass). There is now a pair of slots in the edge of the door a little to one side of centre. This side will open outwards. Cut away a little of the surface planking on this side to accept half the hinge barrel. The door jambs are cut and rebated to the measurements given in each project, and slots to accommodate the hinge are cut into the jamb on the hanging side, allowing about ¹⁄₃₂in (1mm) extra in length for vertical adjustment when hanging the door. The door can now be sealed with one coat of matt varnish, after which the hinges are glued in place with quick-setting epoxy. Take care to remove any surplus, particularly around the barrel, while the glue is still slightly rubbery. The door will be fitted, with the other sides of the hinges being glued into the slots in the door jamb, after decorating is completed.

Stairs *Straight flights* Separate steps are glued to a bearer of ¼in (6mm) ply (Fig 4), leaving a space between them for the tread which is ¹⁄₁₆in (1·5mm)

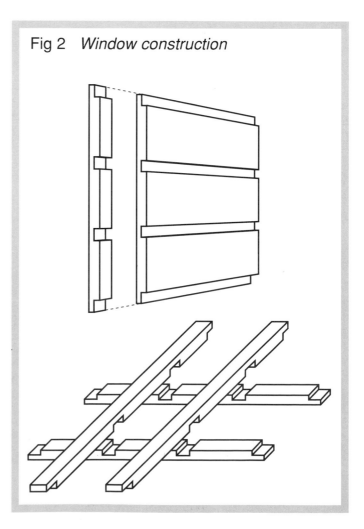

Fig 2 *Window construction*

Fig 3   *Fitting door hinges*

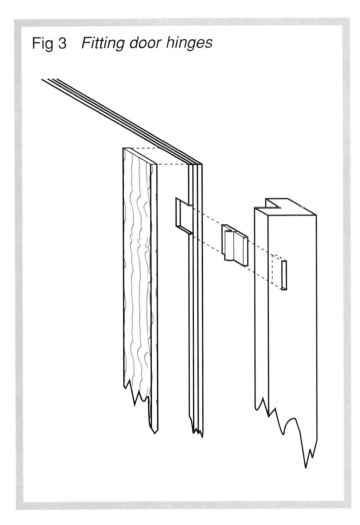

(mahogany for the shop) to cover the exposed end grain of the plywood. Flagstones and other surfaces are discussed in the projects which require them.

Mouldings   All the mouldings (for skirtings, cornices etc) can be made on the router table, if you have a fair selection of profile cutters. Most of the cutters available for full-size joinery are too large to be of any use, but in some cases mouldings can be made by using just a part of the cutting edge, or by a combination of two or more cutters. However, unless you have a full-size application, it is not worth the expense of shaped cutters, as a wide range of mouldings is available from Borcraft. If you do wish to try making your own mouldings, one example is given here, and patterns are given for the remainder where applicable in the projects.

Skirting   It is easier to cut the wood, not to the required width, but much thicker, around 1in (25mm); this will give added stability when routing, and the mouldings can afterwards be sliced off on the circular saw to the required thickness. The sawn edge can then be remoulded and the process repeated several times on the same block of wood.

thick and projects at the front and open side to form a nosing.

Winding stairs   These are more easily made from a series of stacked blocks, each cut to the pattern of the appropriate step. Nosings are formed by routing away the lower part of each step front before assembly. Detailed instructions and measurements are given with each project.

Floor Finishes   Floors can either have the planks scribed on to them with a sharp, pointed tool, or have planks cut from microwood, or wood strip laid on top. If scribing is chosen, the grain of the plywood must run in the same direction as the planking. Concealed wiring and tape runs can be successfully incorporated into floors by routing a channel across the floor from the light position to the supply point (usually on the back wall) and fitting a loose floorboard on top. In this case both the planking and plywood grain should run in the same direction as the channel, and the scribed or overlaid planking will be adjusted so that a plank width coincides with the channel. All front edges of floors are veneered with strips of lime

Fig 4   *The construction of straight flights of stairs*

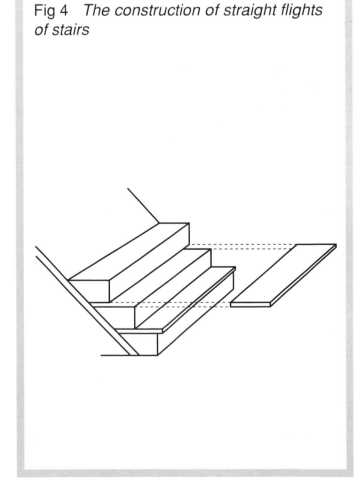

Referring to Fig 5, start with a piece of lime ⅝in (16mm) wide × 1in (25mm) thick, a little longer than the longest length of skirting needed. With a straight cutter, rebate one face ⅜₆in (8mm) wide × ½₂in (1mm) deep. Rebate edge A ⅟₁₆in (1·5mm) wide and a further ½₂in (1mm) deep.

Using a V-cutter, rout a groove ½₂in (1mm) deep, ⅜₆in (5mm) in from edge A.

Round over edges B, C, and D with a fine sandplate and finish with 220 and then 400 grit silicone-carbide paper.

Wiring and Lighting   Use is made wherever possible of self-adhesive copper tape, which is available in rolls either as a single strip or a twin tape. Cir-Kit Concepts produce a twin tape with surface insulation, which is very convenient, as the two conductor strips are already correctly spaced, and additional insulation on crossovers is not required. Where two lengths are to be joined, a small brass brad must be hammered into the overlap to establish contact between the two layers. If solder joints are to be made on the surface, a brad should be inserted, and connection made to this. Outlet sockets are available with pins moulded into them, which can be hammered directly into the tape. Lighting is available in two types: fittings with replaceable bulbs; and fittings with grain-of-wheat bulbs where the bulb and wire tails come as one unit, and in the event of failure the whole unit has to be stripped out and replaced. There are obviously some advantages in having replaceable bulbs, particularly if the light is to be sited in an awkward position and there is no provision for a plug-in ceiling rose or backplate. Cir-Kit Concepts (USA) have a good range of fittings, some with replaceable bulbs, some with grain-of-wheat bulbs. Wood 'n' Wool (UK) have a very attractive range of lighting with a rather more English style — all have grain-of-wheat bulbs. Both firms supply booklets on using their equipment, and both can supply suitable transformers. But please note that due to differences in mains voltage, US transformers cannot be used in Britain and vice versa.

Any of the following methods can be employed for installing fittings with replaceable bulbs. Those with grain-of-wheat bulbs will need to be easily disconnected and removed if a bulb has to be changed. The first two of the following are typical ceiling light installations with grain-of-wheat bulbs. The third has replaceable bulbs.

Cir-Kit   Continue the tape run to the light position, across the ceiling which can be papered or painted over, and use a CK800 canopy. This consists of a pad with moulded pins that is hammered into the tape run, and a cover into which the wires from the light are screwed. The cover is then connected to the pad with a half turn clockwise. A half turn anti-clockwise removes the light.

Wood 'N' Wool   Proceed as above using Wood 'n' Wool's own plug-in ceiling rose, or drill a small hole through the floor and lead the wire tails up through this to be soldered to a tape run either laid directly on top of the floor or in a pre-cut channel covered with a loose floorboard.

Peter Kennedy   All fittings have replaceable bulbs, but no plug-in connectors, so holes must be drilled through the floors for connection to the tape run. Some variations on the above are inevitable and will be discussed in the projects concerned.

Good lighting is available from other manufacturers, but in the projects covered in this book only fittings from the above three have been used.

Decoration   The most important part of the finishing process is surface preparation. Unless this is carried out thoroughly, no amount of paint will ever disguise the defects. You must rub down thoroughly between coats with a progressively finer paper, and vacuum away all dust. Three grades of silicone-carbide abrasive paper should be used — 180, 220 and 400. Stopping or wood filler will be needed to fill screw and nail holes. Where clear varnish is to be applied over light or honey-coloured woods, neutral plastic wood is fine, but for mahogany or elm where a coloured stopping is required, or on wood that is to be painted, Brummer stopping is recommended.

Paints and varnishes   Emulsion should be used for plain walls and ceilings, Humbrol matt or satin acrylic on doors, windows and mouldings. Whitewashed roughcast or cob exterior walls have a coating of textured masonry paint. Most external finishes on natural wood, together with some internal fittings where a slight sheen is required (eg shop counter and shelves) use satin varnish. Doors, windows and timbers in the cottages are finished with matt varnish to give a very dull sheen. Floors are coated with matt varnish both straight from the tin and also mixed with a little walnut varnish stain to produce colour variations on scribed floorboards which would otherwise be a uniform colour. Thatch and stonework, where no sheen is acceptable, are

OPPOSITE PAGE
Lighting and builders' hardware

treated with Humbrol matt varnish as this gives a completely matt finish. Take care when stirring the little tins, that *all* the matting agent is thoroughly mixed in, as failure to do this will result in a satin finish at first which gradually becomes matt white when you reach the bottom of the tin.

Wallpapers All the patterned papers are from the wide choice available from The Singing Tree. Normal household wallpaper paste is used but the walls should be sized first to limit absorption, and the paper applied with a generous overlap at openings and front edges. Only when thoroughly dry should these be trimmed using the Swann-Morton knife *with a new blade*. Always start on the back wall and work outwards. Where wires from a wall light have to be soldered to a tape behind the wallpaper it is better to paper on to card which has

been cut to the pattern of the wall, then glue the light fitting to the card, pass the wire through, solder the connections and let the wires drop down behind the card which is then glued to the wall. This is *no place* to use a fitting where the bulb cannot be changed (see Wiring and Lighting above). Skirting, picture rails and dummy doors are best pre-painted and applied over the paper. This saves having to cut the paper.

Decorating tips Parts of the houses will be very difficult, if not impossible to reach once assembly is finished. Wherever possible you should paint sections before or during assembly, so that the internal paintwork needs no more than a touch-up after construction is completed. Painting special effects, like the stonework in the Fisherman's Cottage, is covered in the relevant chapter.

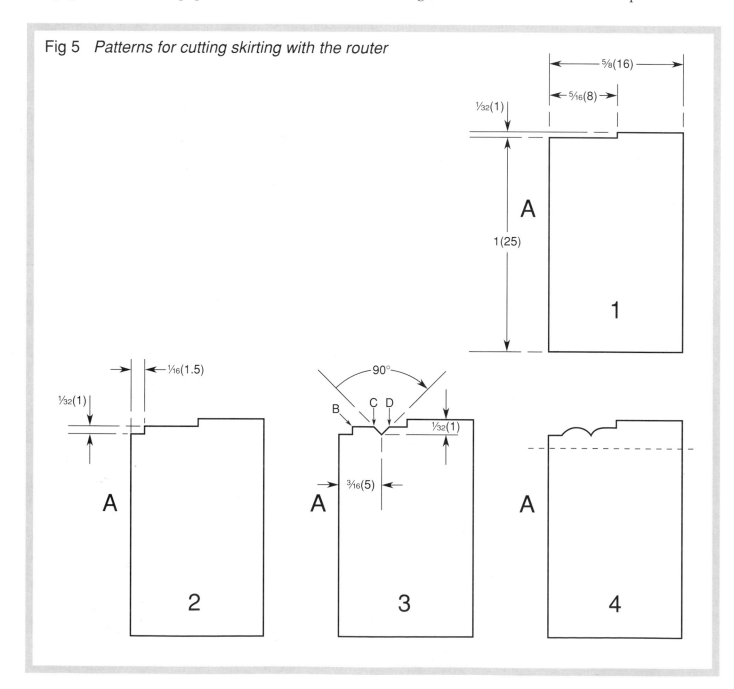

Fig 5 *Patterns for cutting skirting with the router*

2
THE
VICTORIAN
SHOP

*The design of this shop owes much to the
Dutch houses at Topsham, Devon.
Where space is at a premium it is small and light
enough to be wall mounted.
Although shown as a Victorian grocer's shop, it lends itself
to a wide variety of themes. For example, if arranged as
a bric-à-brac or antiques shop it makes a good starting point
for the beginner, as a wide assortment of furniture
and accessories can be displayed together
without appearing incongruous.*

This model has a simple carcase with a hinged front panel. The front gable has a scrolled top, with a ¾in (19mm) wide surface overlay of ⅛in (3mm) plywood, forming a contrasting border when applied over the mahogany-faced plywood of the main structure. This arrangement lends itself to a clear varnish finish. The exposed end grain of the plywood around the scroll and at the edges of the floor and side panels is faced with lime or mahogany strip. To save space internally, no stairs are fitted; instead dummy doors are provided which lead to an imaginary stairway.

CARCASE
Referring to Figs 6 and 7, cut one back, two sides, three floors, and two roof panels from ⅜in (9mm) mahogany-faced plywood. Note that the roof

The Victorian Shop

panels are of different depths to allow for the overlap at the ridge. Birch plywood can be used if the shop is to be painted rather than varnished. It should also be used for the floors if these are to have scribed boards. Cut the ⅜ × 3⁄16in (9 × 5mm) rebates and grooves on the inside faces of the side panels where shown in Fig 7. Before assembly drill two 1⁄16in (2mm) diameter holes through the middle floor 7in (178mm) from the back edge, and 4¼in (108mm) from each side. Drill a similar hole centrally through the upper floor 7in (178mm) from the back edge. These holes will later be used for lighting. Apply a 25in (635mm) length of Cir-Kit twin wiring tape up the centre of the inside face of the back panel, and hammer a small brass brad into each conductor line ½in (13mm) below the apex and ½in (13mm) above the bottom edge of the panel. Temporarily tack the carcase together *without glue* and check that the parts fit correctly. When satisfied, the carcase should be dismantled and re-assembled with glue and ¾–1in (20–25mm) panel pins, in the following order.

Glue and pin the floors into the rebates on the side panels, ensuring that their back edges are flush with the inside of the rebates for the back panel. Glue and pin the back panel in place with

TIMBER REQUIREMENTS

WOOD	THICKNESS in	THICKNESS mm	WIDTH in	WIDTH mm	LENGTH ft/in	LENGTH m
Mahogany	1/16	1.6	1/16	1.6	9in	0.23
			7/16	11	5ft	1.53
			⅝	16	4ft	1.22
	⅛	3	3/16	5	9in	0.23
			⅜	10	9ft	2.75
			⅞	22	9in	0.23
			1	25	4ft	1.22
			1 5/16	33	6in	0.16
			2¼	57	18in	0.46
	¼	6	¼	6	12in	0.31
			⅜	10	3ft 3in	1.0
			¾	19	18in	0.46
			⅞	22	2ft	0.61
			1	25	3in	0.92
	5/16	8	⅜	10	18in	0.46
	⅜	10	⅜	10	6in	0.16
			¾	19	6in	0.16
			1⅛	29	9in	0.23
	½	13	¾	19	6in	0.16
	¾	19	1	25	18in	0.46
			1⅞	48	9in	0.23
	⅞	22	1½	38	18in	0.46

WOOD	THICKNESS in	THICKNESS mm	WIDTH in	WIDTH mm	LENGTH ft/in	LENGTH m
Lime	1/32	1	⅝	16	3ft	0.92
	⅛	3	7/16	11	4ft	1.22
			⅝	16	3ft 6in	1.07
	¼	6	5/16	8	12in	0.31
Lime or Beech	¾	19	1½	38	15in	0.38
Pine	1½	38	1½	38	2ft	0.61

WOOD	THICKNESS in	THICKNESS mm	AREA sq ft	AREA sq m
Mahogany or Birch-plywood	⅜	9	15	1.39
Birch-plywood	⅛	3	1½	0.14
	1/16	1.5	½	0.05
	1/32	0.8	3	0.3

additional pins into the back edges of the floors, spaced to avoid damaging the copper tape on the inside. Glue a strip of ⅜in (9mm) plywood, ¾in (19mm) wide, along the inside of each side panel above the top floor (Fig 8). This provides additional support for the bottom of the roof and sufficient internal height for skirting.

When the glue has set, plane a bevel at the top of each side panel to conform with the roof slope. Now glue and pin the roof sections in place with a simple overlap at the ridge, allowing the bottom edges to overhang at the eaves. When the glue has dried, plane this overhang flush with the carcase sides.

Now plane all the joints at the front and back of the carcase true and square.

FRONT PANEL

Following the outline and dimensions in Fig 9, cut the front panel from ⅜in (9mm) mahogany-faced plywood. Also cut out the window and door apertures. Cut a 17¾in (451mm) length of piano hinge (preferably brass, rather than plated steel) to fit from the underside of the ground floor to the top of the upper floor, and temporarily fasten this with three screws (top, middle and bottom) to the front edge of the right-hand carcase side so that the edge of the hinge flap is flush with the inside face of the side panel, leaving approximately ⅛in (3mm) of hinge and barrel projecting at the outside face. Centre the front panel over the carcase with the bottom edges flush and an equal overhang of approximately 1/16in (2mm) at each side. Mark the

Fig 6 *Measurements for the carcase panels of the Victorian Shop*

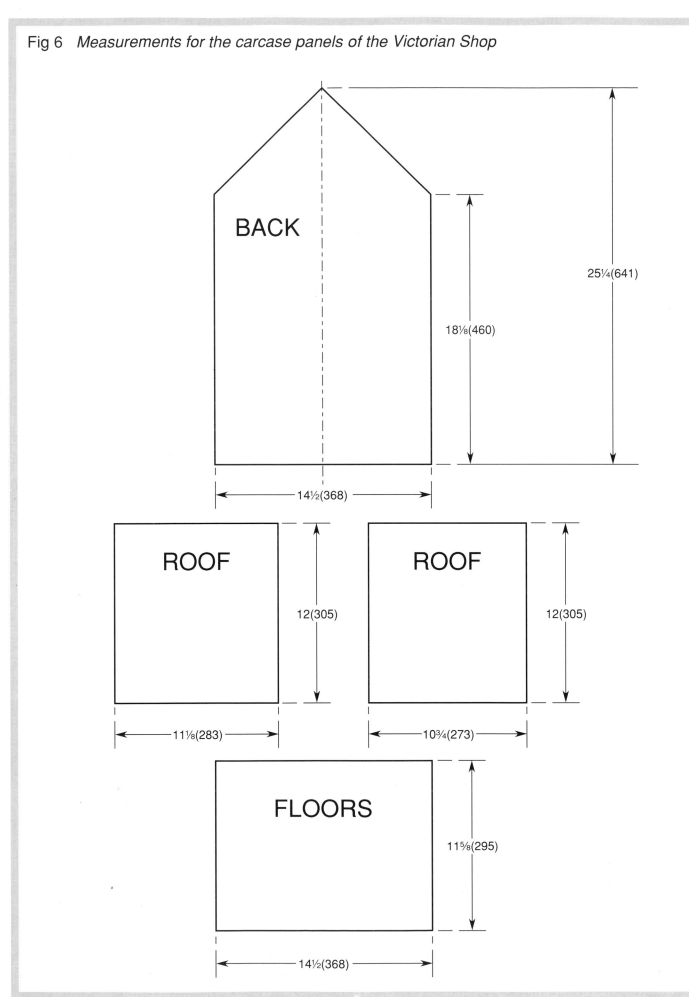

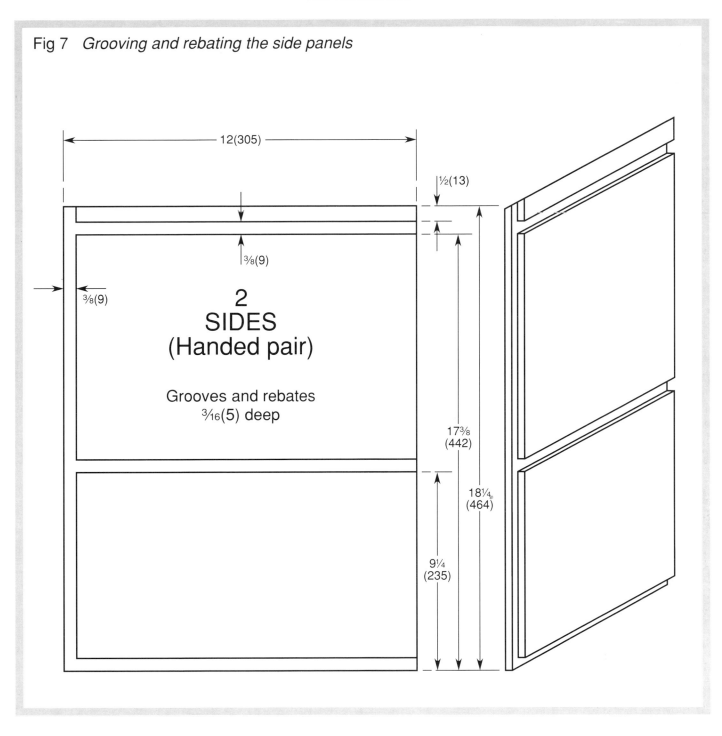

Fig 7 *Grooving and rebating the side panels*

12(305)

½(13)

⅜(9)

⅜(9)

2
SIDES
(Handed pair)

Grooves and rebates
³⁄₁₆(5) deep

17⅜
(442)

18¼
(464)

9¼
(235)

position of the hinge on the back of the front panel. Temporarily screw the hinge to the front panel, and adjust if necessary for even closure with the bottom edges level. (Don't worry if the screws break through to the outside of the front panel, as the surface overlay to be applied later will cover this.)

CARCASE TRIM
Remove the front panel, leaving the hinge attached to the carcase. Fold the hinge into the closed position and glue a ⅜ x ⅛in (10 x 3mm) mahogany facing to all the exposed front edges of the carcase, starting with the left-hand side, moving to the roof,

then the right-hand side down to the top of the hinge, and finally across the three floors. Now plane all these facings back to the thickness of the folded hinge. (This ensures flat and even closure of the front panel.) Face the edges of the roof panels at the eaves with ⅝ x ¹⁄₁₆in (16 x 2mm) mahogany, planing the top edge of the facing to conform with the roof slope. A similar facing should be glued along the bottom of the side panels. Its purpose here is solely to balance the facing at the eaves. A 12in (305mm) length of Ramin moulding (approximately ⅞in/22mm across the face) is glued along the ridge. Glue and screw two 1½ x ½in

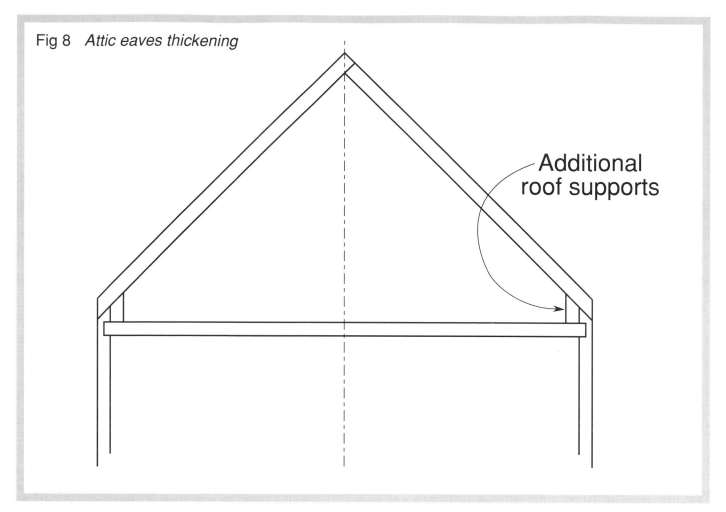

Fig 8   *Attic eaves thickening*

Additional roof supports

(38 × 13mm) bearers, each 12in (305mm) long, under the bottom of the carcase, inset ¼in (6mm) at each side. These lift the house, allowing the front to pivot without rubbing on the table top. The shell of the shop is now complete, and work can begin on the detailing of the front panel.

SHOP FRONT
Referring to Fig 10, glue and screw the 1½ × ⅞in (38 × 22mm) mahogany fascia block A, 15in (381mm) long, across the front panel, its bottom edge flush with the top of the shop window/door cutout. The ⅞in (22mm) face butts against the front panel. Glue and screw the sill B across the bottom of the front panel. This is made from beech or lime 1½ × ¾in (38 × 19mm) moulded to the profile shown, and 15in (381mm) in length. Glue side posts C of 1 × ¾in (25 × 19mm) mahogany 8⅜in (213mm) long on to the outside of the front panel between the sill and fascia block. Their inner edges should be flush with the window/door cutouts. Glue a facing block D of mahogany 1⅞in (48mm) deep and ¾in (19mm) thick to the panel front. Resting on top of the sill with its top edge flush with the bottom of the window aperture, it should butt against the post at the right-hand side and reach to the door opening at the left-hand side. A mahogany post E 1⅛ × ⅜in (29 × 10mm) and 8⅜in (213mm) long is now glued

between the sill and fascia at the right-hand side of the door opening with the lower part of one 1⅛in (29mm) face butting against the open edge of the facing block previously fitted. The ⅜in (10mm) face at the back should be flush with the plywood panel.

A shelf of mahogany 2¼in (57mm) wide, ⅛in (3mm) thick, and 8½in (216mm) long, is glued on top of the facing block D and the edge of the plywood panel at the bottom of the shop window aperture, with a ⅛in (3mm) projection over the facing block D at the front.

SHOP WINDOW
Referring still to Fig 10, cut two pieces F of mahogany ⅜ × ¼in (10 × 6mm) and 8½in (216mm) long to fit horizontally between the right-hand side post C and the post E at the side of the doorway. Do not glue yet. Following Fig 11, these are slotted at the back ⅜in (10mm) wide and ⅛in (3mm) deep for the two vertical centre bars which are halved into them. Make two moulded window bars G from mahogany, each 6⅜in (162mm) long, and remove the moulded face for ⅜in (10mm) at each end to

The shop front

Fig 9 *Pattern for the front panel of the shop*

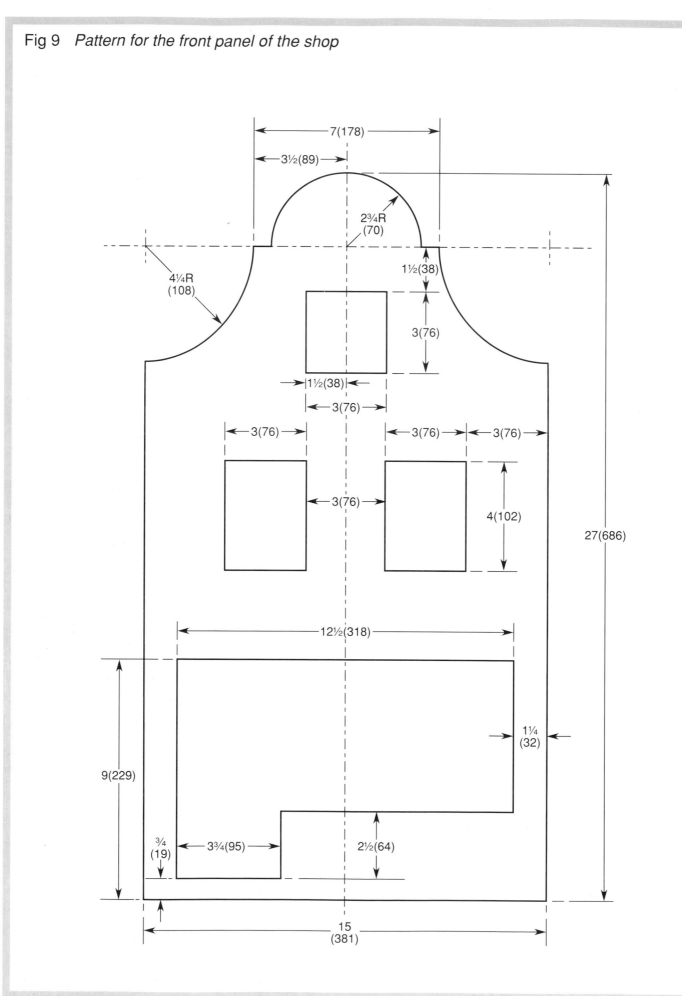

Fig 10 *Shop front detail*

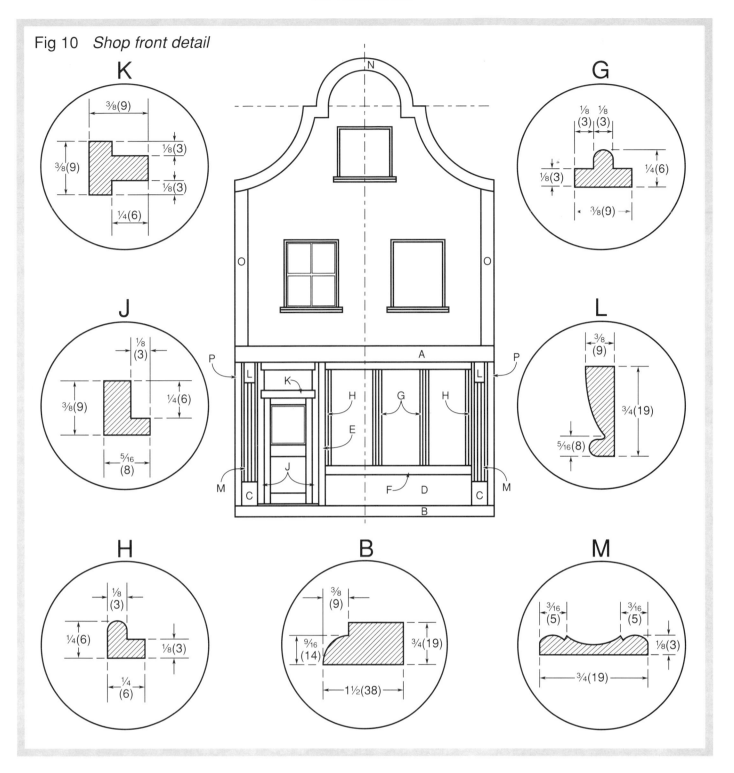

leave a flat surface ⅜ × ⅜in (10 × 10mm), ⅛in (3mm) thick for crosshalving into F. Màke two further window bars H, each 5⅝in (143mm) long to butt between the two horizontal bars F, and fit against the posts C and E. Now glue the horizontal bars F in position with their outer faces flush with the outer faces of the door-post E and the side post C. Ensure that the slots are at the back. When the glue has set, the vertical bars G and H can be added, taking care that all the back faces are level. (Glazing will later be fitted behind them.)

EXTERNAL DOOR

For details of construction see Chapter 1. Cut the core to the dimensions given in Fig 12, and remove the surface veneer to recess the hinges on the back face. The door hangs from the right when viewed from the front, and opens inwards. Glue rails and stiles to both faces; all are ¹⁄₁₆in (1·5mm) thick mahogany, the bottom and middle rails being ⅝in (16mm) wide and the top rail and stiles ⁷⁄₁₆in (11mm) wide. The door should finish between ³⁄₁₆in (5mm) and ⁷⁄₃₂in (6mm) thick. Glue ¹⁄₁₆in (1·5mm) mahogany, either square in section or quadrant, mitred at the corners, into the window aperture, flush with the outer faces of the rails and stiles.

Fit 2mm glass or Glodex acrylic sheet behind this, and then repeat the framing at the back to hold the glazing in place. (Glass is preferable here unless the shop is being made for a young child. If Glodex or a similar acrylic material is used, the door should be painted or varnished before the glazing is fitted as it will be impossible to remove stray paint or varnish without leaving unsightly scratches.)

Brass knobs should be fitted on each side of the door.

For the jambs cut two pieces of mahogany ⅜ × ⁵⁄₁₆in (10 × 8mm), 8⅜in (213mm) long, rebated to the dimensions in Fig 10 (J). Dry fit these between the fascia and sill with a plain ⅜in (10mm) face of each against the left-hand post C and the

door-post E, with the rebate facing the back. Position them so that the back edges are flush with the back of the plywood front panel. Place the door in position and mark the right-hand jamb (viewed from the front) with the position of the hinges. Remove the jamb, and then drill and file the slots for the hinges. With the door and jambs temporarily replaced, cut two headers of mahogany ⅜in (10mm) square, and 1½in (38mm) long. Rebate one piece to the dimensions given in Fig 10 (K). The other piece should have a similar rebate *on one face only*.

Place the section K across the door frame with one rebate resting on top of the door, and mark where it crosses the jambs. This should be 6¼in (159mm) above the bottom of the jambs. The remaining L-shaped section should be placed, rebate downwards, across the jambs with its plain face butting the underside of the fascia. Again, mark where it crosses the jambs. Remove ⅜in (10mm) of the short ⅛in (3mm) return on each jamb in both positions to let the headers fit securely between them.

When satisfied with the fit, re-assemble with glue, using the door as a wedge to keep the jambs tightly pressed against the left-hand post C and the door-post E. (If the door is a little too slack for this, push a sliver of veneer into the gap to maintain pressure.) Ensure that all back edges are flush with the back of the front panel, and *avoid getting glue in the hinge slots*. The door should now be removed and put aside.

MOULDINGS AND BRACKETS

Cut two pieces of mahogany 1 × ¼in (25 × 6mm) and 1⅜in (35mm) long and glue them at the bottom of the front faces of the side posts. Cut a 6in (152mm) length of ¾ × ⅜in (19 × 10mm) mahogany, and carve two brackets to the pattern in Fig 10 (L), one at each end. Cut them off 1½in (38mm) long. (The extra length of wood is used as a handle while working on the ends.) Glue these in place centrally at the top of the front faces of the posts, below the fascia. Cut a 6in (152mm) length of ¾ × ½in (19 × 13mm) mahogany, and machine two opposing ¾in (19mm) faces to the moulding pattern in Fig 10 (M). Slice off the two mouldings ⅛in (3mm) thick. Cut both pieces 5¾in (146mm) long to fit snugly between the brackets and bottom pads, and glue them centrally to the front faces of the side posts.

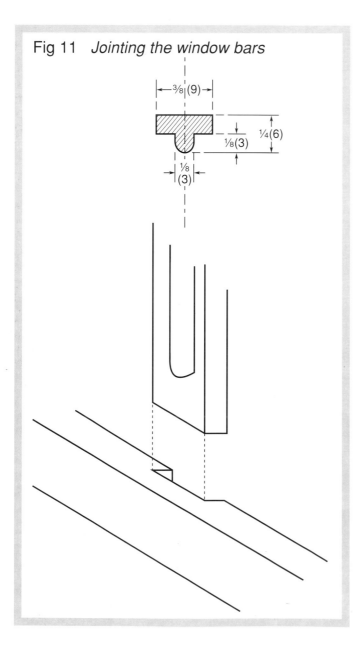

Fig 11 *Jointing the window bars*

⅜(9)

¼(6)
⅛(3)

⅛(3)

OPPOSITE *Unfurnished interior of the Victorian Shop*

Fig 12 *Making the external shop door*

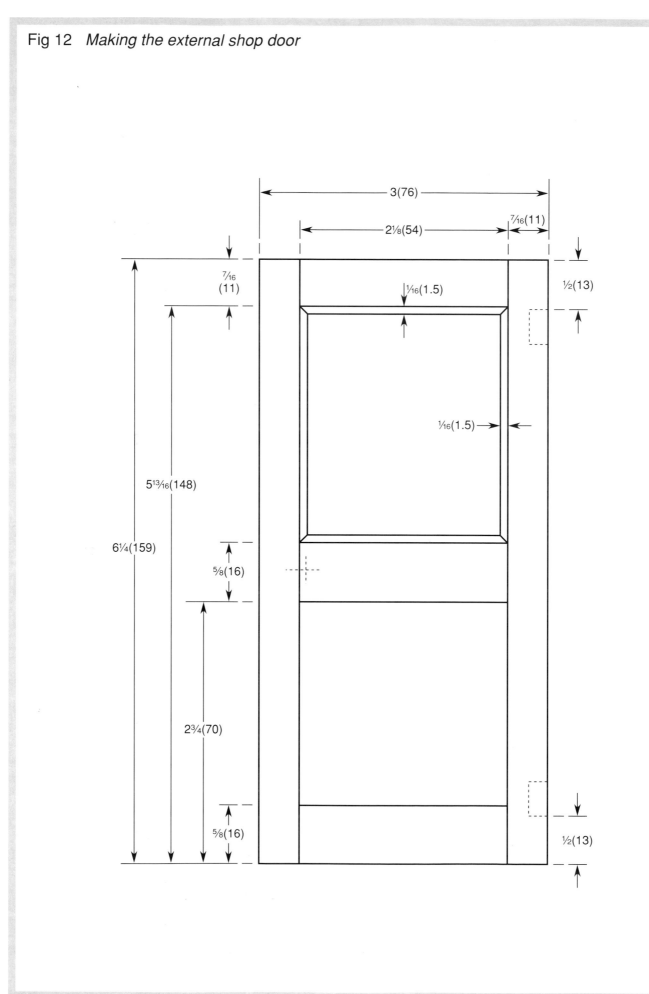

Fig 13 *Constructing the upper windows and linings*

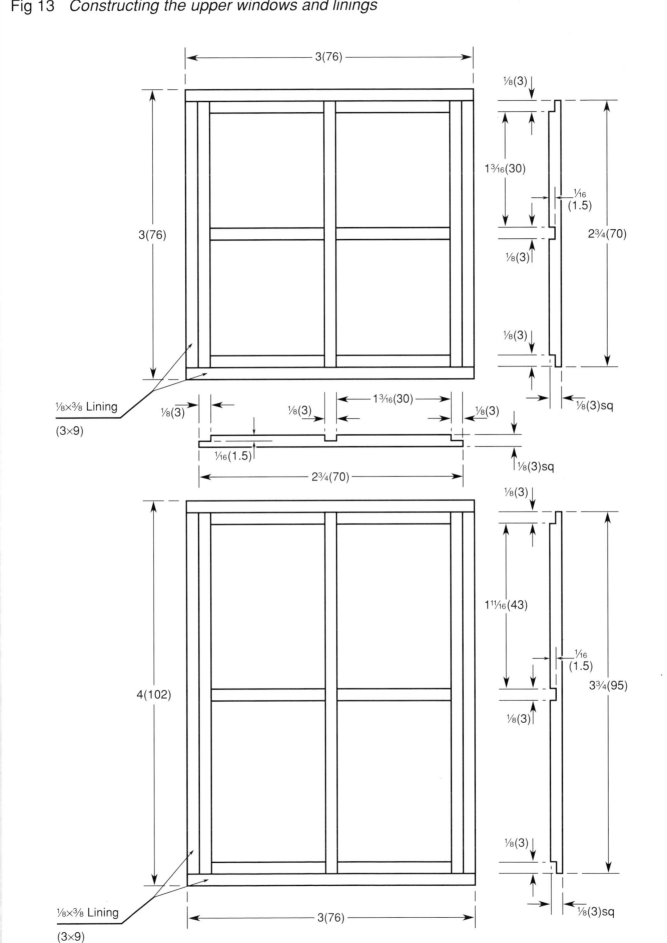

UPPER WINDOWS

Following the method described in Chapter 1 and the dimensions in Fig 13, make two large first-floor windows and one smaller window for the attic, all from lime. They should each have two coats of varnish except at the outer edge where they will later be glued. Put them aside until the remainder of the construction is completed.

Linings Line the window openings with $7/16 \times 1/8$in (11×3mm) lime, starting with the horizontal sections at the top and bottom, and then fitting the vertical sections between them. Glue and wedge them in position taking care not to damage the surface of the lining. When dry, plane both sides flush with the plywood panel.

Sills Cut three pieces of lime $5/16 \times 1/4$in (8×6mm) each $3\frac{5}{8}$in (92mm) long. Bevel the top edge of each to leave $3/32$in (2·5mm) thickness at the front edge rising to $1/4$in (6mm) at the back. Glue these to the front panel under the window openings so that the tops of the sills are level with the top edge of the lower lining, overlapping $1/4$in (6mm) at each side of the window.

SCROLL AND BORDER

Referring to Fig 10, cut the scroll facing N from $1/8$in (3mm) birch plywood, $3/4$in (19mm) wide, with its outer edge conforming to the profile of the plywood front panel, and glue it in place. When the glue has set, cut two straight sections O from $1/8$in (3mm) birch plywood, each $3/4$in (19mm) wide, and glue them at either side of the front panel between the scroll and the fascia — note that their top edges will need to be shaped (slightly concave) to fit under the scroll.

The two narrow lower sections P, each $5/16$in (8mm) wide, should now be cut from $1/8$in (3mm) plywood and glued to the front panel outside the posts, extending from the underside of the fascia to the top of the sill.

When the glue is dry, carefully plane and sand all the outer edges of the border flush with the edge of the plywood panel, taking care not to round over the edges. (If the edges are not sharp and square, there will be a gap between the border and the edge veneer to be applied next.)

EDGE VENEER

Prepare a strip of lime $5/8$in (16mm) wide, $1/32$in (1mm) thick and about 30in (762mm) long. Carefully bend one end of this around the top curve of the scroll to find the length required. Cut off and glue in place with contact adhesive. Now veneer the two lower curves, followed by the two short straight sections above them. Trim the veneer flush with the face of the border, and the back of the front panel. Cut two strips of lime $5/8$in (16mm) wide and $1/8$in (3mm) thick, both $18\frac{1}{2}$in (470mm) long, and glue to the vertical edges at the right and left of the front panel. Plane the outer edge of the strip at the right-hand side so that it extends fractionally beyond the hinge barrel. A similar amount should be planed off the left-hand side. Trim the veneer flush at the front and back of the panel.

WINDOW COMPLETION

The upper windows should now be glued in place, inset $3/32$in (2·5mm) from the back face of the panel. Apply three coats of satin varnish to the front panel, leaving the sides of the shop window cutout bare, as further framing must be glued in and varnished after the glazing is fitted.

Glazing Cut one piece of 2mm glass or Glodex $8\frac{1}{2} \times 6\frac{3}{8}$in ($216 \times 162$mm) to fit behind the shop-window frames and bars. Cut a piece of mahogany $3/8 \times 1/4$in (10×6mm) and $8\frac{1}{2}$in (216mm) long to fit behind the glazing and rest on the top of the shelf with a $3/8$in (10mm) face vertical to match the frame on the outside of the glazing. Cut the remainder of the internal shop-window framing from $7/8 \times 1/4$in (22×6mm) mahogany to fill the total depth from the back of the glazing to the back face of the plywood panel. One piece is $8\frac{1}{2}$in (216mm) long to fit across the top of the window, the other two are $6\frac{1}{8}$in (156mm) long to fit down each side. Glue them in place behind the glazing and, when dry, plane off any surplus flush with the back of the front panel. (If glass is used it is better to fasten this internal framing with veneer pins only, to facilitate removal in the event of broken glass.)

Cut a piece of glass or Glodex $3 \times 1\frac{5}{8}$in (76×41mm) to fit between the rebated jambs and headers over the doorway. Glue a frame of $1/16 \times 3/32$in ($1\cdot5 \times 2\cdot5$mm) mahogany behind it. Both this frame and that behind the shop window can now be varnished. Glazing can now be fitted to the three upper windows. This is held in place at the back by a mitred surround of microwood self-adhesive veneer $5/16$–$3/8$in (8–10mm) wide.

FINAL ASSEMBLY

Glue the hinges into the slots in the front door with epoxy resin. Let this set and clean off any surplus before gluing the other side of the hinges into the door jamb. Re-hang the front panel with three screws, and check again that it closes squarely.

The Victorian Shop, fully furnished

Fig 14 *Dimensions and outlines for the fireplace*

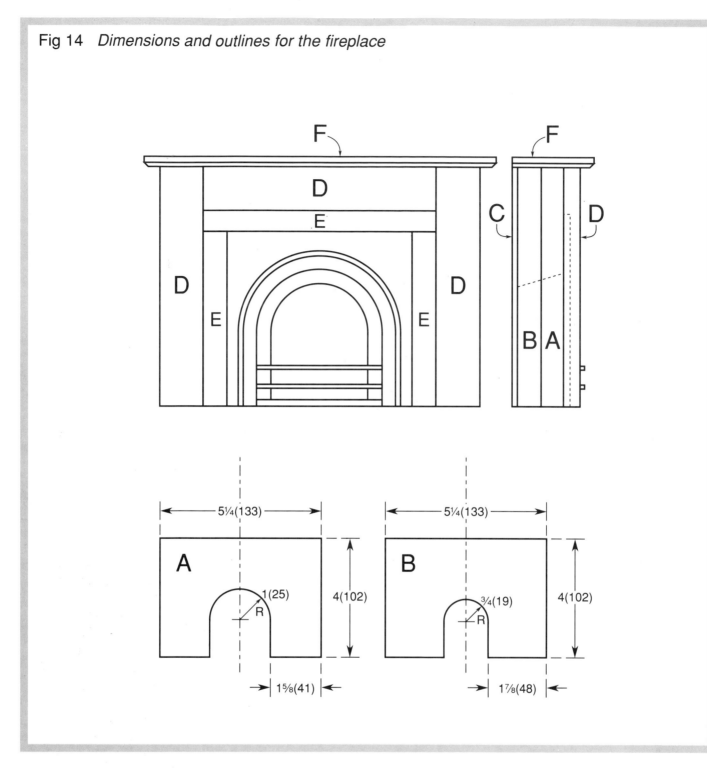

Make any adjustments needed before inserting the rest of the screws. A side hook is fitted in the centre of the veneered left-hand edge of the front panel in line with the centre of the middle floor. Insert a small round-headed brass screw through the left-hand side of the carcase centrally into the middle floor. The distance back from the front edge will be determined by the radius at the inside of the hook. The hook must be cranked slightly to allow for the overlap of the front panel. The shop is now complete, and work can start on internal fittings, lighting and decorating.

FIREPLACE
Referring to Fig 14, cut two pieces of ⅜in (9mm) plywood 4 × 5¼in (102 × 133mm). Cut out the arched shape B from both pieces, and glue them together. Now mark the outline A on one face which will become the front. Using a rasp, and then a small sanding drum (Dremel) fitted in a Minicraft drill, fair the edges of the arch from profile B at the back to A at the front. Cut a piece C of 1⁄16in (1·5mm) plywood 4 × 5¼in (102 × 133mm) and glue this to the back of the assembly. Glue on a facing border D of mahogany ¾in (19mm) wide and ¼in (6mm)

Fig 15 *Plans for the shop counter*

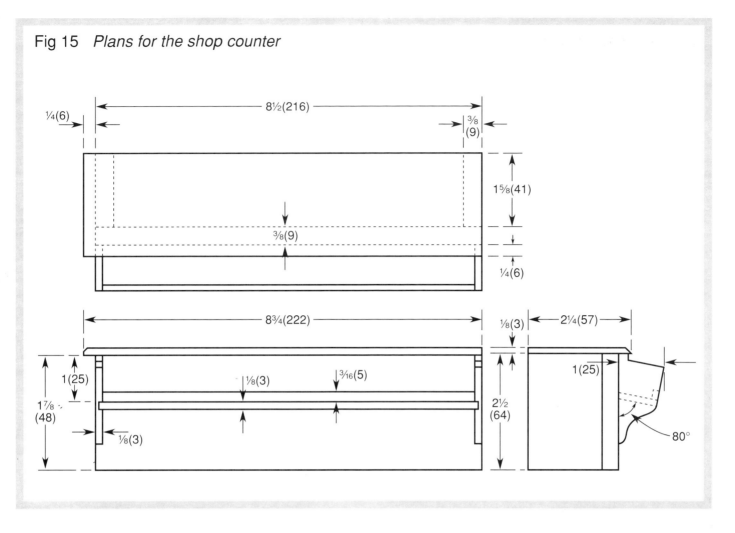

thick. The model shown has an inner surround E of
$\frac{3}{8} \times \frac{3}{32}$in (10 × 2mm) marble. This may be difficult
to obtain, and ceramic tiles are a good alternative. If
tiles are to be used, adjust the width of the
mahogany border accordingly.

Cut the shelf F from mahogany $\frac{1}{8}$in (3mm) thick,
$1\frac{5}{16}$in (33mm) wide and $5\frac{5}{8}$in (143mm) long. Glue
this on top with the back edge flush with the
fireplace backing C. Glue smooth string with a
diameter of approximately $\frac{1}{16}$in (2mm) around the
arch, and again parallel to this but $\frac{1}{4}$in (6mm)
further out. Cut the hearth from $\frac{1}{8}$in (3mm)
plywood, angled at each end to fit between the
sides of the arch and against the backing C. Drill
two $\frac{1}{16}$in (2mm) diameter holes on each side of the
arch $\frac{1}{16}$in (2mm) in from the front edge and $\frac{1}{8}$in
(3mm) deep, spaced at $\frac{1}{4}$in (6mm) centres above the
hearth. Paint all surfaces inside the marble
surround matt black. Two lengths of $\frac{1}{16}$in (1·5mm)
diameter brass rod, cut $\frac{1}{4}$in (6mm) longer than the
width of the arch, are bent into a slight bow and
sprung into the holes already drilled.

SHOP COUNTER
Cut one piece of $\frac{3}{8}$in (10mm) thick mahogany or
mahogany-faced plywood $2\frac{1}{2} \times 8\frac{1}{2}$in (64 × 216mm),

and two pieces $2\frac{1}{2} \times 1\frac{5}{8}$in (64 × 41mm). Glue these
together as shown in Fig 15, with the longer piece
overlapping the short return section.

The counter top is made from $\frac{1}{8}$in (3mm) thick
mahogany $8\frac{3}{4}$in (222mm) long and $2\frac{1}{4}$in (57mm)
wide with the front and left-hand edges either
chamfered or moulded with the router. This should
be glued on top with a $\frac{1}{4}$in (6mm) overhang at the
front and left-hand edges.

The two shelf brackets are cut from $\frac{1}{8}$in (3mm)
thick mahogany with a housing $\frac{1}{8}$in (3mm) wide
and $\frac{1}{16}$in (2mm) deep, cut where shown in Fig 15.
Cut the shelf from $\frac{1}{8}$in (3mm) mahogany $8\frac{3}{8}$in
(213mm) long and $\frac{7}{8}$in (22mm) wide, with the back
edge bevelled to fit against the counter front, and
glue it into the bracket housings. A further piece of
mahogany $\frac{3}{16} \times \frac{1}{8}$in (5 × 3mm) and $8\frac{1}{4}$in (210mm)
long is glued on top of the outer edge of the shelf.
Now glue the whole shelf assembly to the counter
front, with the brackets flush at each end and tight
against the underside of the counter top.

INTERNAL DOORS
Make two dummy doors to the pattern in Fig 16.
The rails and stiles are applied to one face only of
the $\frac{1}{16}$in (1·5mm) plywood backing, which should

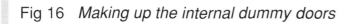

Fig 16   *Making up the internal dummy doors*

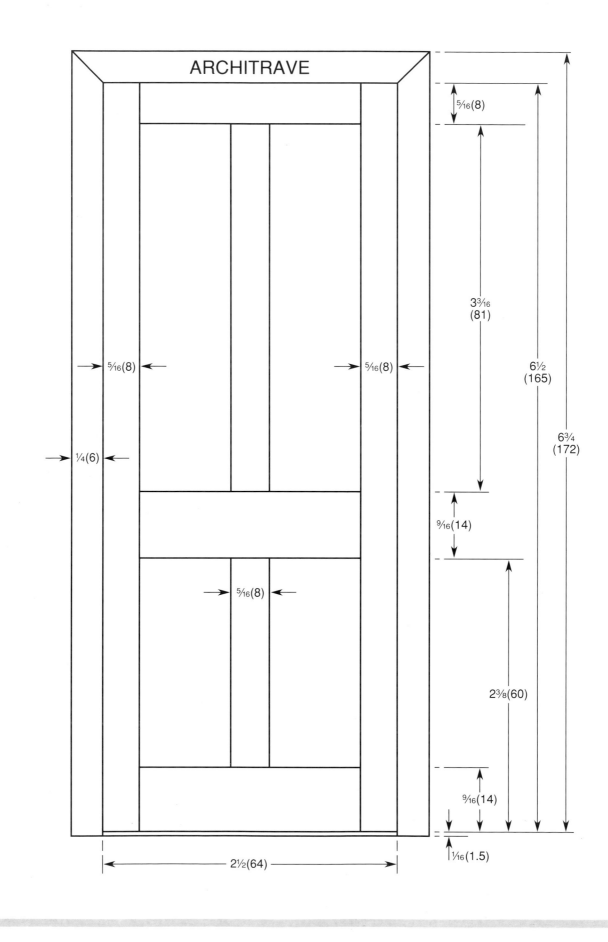

extend a further ¼in (6mm) at each side and at the top, to take the architrave. These doors should be painted or varnished now, and glued inside the house *after* decorating.

SHOP SHELVES

Make one assembly of three back shelves A from ⅛in (3mm) thick mahogany to the dimensions given in Fig 17, noting that the shelves are housed into the end support brackets. The two side shelf assemblies B and C are made from mahogany of a similar thickness. Note that the shelf to be fitted at the right-hand side of the shop is shorter than that on the left. The shelves are glued above and below the 1⅛ × ⅛in (29 × 3mm) backing with 1 × 1⅛in (25 × 29mm) spacers fitted where shown. Both side shelves are radiused on the inside edge at the front. After decorating, shelf assembly A will be glued to the back wall of the shop with its *middle shelf* 5½in (140mm) above the floor, and the right-hand bracket against the right-hand wall of the shop. The side shelf assembly B is glued to the right-hand shop wall with its two shelves in line with the upper two shelves of the back unit A. Shelf assembly C is glued to the left-hand shop wall at the same height with its back edge butting the back wall.

LIGHTING

All the light fittings used here are from Peter Kennedy, and have replaceable bulbs. The tape run is applied to the back wall before carcase assembly, and the holes drilled through the appropriate floors. For simplicity on this model, the tape connections from the ground- and first-floor lights to the back wall are applied on top of the floors above them with carpets hiding the tape. If you wish to have exposed flooring with hidden wiring, refer back to Chapter 1 for details of scribing floors and fitting tape or wire under loose boards. Start by drilling one 3⁄32in (2mm) diameter hole through the back wall of the shop area just to the right of the tape and ⅛in (3mm) above floor level. Thread through a 36in (915mm) length of twin wire, and solder the ends to the brass brads at the bottom of the tape. The other end of this wire will be connected to a transformer.

Ground Floor Apply tapes on top of the first floor to run from each lighting position to the tape on the back wall, and overlap it above floor level. Ensure that each conductor line to be connected is directly over its counterpart, and insert brass brads to make the connection. (Insulation is built in on the tape surface, and a connection cannot be made without the brads.) Hammer further brads into the floor tapes ½in (13mm) behind each light position. The

wire tails from the light fittings will be soldered here.

First Floor Apply tape from the single light position and connect it to the back wall in the same manner.

NOTE: It is worth having a transformer available, together with a light fitting, so that the circuit can be tested as you progress. The lights will not be fitted until the interior has been decorated.

Bedroom Cut a block of wood ¾in (19mm) square and ½in (13mm) thick. Bevel two opposing sides to 45° leaving a flat area ⅛in (3mm) wide at the top. Drill a 1⁄16in (2mm) diameter hole centrally through the block, and paint it white. The wire tails from the light are threaded through the block and soldered to the brads at the top of the back wall tape. The block is then glued under the roof 7in (178mm) from the back wall. (This light should be installed before papering the back wall, so that the solder connections can be covered.)

DECORATING

The front panel has already had three coats of varnish. The remainder of the carcase exterior should now be similarly varnished.

All the floors are finished with two coats of matt varnish.

The bedroom roof sections are painted with white emulsion down to skirting level, and the back wall is papered. In the living-room the ceiling and frieze down to the top of the doorway are painted white, with the remainder of the walls papered. The top edge of the wallpaper is covered by a white picture rail, with dark brown skirting at the bottom. The door and surround are white. In the shop both the walls and ceiling are covered with 1⁄32in (0·8mm) plywood and given two coats of matt varnish. A cove moulded from 3⁄16in (5mm) square lime is fitted around the room at the junction of the walls and ceiling. The door is varnished, with mahogany rails and stiles, and lighter-coloured panels (natural plywood). All the shelving and the counter have two coats of satin varnish. The skirting throughout this model is made as described in Chapter 1 (Fig 5), but a wide range of mouldings is available from Borcraft (see Acknowledgements) if you do not wish to make your own.

Fig 17 *Plans for the shop shelf assemblies*

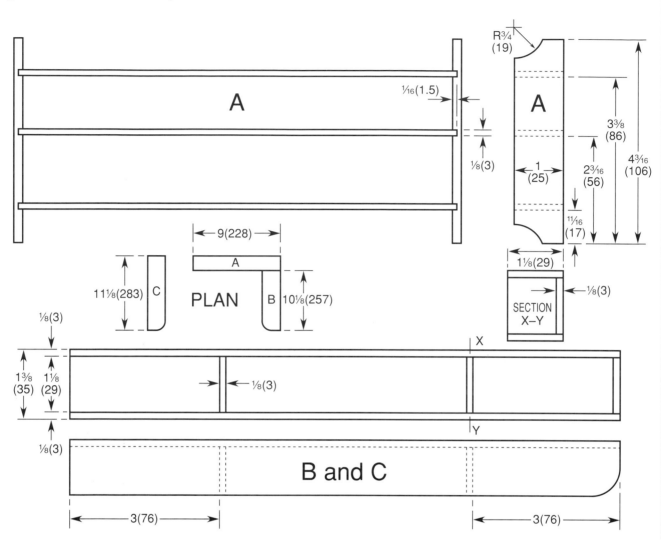

THE VICTORIAN SHOP – LIST OF SUPPLIERS

The furniture and accessories used in the Victorian Shop are from the following suppliers; see Acknowledgements for addresses.

Avon Miniatures: Jug.
Peggy Birrell: Potted plant.
Blackwells: Picture frames, books (kit).
Rohanna Bryan: Apples.
Bryntor: Post box, cream and marmalade jars.
C & D Crafts: Baskets.
Irene Campbell: Washbasin, jug, soap bowl and chamber pot.
Copycats: Clock, pedestal table, low table.
Dijon: Brass bed, small chest of drawers, desk, upholstered chairs, small circular table, tin bath.
Dolls & Miniatures: Till, cheese, bread, storage jars and ginger beer.
Dolphin Miniatures: Windsor chair, toy box, slop pail, beer crates and barrel.
Dorking Dollshouse Gallery: Tea chest.

Marie Theresa: Lady shop customer, hat and shawl.
Hobbys: Picture frames, shopkeeper (re-dressed).
Tony Hooper: Brass curtain rails.
Marions Miniature Millinery: Cat and kitten.
John and Pauline Meredith: 'Staffordshire' figurines.
Miniature Curios: String of onions.
Miniature Model Imports: Sewing table.
Phoenix Model Developments: Sewing machine (kit).
Quality Dollshouse Miniatures: Flour and potato sacks, shovels, dustpans and brush, scoops and brooms.
The Singing Tree: Wallpapers.
Sunday Dolls: Lady at desk (kit).
Thames Valley Crafts: Grocery stock and scales.
Wentways Miniatures: Carrots and lorgnettes.

The gramophone is from the author's own collection. The shop sign is cut from a magazine.

3
THE
GEORGIAN
HOUSE

*Many people are attracted by the elegance and
proportion of Georgian architecture. Variations on Georgian themes
are probably the most popular designs for dolls' houses, and a
wide range of furniture and accessories is available for them.*

Because of its size, it is easier to build the carcase of this house in two sections, starting with the lower section up to top-floor level, and adding the more complex gable ends and chimneys afterwards. To add more interest, the rooms to the right of the hall and landing are wider than those to the left. The closing joint between the two hinged front panels has been arranged to lie over the centre of the right-hand partition wall, leaving enough of the left-hand panel at the right of the front door and landing window to maintain adequate strength. Note that both the window and door are offset slightly to the left to allow for this, and that part of the right-hand door pillar, pediment and step overlap the join in the front panels to disguise the break. They also hold the right-hand panel when closed. Stairs are

Front of the Georgian House

fitted to the first floor only, but could be continued to the top floor with the loss of the bathroom.

LOWER CARCASE CUTTING

From the patterns in Figs 18 and 19, cut one back A, two sides B, two partition walls C and one ground floor D, from ⅜in (9mm) birch plywood. Cut the top floor E and the three first-floor sections F, G and H from ¼in (6mm) birch plywood. Cut out the window openings in the back A, and the door openings in the two partition walls C. Cut a rebate ⅜in (9mm) wide and ³⁄₁₆in (5mm) deep down each inside vertical edge of the back A, and across the inside of the bottom edge. To avoid resetting the router, cut a similar rebate across the inside bottom edges of the two sides B. Cut two grooves ⅜in (9mm) wide and ³⁄₁₆in (5mm) deep, on the inside face of the back A, where shown in Fig 18, noting that they are stopped 2⅝in (67mm) from the top. Cut two similar grooves right across the ground floor D. Cut a groove ¼in (6mm) wide and ³⁄₁₆in (5mm) deep across the inside faces of the two sides B, 1⅛in (29mm) from the top. With a sharp-pointed

TIMBER REQUIREMENTS

WOOD	THICKNESS in	mm	WIDTH in	mm	LENGTH ft/in	m
Lime	1/32	1	1/4	6	5ft	1.53
			5/16	8	12ft	3.65
			3/8	10	4ft	1.22
			1/2	13	126ft	38.4
			9/16	14	3ft	0.92
			3/4	19	12in	0.31
			1 7/8	48	2ft	0.61
	1/16	1.6	3/8	10	15ft	4.57
			1/2	13	6ft	1.82
	3/32	2.5	1/4	6	12ft	3.65
			2	51	6ft	1.82
	1/8	3	1/4	6	6ft	1.82
			3/8	10	6ft	1.82
			1/2	13	3ft	0.92
			2 1/8	54	12in	0.31
	3/16	5	5/16	8	14ft	4.27
			3/8	10	18ft	5.48
			9/16	14	6ft	1.82
			3/4	19	10ft	3.04
			1	25	5ft	1.53
	1/4	6	5/8	16	18in	0.46
	7/16	11	7/16	11	22ft	6.70
			3/4	19	6in	0.16
			1 1/2	38	12ft	3.65

WOOD	THICKNESS in	mm	WIDTH in	mm	LENGTH ft/in	m
Lime	1/2	13	1/2	13	3ft	0.92
			3/4	19	18in	0.46
	5/8	16	5/8	16	7ft	2.14
	3/4	19	3/4	19	12in	0.31
			1 3/4	45	6ft	1.82
Mahogany	1/16	1.6	1/16	1.6	20ft	6.09
			1/8	3	18in	0.46
			13/16	21	4ft	1.22
			1 1/16	27	4in	0.10
	3/32	2.5	3/16	5	30in	0.76
	1/4	6	1/4	6	3ft	0.92
	3/4	19	3/4	19	4ft	1.22

WOOD	THICKNESS in	mm	AREA sq ft	sq m
Birch-plywood	3/8	9.0	30	2.8
	1/4	6.0	15	1.4
	1/8	3.0	2	0.18
	1/16	1.5	1	0.09

tool scribe planking ½in (13mm) wide, lengthwise on the top face of the upper floor E. (All the other floors will be finished with stripwood or tile paper.)

ELECTRIFICATION

Some of the wiring is best done now, before the carcase is assembled.

Mark the positions for the landing and drawing-room lights on the underside of the top floor 7⅝in (194mm) from the back, and 19⁵⁄₁₆in (491mm) and 7¾in (197mm) respectively from the right-hand end.

Apply Cir-Kit tape from each light position to the back of the floor plus 2in (51mm) extra, which is doubled back on itself to form a flap 1in (25mm) long.

Cut two notches in the back edge of the floor, ¾in (19mm) wide and ¹⁄₁₆in (1·5mm) deep, centred on the tapes, so that the flaps can be folded upwards and the floor butted against the back wall without damage.

Fit a Cir-Kit CK800 canopy pad at each light position. Apply tape on the inside face of the back panel, running from the top to the upper edge of the rebate at the bottom, parallel to, and ½in (13mm) to the right of the left-hand groove. Hammer a brass brad into each conductor strip ½in (13mm) above the rebate at the bottom.

Mark the position of the upper faces of both top

Fig 18   *Patterns for the lower section carcase panels*

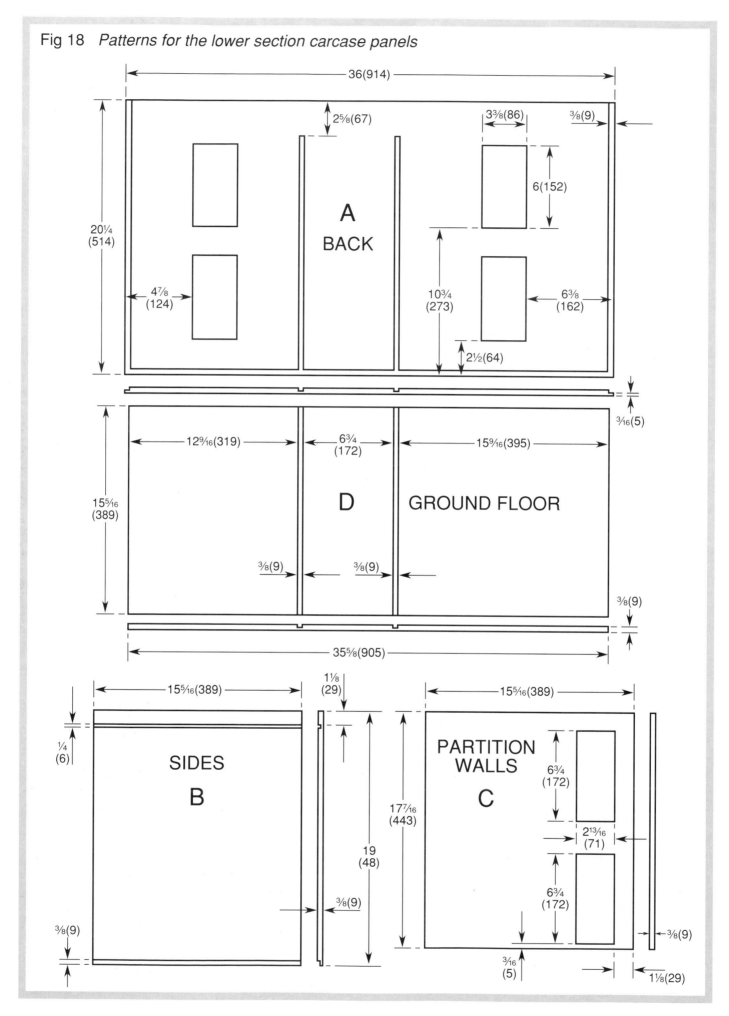

Fig 19 *Patterns for the first- and top-floor sections*

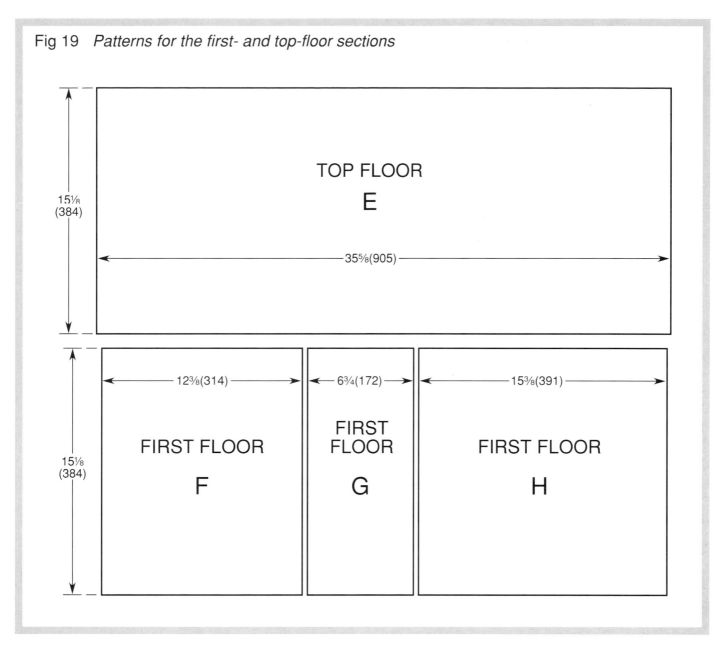

and first floors on the back panel and apply a horizontal tape for the full width of the back, in each position, with the lower edge of the tape just above the line, *having first* glued a small fillet of wood ¾in (19mm) wide, ³⁄₁₆in (5mm) deep and ⅝in (16mm) long into each groove, as a support where the tape crosses.

Connect both horizontal tapes to the vertical tape with brass brads. The upper conductor strip of each horizontal tape should be connected to the left-hand conductor of the vertical tape, and the lower conductor of the horizontal tape to the right-hand side of the vertical tape. The remainder of the wiring will be completed after assembly.

TRIAL CARCASE ASSEMBLY
Assemble the carcase without glue using two or three screws in each joint line.

Start by fitting the back panel to the ground floor ensuring that the grooves in each line up. Fit the sides to the ground floor, and to the back panel.

Place the partitions in the floor grooves and mark their back edges where they meet the fillets in the back grooves, behind the tape. A notch ³⁄₁₆in (5mm) deep is cut from each partition at this point so that the partitions can engage with the back panel.

Fit the upper floor between the two side grooves and butting the back wall. Note that the tape flaps when bent upwards can later be connected to the horizontal tape run. Mark a pencil line all round the

OVERLEAF
Unfurnished interior of the Georgian House, showing the removable stairs and landing

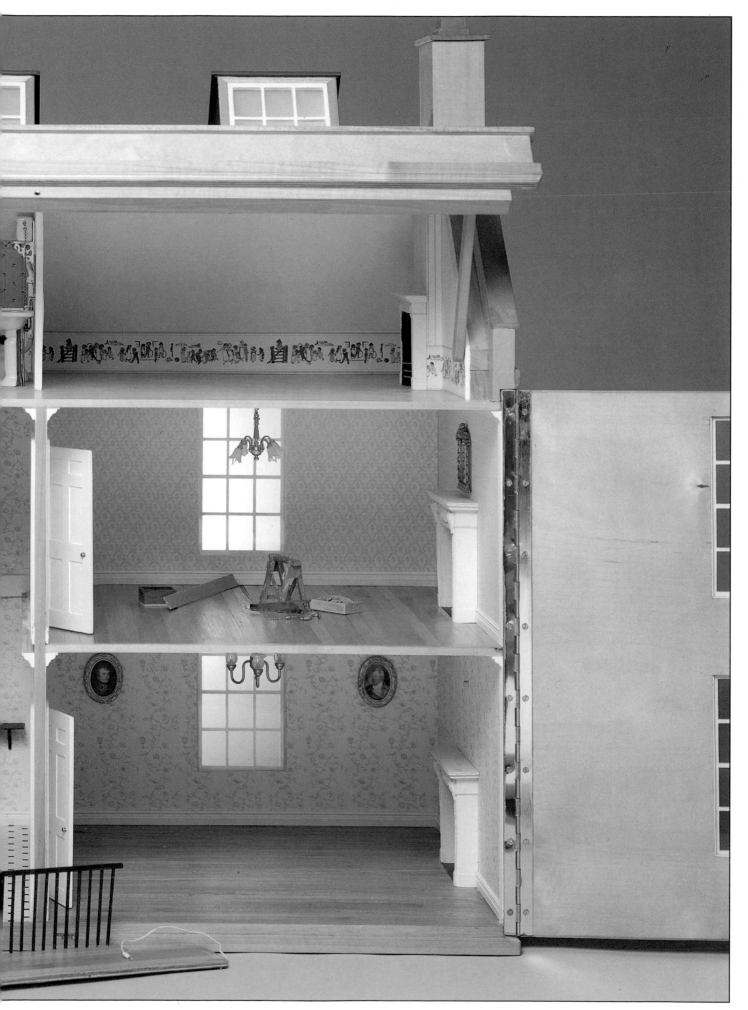

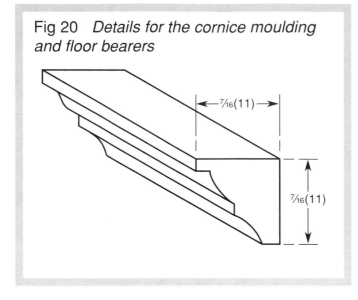

Fig 20 *Details for the cornice moulding and floor bearers*

inside of the carcase, below the top floor. Using a 9in (229mm) plywood spacer, mark the position of the lower face of the first floors on all the inside faces of the carcase.

CORNICE AND FLOOR BEARERS

Referring to Fig 20, make sufficient cornice moulding to fit right round the inside of the carcase below each floor. The cornice at the lower level acts as a bearer for the first floors, but is purely decorative when fitted below the upper floor. Note that the cornice is omitted from the back of the centre section below the first floor, but fitted for 5in only (127mm) from the front of the left-hand wall; this will allow the stairs to be fitted.

All the corner joints should be mitred, and the cornice glued to the walls using contact adhesive, ensuring that all the top edges are level and just butting the pencil lines previously marked.

The section below the first floor on the left-hand side wall of the carcase (the kitchen), should have a gap 5⅝in (143mm) wide in the centre, but with mitres cut on the open ends — this will receive the chimney breast which will be made and fitted later. Dismantle the carcase and pin through the cornice into the walls, to back up the glue joint. To avoid the pins breaking through to the outside, they should be cut shorter where necessary.

INTERNAL DOORS AND FRAMES

Following the method described in Chapter 1 and the pattern in Fig 21, make and fit the four internal doors, together with their frames and architraves. This is more easily done while the partitions are separated from the carcase. Note that all the doors are hung with their hinged side towards the back of the house, and open from the hall or landing into the adjacent rooms. Do not yet fix the doors.

FLOOR AND PARTITION EDGES

Glue a strip of lime ⅛in (3mm) thick and a little over ⅜in (10mm) wide to the front edge of the ground floor. Glue a similar strip to the front edge of both partitions, leaving ³⁄₁₆in (5mm) uncovered at the bottom. A strip ⅛in (3mm) thick and a little over ¼in (6mm) wide is glued to the front edges of the top and first floors. Plane these strips flush with the faces of the plywood once the glue has set. Do not apply edging to the carcase sides.

SIDES

The front edges of the carcase sides need thickening before the hinges for the front panel are screwed to them. Lime ½in × ⅛in (13 × 3mm) should be glued to the inside front edges of the side panels below the cornice mouldings. Leave a ¼in (6mm) gap below the upper section for the first floor, and stop the lower section at the rebate for the ground floor.

FINAL CARCASE ASSEMBLY

Re-assemble the carcase with glue and screws, adding panel pins at 2in (51mm) centres. Take care that the Cir-Kit tape flaps on the top floor are bent upwards. The top floor rests on top of the partitions; check that these are square with the back panel and evenly spaced 6¾in (172mm) apart at top and bottom. Fasten the top edges by pinning through the top floor. The first floors are not fixed and should be removed for further work.

BASE FRAME

When the glue has set, a light framework of lime 1½in (38mm) wide and ⁷⁄₁₆in (11mm) deep should be glued and screwed to the underside of the carcase with its outer edge flush with the outside face of both side and back panels. At the front it should project ⅝in (16mm) beyond the ground floor. A further piece should be fitted centrally from front to back between those already placed.

GABLES AND CHIMNEYS

From the patterns in Fig 22, cut two gable ends A, four inner gables B, four chimney sides C, and two chimney ends D, all in ⅜in (9mm) thick plywood.

This model has a small fireplace, made from a Phoenix kit, in the attic bedroom. Unlike the other fireplaces used, this one has a projection at the back and needs a cutout in the chimney. The chimney end D to be used at the left-hand end must therefore have a cutout 1½in (38mm) wide and 2¼in (57mm) high, centrally at the bottom.

Assembly Assemble the chimneys on the inside faces of the gable ends, as shown in Fig 23, ensuring that each chimney extends 1⅛in (29mm) below the base of each gable end A. With the base of the gable

Fig 21   Constructing the internal doors and frames

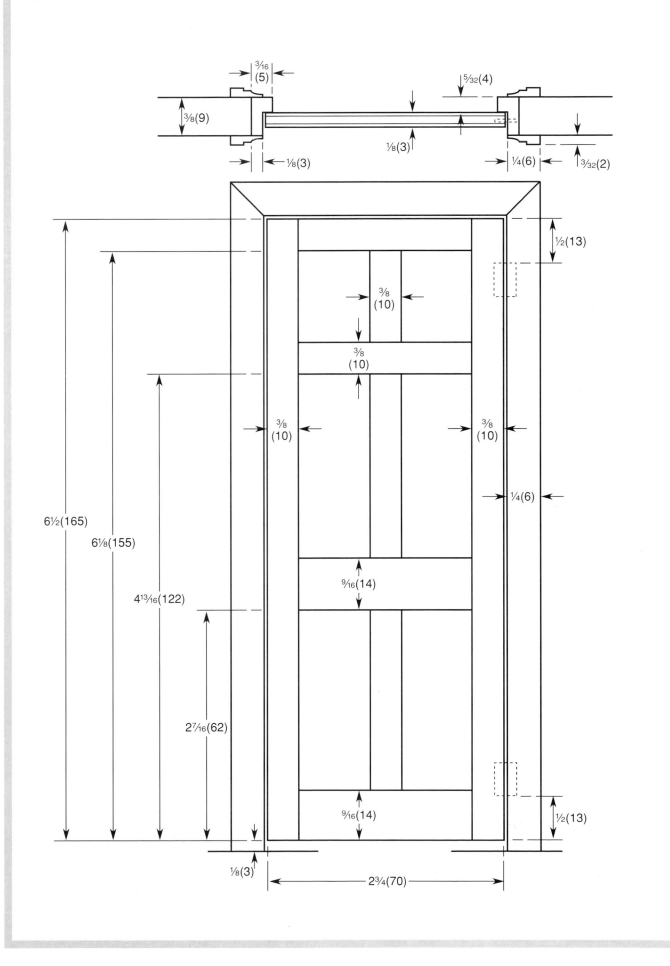

end resting on top of the lower carcase side, the chimney should reach down to the top of the floor. The back edges of the gable ends, which are extended by ³⁄₁₆in (5mm), locate in the side rebates at the top of the back panel. Glue the inner gables B to the inside faces of both outer gables, on each side of the chimney. The top profiles should match those on the outer gables, and the bases extend to floor level inside.

Fixing to Lower Carcase Fasten both gable/chimney assemblies to the lower carcase, by gluing and screwing through the 1⅛in (29mm) upstand of the lower carcase sides into the lower part of the inner gable, and also through the rebate in the back panel. The horizontal joint on the outside will later be concealed by a moulding.

RIDGE BEAM AND ROOF SUPPORTS

Cut two ridge supports from ¼in (6mm) plywood both 3½in (89mm) wide by 8½in (216mm) long, with their tops cut at 45° on each side of the centre, to conform with the roof slope. A notch ½ × ½in (13 × 13mm) should be cut in the top centre, square with the roof slope, to accept the ½ × ½in (13 × 13mm) ridge beam (see Fig 24). Temporarily screw these supports to the inside faces of the chimneys with their bases resting on top of the upper floor.

Cut a ridge beam ½in (13mm) square and 32¼in (819mm) long, to fit between the chimneys, resting in the notches. Drill ¹⁄₁₆in (2mm) diameter holes through the ridge beam, from the centre of one face to the centre of an adjacent face, in three positions: 7⅛in (181mm) and 17½in (445mm) from the right-hand end, and 5½in (140mm) from the left-hand end. A groove ⅛in (3mm) wide and ⅛in (3mm) deep should be cut on the back face, connecting these three holes, and extending to the right-hand end. (These holes will later have lighting wires threaded through, to be run in the groove to a connection at the top of the right-hand ridge support.)

Cut two eaves supports from lime 1¹¹⁄₁₆ × ¾in (43 × 19mm), each 34½in (876mm) long. Bevel one ¾in (19mm) face of each to 45° (see Fig 25). Put one aside for later use on the front roof, and fit the other along the inside of the back panel above the floor, to fit snugly between the inner faces of the gables at each end, with the high side of the bevel inwards, so that the slope conforms with that of the roof.

Busy in the kitchen — 'rhubarb pie'

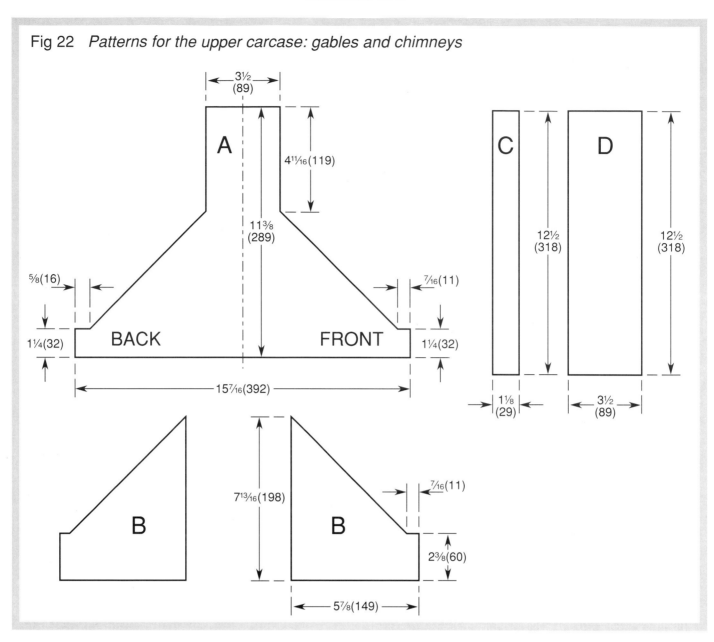

Fig 22 *Patterns for the upper carcase: gables and chimneys*

Mark where the tape flaps come up through the back edge of the floor, and also mark the point directly above the centre of each of the two lower carcase partitions.

Remove the eaves support and to accommodate the tapes, cut out the bottom edge to a height of 1in (25mm) extending ¾in (19mm) either side of the tapes, and additionally 1in (25mm) high and 1in (25mm) wide at the right-hand end. (This provides access to the upper horizontal tape on the back wall for connection of the floor tapes and the attic lights.) Now cut two ¼in (6mm) wide grooves ⅛in (3mm) deep vertically on the inside face, centred over the lower partitions, to locate the attic partitions. Temporarily replace the eaves support.

Cut four side roof supports from ⅛in (3mm) plywood, 5⅛in (130mm) wide and 6¾in (172mm) high, to fit against the inside faces of the gables at

the front and back of the chimneys. The tops should be cut at 45° to line up with the slope on the ridge support. Assemble them in handed pairs with a backing framework of ⅝in (16mm) square lime (see Fig 26). Place them in position against the inside of the gables with the ⅛in (3mm) plywood face outwards.

Check that the top edges of all three components (ridge, side, and eaves supports) form a straight line from ridge to eaves, and adjust if necessary. They can now be permanently fastened with glue and screws or veneer pins. The eaves support should be fastened with four screws through the back wall from the outside at a level just below that of the horizontal joint between the gables and lower carcase sides, so that a moulding can later cover the screw holes. The side supports are pinned in place from the outside, taking care not to dent the surface

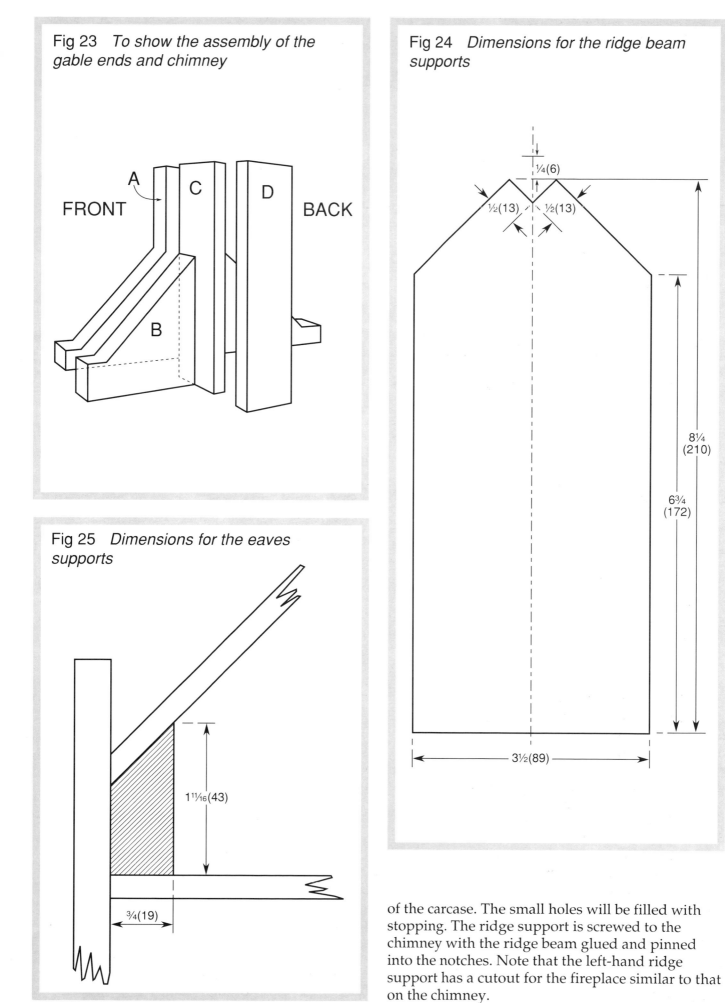

Fig 23 *To show the assembly of the gable ends and chimney*

FRONT   A   C   D   BACK

B

Fig 24 *Dimensions for the ridge beam supports*

¼(6)

½(13)   ½(13)

8¼ (210)

6¾ (172)

3½(89)

Fig 25 *Dimensions for the eaves supports*

1¹¹⁄₁₆(43)

¾(19)

of the carcase. The small holes will be filled with stopping. The ridge support is screwed to the chimney with the ridge beam glued and pinned into the notches. Note that the left-hand ridge support has a cutout for the fireplace similar to that on the chimney.

49

FURTHER ELECTRIFICATION

Before proceeding further, the wiring can be extended while still reasonably accessible. Connect the tape flaps from the upper floor to the horizontal tape, with brass brads. Using a similar connection, extend the horizontal tape at the right-hand end across the roof side-support panel and up the face of the ridge support to a point just behind the ridge beam. Insert a brad into each conductor strip at the top, close to the ⅛in (3mm) groove in the back of the ridge beam. Now extend the tape in the main bedroom (first floor, left-hand side) along the left-hand side wall for 12in (305mm) and from this run two further tapes 7in (178mm) apart, and inset equally from the front and back of the wall, vertically to a point 6in (152mm) above floor level. Remember to brad each connection, and also the tops of the vertical tapes.

ATTIC PARTITIONS

Cut two partitions from ¼in (6mm) plywood 10¼in (260mm) wide and 8½in (216mm) long, to the pattern in Fig 27, noting that ⅛in (3mm) of the back edges will be recessed into the vertical grooves in the eaves support, and that the tops are notched to fit under the ridge beam. Mark the bottom edges of the partitions 1in (25mm) in from front and back, with a corresponding mark on the floor. Set the partitions square with the back wall then mark the floor along both sides of the bases. Holes ³⁄₃₂in (2mm) in diameter can now be drilled centrally between these lines to a depth of ³⁄₁₆in (5mm) into the floor, with corresponding holes drilled into the bottoms of the partitions. Bamboo dowels ³⁄₃₂in (2mm) in diameter, cut from barbecue skewers, are used to locate the partitions on the floor. A drawplate will be useful here to skim the dowel to the correct diameter. If you do not have one, adjust the hole size to suit the size of dowel available. Check that the sloping edges at the top conform with the line between the ridge and eaves before gluing in place.

BACK ROOF

Cut two roof panels from ¼in (6mm) plywood, both 34½in (876mm) long, one 11¼in (286mm) deep for the front, and the other 11in (279mm) deep for the back. A little extra has been allowed on the depth for trimming at the ridge and eaves. Lay the back panel between the gables with its top edge against the backs of the chimneys, and mark the width and

Main bedroom of the Georgian House

Fig 26 *Dimensions for the side roof supports*

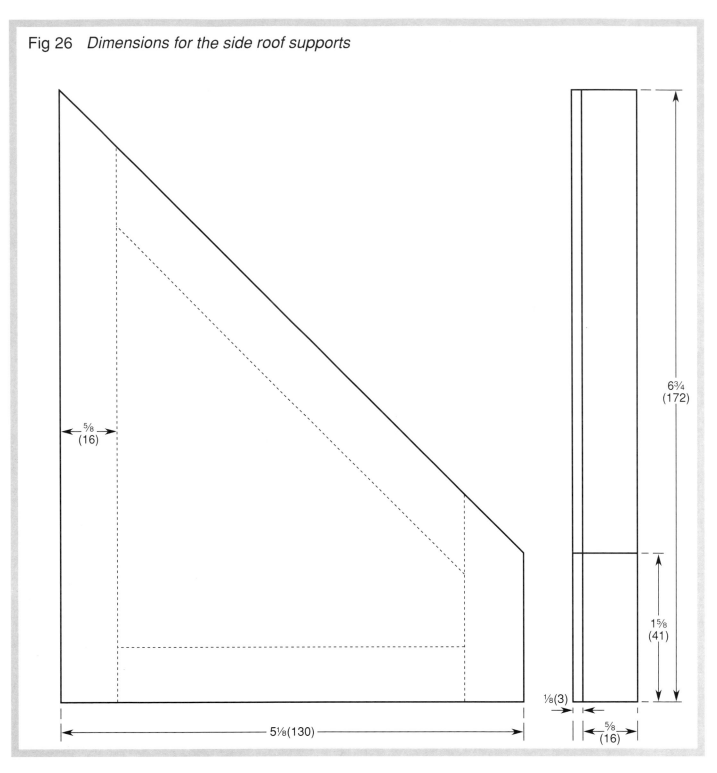

depth of the cutouts required to fit round the insides and backs of the chimneys, and allow the top edge to overlap the ridge beam. The cutouts should be approximately 1⅛in (29mm) wide and 2½in (64mm) deep, with the edges that butt the backs of the chimneys bevelled to 45°. Plane the top edge of the panel fair with the ridge beam, and plane the bottom at 45° to drop on to the eaves support inside the back of the carcase. Cut a shallow rebate ½in (13mm) wide and 1/32in (1mm) deep along the top edge of the upper face of the roof. Extend this to ⅛in (3mm) deep and ⅛in (3mm)

wide at the top edge. This rebate will later take the barrel and back flap of the piano hinge (used upside down) which will pivot the front roof (see Fig 28). The back roof can now be glued and pinned to the ridge beam and eaves and side supports. Glue alone will suffice between the roof and the attic partitions, to avoid splitting the plywood.

FRONT ROOF
Fit the front roof panel in the same way as the back, with its top edge overlapping the back roof. Cut a rebate ½in (13mm) wide and 1/32in (1mm) deep, this

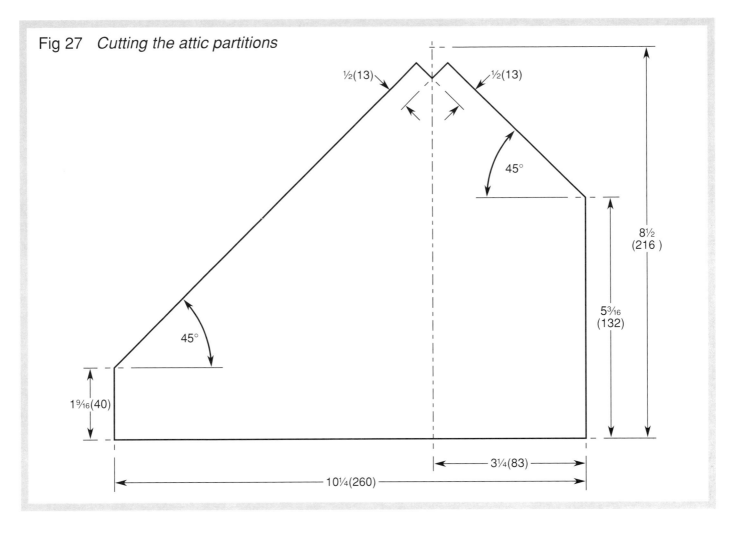

Fig 27 *Cutting the attic partitions*

½(13)   ½(13)

45°

45°

8½ (216)

5³⁄₁₆ (132)

1⁹⁄₁₆(40)

3¼(83)

10¼(260)

time on the underside of the top edge, and screw on a 32¼in (819mm) length of piano hinge, 1in (25mm) wide when fully opened. Replace the roof with the loose hinge flap in the rebate at the top of the back roof (see Fig 28) and temporarily fix with three screws (one at each end and one in the middle). Note that the barrel of the hinge is underneath and fits in the ⅛in (3mm) rebate at the top edge of the back roof; also that the back flap of the hinge must be recountersunk as the screws will enter from the plain face. Trim the front roof edges and cutouts so that the front roof pivots freely — it will need about ⅟₃₂in (1mm) clearance at the sides and round the chimneys.

Now, take the other bevelled eaves support and rest this on the floor with its high side inwards and butted against the front edge of the side roof support panel at each end. Lower the roof on to the eaves support and check that it bears evenly on both this and the side supports. Adjust if necessary and then fasten the roof to the eaves support with glue and screws (Fig 29). When the glue has set, plane the roof overhang flush with the outside face of the eaves support. The support is now free to lift with the roof, and will later have the front parapet added to its outside face.

DORMER WINDOW CARCASES
Referring to Fig 30, make three dormer window carcases from ⅜in (9mm) plywood, rebated at the front for both window and glazing. Remove the roof and mark the dormer openings on to it, as shown in Figs 31 and 32. Cut these openings and glue and screw the dormer carcases to the roof.

Fig 28 *To show the rebate and hinge assembly of the lifting front roof*

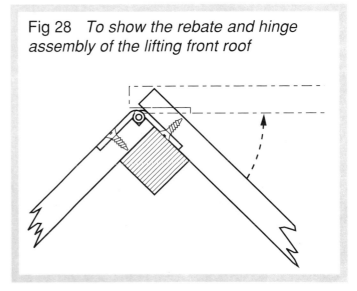

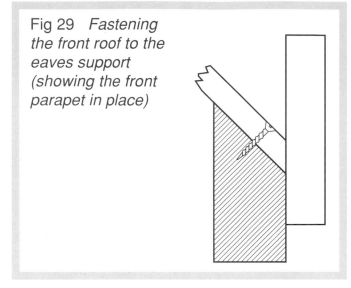

Fig 29 *Fastening the front roof to the eaves support (showing the front parapet in place)*

³⁄₁₆in (5mm) length of the ground-floor edging at each side where it crosses the bottom of the side panels. Cut two lengths of piano hinge to fit exactly from top to bottom of the front panels, and screw these in place in the rebates. Temporarily hang the front panels with three screws into the edge of each side panel. Check for even closing, and if necessary adjust the screw positions and the thickness of the edging on the floors and partitions.

When the glue is dry, clean up the inside of the openings with a sanding plate. Make three dormer roofs from ⅛in (3mm) plywood, 4¼in (108mm) wide and 4⅛in (105mm) deep, and bevel the back edges to fit the roof. Glue these on top of the dormer carcases with ⅛in (3mm) overhang at the front and sides.

FRONT PANELS

Cut the front panels as one piece from the pattern in Fig 32. Mark and cut out the window and door openings first, then cut the panel in two at the break line (the loss in length — about ⅛in (3mm) — caused by the saw-cut, will be restored by an edging strip). Plane the bottom edges of both sections, and also the vertical edges where the panels will meet, so that they are square to each other. Glue an edging strip of ⅜ × ¹⁄₁₆in (10 × 1·5mm) lime to each of these edges with contact adhesive, and plane them flush on both the front and back faces of the panels. Do not yet edge the outer ends or the top. Place the two sections against the front of the carcase, with the two inner edges butting each other exactly over the centre of the right-hand partition, and the bottom edges resting on the base frame projection. Mark the back of both panels at the ends where they overhang the carcase front, and also on the top, ⁵⁄₁₆in (8mm) above the top floor. Plane the panels back to these marks and then glue a ⅜ × ¹⁄₁₆in (10 × 1·5mm) lime edging strip to the top of both sections. The outer edges will be left until the hinges and quoins are fitted.

Cut a ½ × ¹⁄₃₂in (13 × 1mm) rebate for the hinge on the back of each panel at the outer edge. Remove a

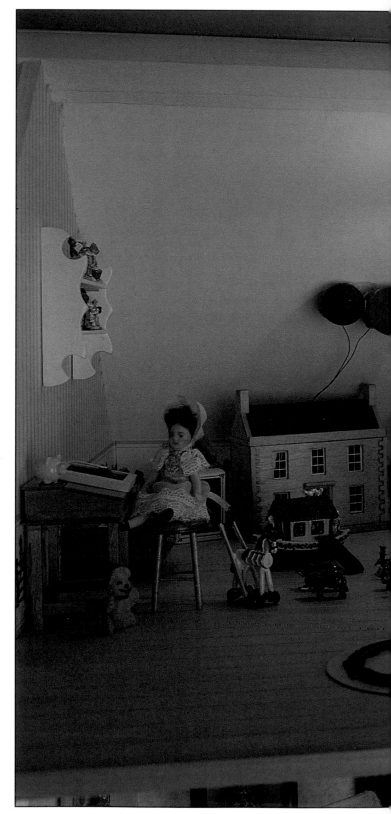

The Nursery of the Georgian House

FRONT PARAPET

Cut this from ⅜in (9mm) plywood, 35⅞in (911mm) long and 2in (51mm) wide. Edge both ends with ¹⁄₁₆in (1·5mm) lime to bring its length to 36in (915mm). Lay the parapet along the top of the front panels with its back against the outer face of the front roof and eaves support, and the ends flush with the outer faces of both gables. Glue and screw the parapet to the roof edge and eaves support (see

Fig 33). The four screws required should be ⅜in (10mm) above the bottom of the parapet where they will later be hidden by a moulding. Note that the bottom of the parapet is ⅜in (10mm) above the bottom of the eaves support.

FRONT ROOF STRUTS

Two struts are now made from ⅝ × ¼in (16 × 6mm) lime, each 7in (178mm) long. Measure off ⅜in

(10mm) from one end only of each strut, and drill a ⅛in (3mm) diameter hole at this point. These ends should be rounded, and a screw inserted through the hole into the lower front of the side roof support where this is backed by the lime framework. The other end of each strut is cut at an angle so that it lies snugly against the front edge of the chimney when folded back. The top edge of the strut, when thus folded, should be slightly below the top edge of the side roof support. When pivoted upwards these struts support the roof in the open position.

CHIMNEY-FACE VENEER
Both the front and back faces of the chimneys show end-grain plywood, which must be covered. Cut four pieces of lime 1⅞ × 1/32in (48 × 1mm), each 5¾in (146mm) long, and glue these to the chimney faces reaching to the top of the side roof supports at the front. A ¾in (19mm) wide notch must be cut from the outside edge of each to fit over the gable. The front roof should now be eased slightly where it meets the front face of the chimneys.

GABLE AND PARAPET COPING
Cut two pieces of lime 9/16in (14mm) wide, 3/16in (5mm) thick and 36⅜in (924mm) long. Glue one on top of the front parapet with a 3/16in (5mm)

overhang at each end, and at the front. The back edge should be flush with the inside of the parapet (see Fig 33). The other piece should be fitted similarly on top of the back panel where the additional height forms an integral parapet above floor level. Cut four pieces of lime 15/16in (24mm) wide, 3/16in (5mm) thick and 8¾in (222mm) long. Bevel one end of each piece at 45° and cut those ends off approximately ¾in (19mm) long, to fit on top of the gable steps behind the front and back coping. Trim to the exact length required, and then glue and pin them to the top of the gable step, flush on the inside edge, and with a 3/16in (5mm) overhang at the outer edge.

Bevel one end of each of the four remaining 8in (203mm) lengths to 45°. Place these ends on top of the coping just fitted and mark the other ends where they pass the chimney. Cut a further 45° bevel so that the coping will sit down on top of the gable. Glue and pin them in place on the gables to the front and back of each chimney with their inside edges flush and a 3/16in (5mm) overhang at the outside edges.

GABLE AND PARAPET MOULDING
Cut a 9ft (3m) length of lime ¾in (19mm) wide and 3/16in (5mm) thick. From the pattern in Fig 33 apply

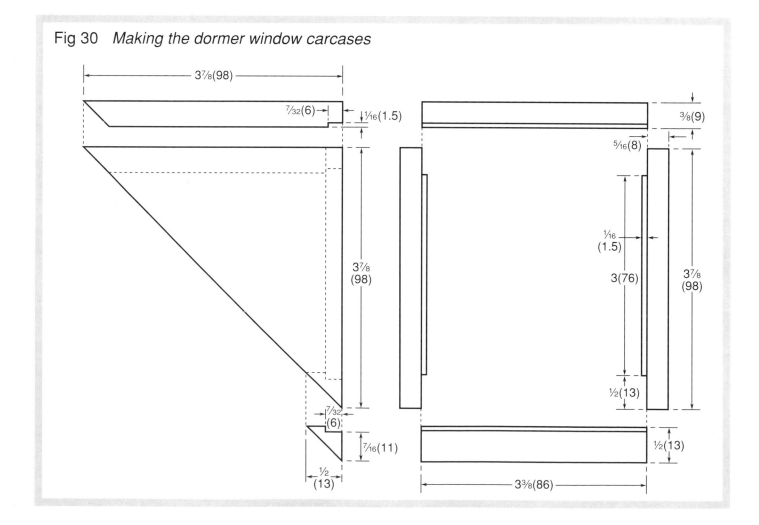

Fig 30 *Making the dormer window carcases*

Fig 31 *Measuring the roof cutout for the dormer windows*

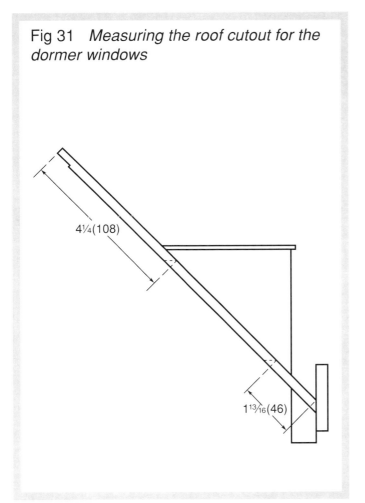

4¼(108)

1¹³⁄₁₆(46)

the moulding to one edge. Cut two pieces 36⅜in (924mm) long and mitre each end on the back face. Glue and pin one across the front parapet, with the moulded edge flush at the bottom, and with a ³⁄₁₆in (5mm) overhang at each end. Glue and pin the other across the back panel at the same level. Cut two further pieces 15³⁄₁₆in (386mm) long and mitre the opposite ends of each to make a handed pair with one end cut square, and one mitred. Glue and pin these along the side walls of the carcase from back to front at the same level as the front and back mouldings. Now cut a further handed pair ⁹⁄₁₆in (14mm) long with one mitred end, and one plain. Glue and pin these to the short return on either side of the front parapet.

QUOINS
Remove both front panels. Cut a 5ft (1·6m) length of ⅛in (3mm) plywood, ¾in (19mm) wide, and bevel both edges. Cut this into twenty-four pieces 1⅜in (35mm) long, and twenty-four pieces ¹¹⁄₁₆in (18mm) long. Bevel one end of each piece. Using contact adhesive, start from the bottom of the front panels and glue them alternately first long, then short, up each side (see Fig 34). The plain ends should be flush with the outer edges of the panels. Any overlap or shortfall at the top can be adjusted with a

Fig 32 *Pattern and measurements for the front panels of the house*

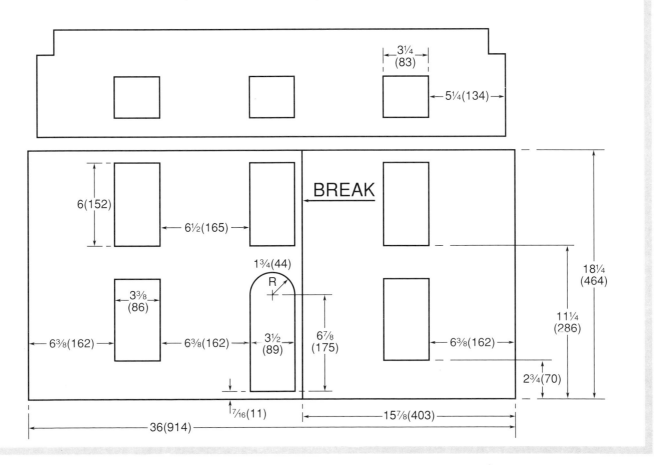

3¼ (83)

5¼(134)

6(152)

6½(165)

BREAK

1¾(44)
R

3⅜ (86)

3½ (89)

6⅞ (175)

6⅜(162)

6⅜(162)

6⅜(162)

18¼ (464)

11¼ (286)

2¾(70)

⁷⁄₁₆(11)

15⅞(403)

36(914)

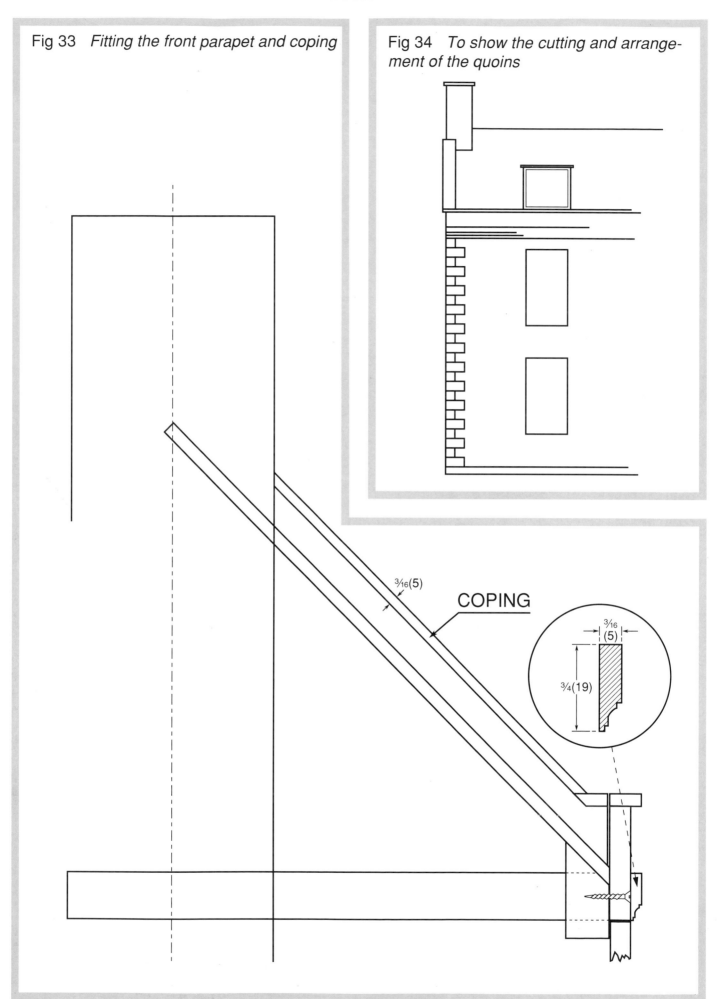

Fig 33   *Fitting the front parapet and coping*

Fig 34   *To show the cutting and arrangement of the quoins*

COPING

³⁄₁₆(5)

³⁄₁₆
(5)

³⁄₄(19)

wider or narrower top quoin on each side. If the finished house is to be varnished, take particular care to keep the adhesive within the bounds of the area to be covered by the quoins.

Glue lime edging to the right and left sides of the front panels ½in (13mm) wide and ¹⁄₁₆in (1·5mm) thick to cover both the ends of the quoins and the hinge barrels.

WINDOWS AND SURROUNDS
Following the method described in Chapter 1, and the patterns in Figs 35a and 35b, make nine large windows and three dormer windows. These should all then have two coats of Humbrol satin finish white acrylic paint before being fitted. On this house, no window linings are required. Clean up the insides of the window openings with a fine sandplate, and then with the same tool trim the outer edges of the windows so they are a good push fit in the openings. For the large window surrounds, make 13½ft (4·2m) of lime moulding to the pattern in Fig 35b, ⁵⁄₁₆in (8mm) across the face and ³⁄₁₆in (5mm) deep; and 42in (1·08m) of window sill from lime ⅜in (10mm) wide and ³⁄₁₆in (5mm) deep. This should have one face bevelled to leave ³⁄₁₆in (5mm) flat at the top, and the outer edge ⅛in (3mm) deep. Cut nine window sills 4⅝in (118mm) long, and glue them with their top edges flush with the bottoms of the window openings, and overlapping ⅝in (16mm) at each side. Cut the window surround, mitred at the top corners, to fit round the remaining three sides of each window, and rest on top of the window sills. The inside of the surround should overlap the window opening by about ¹⁄₆₄in (0·5mm). Glue in place. Do not glue the windows yet.

FRONT DOOR AND SURROUND
Referring to Figs 36 and 37, make the front door, jambs and header. Having first slotted the left-hand jamb (when viewed from the front) for the door hinges, glue the jambs and header into the door opening. The fanlight area will later be glazed with a semi-circular piece of 2mm glass or Glodex, with the glazing bars and surround cut as one piece from 0·04in (1mm) white plastic sheet and glued to the outside. Make the step, pillar bases, pillars and pediment from the patterns given in Fig 37, and glue these to the front panel. The inside edges of the pillars should be in line with the joint between the door jambs and the front panel; the outer edge of

PREVIOUS PAGE
Bathroom of the Georgian House

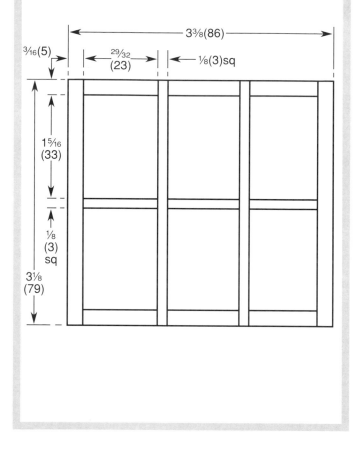

Fig 35a *Pattern for the dormer windows*

3⅜(86)

³⁄₁₆(5)

²⁹⁄₃₂ (23)

⅛(3)sq

1⁵⁄₁₆ (33)

⅛ (3) sq

3⅛ (79)

the right-hand pillar overhangs the panel by ³⁄₁₆in (5mm).

KITCHEN CHIMNEY BREAST
The kitchen range in this house has been made from a Phoenix kit; if any other make is to be used, the internal opening in the chimney breast must be adjusted accordingly. The shell is made from ⅜in (9mm) plywood, as shown in Fig 38, with a backing of ¹⁄₁₆in (1·5mm) plywood.

Cornice moulding is glued round the top edge, with the back edges mitred to fit the open ends of the cornice already fitted in the kitchen. There is a moulded facing of lime round the chimney breast opening, similar to that used on the parapet, but this time 1in (25mm) wide. A shelf is fitted above the facing, supported by four brackets. The inside of the opening has been covered with a blue and white tile paper. The drying rack is constructed from three lengths of ¹⁄₁₆in (1·5mm) brass rod fitted into end blocks of lime ⅛in (3mm) square and 1¼in (32mm) long; the rack is glued into the opening 4⅛in (105mm) above the floor.

FIRST FLOOR
Fit the three loose first-floor sections by sliding them into the carcase above the cornice/bearers; trim the front edges flush with the front of the carcase. The right- and left-hand sections should be

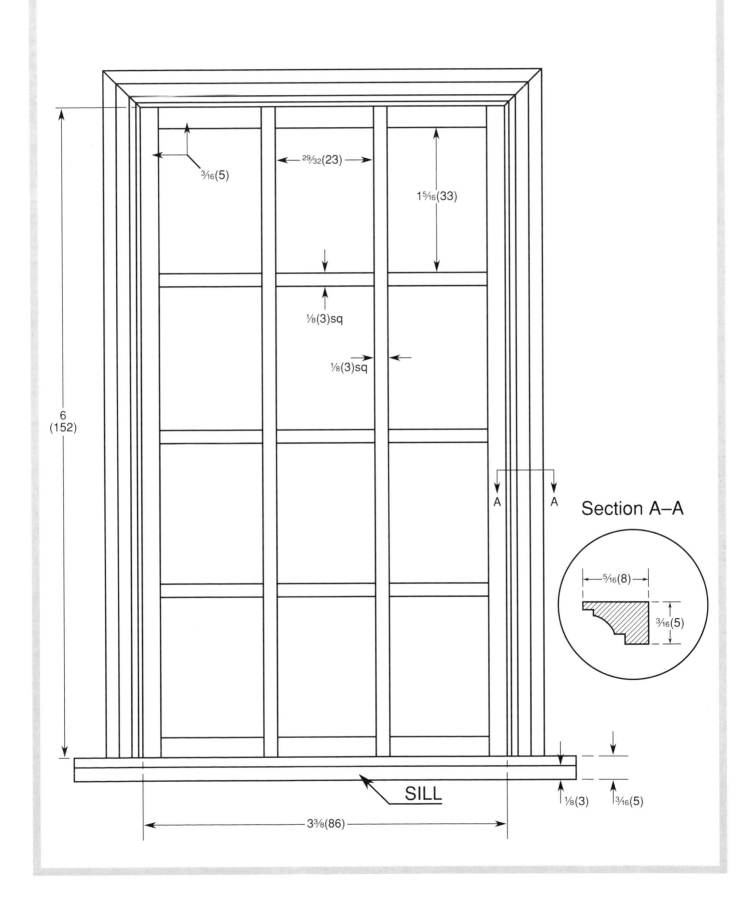

Fig 35b *Pattern and details for the main windows and surrounds*

Section A–A

a fairly tight fit between the side walls and partitions, but the centre section (which will remain portable) should have about ¹⁄₃₂in (1mm) lateral clearance. Do not yet glue in place, as holes will be required for the ceiling lights in the kitchen and dining-room.

Drill these ¹⁄₁₆in (2mm) in diameter, centrally in each section, 7½in (191mm) from the front. No hole is required on the landing floor. In this model, both the kitchen and dining-room have light fittings from Wood 'n' Wool (see List of Suppliers p80) with fixed bulbs, which therefore need to be easily removable in case of failure. The floors above both these rooms should each have a shallow groove ⁵⁄₈in (16mm) wide and ¹⁄₁₆in (2mm) deep, cut on the top surface from the hole to the back edge. Apply a length of Cir-Kit twin tape in each of these grooves, long enough to reach the back wall and to turn up for connection to the horizontal tape on the wall. Leave the backing strip on the tape for the last 2in (51mm). Brad each tape through the conductor strips, ½in (13mm) from the holes. Replace both floors in the carcase with glue at the edges, and if necessary pin them at the extreme edges into the cornice to ensure that the floor is held down; the heads of the pins should be left projecting so that they can be removed once the glue has set. The

floors will later be held down by the skirting. Remove the remaining backing strip from the tapes, and connect them to the horizontal tape. The landing floor is not glued so that both it and the staircase can be removed at any time for decoration.

STAIRWELL

Cut the stairwell opening from the landing floor (see Fig 39), and mark the position of the hall ceiling light on the underside in the centre, 3in (76 mm) back from the front edge. Starting at the back edge, apply Cir-Kit tape along the underside of the floor for 12½in (318mm), keeping 1⁵⁄₁₆in (33mm) inside, and parallel to, the long edge; then turn at right angles to finish at the light position, and fix the pad for a CK 800 canopy (Fig 39). Brad the back end of the tape just inside the floor edge. Fix a Cir-Kit 1003 socket to the vertical tape on the back wall, with its top 6³⁄₈in (162mm) above the ground floor.

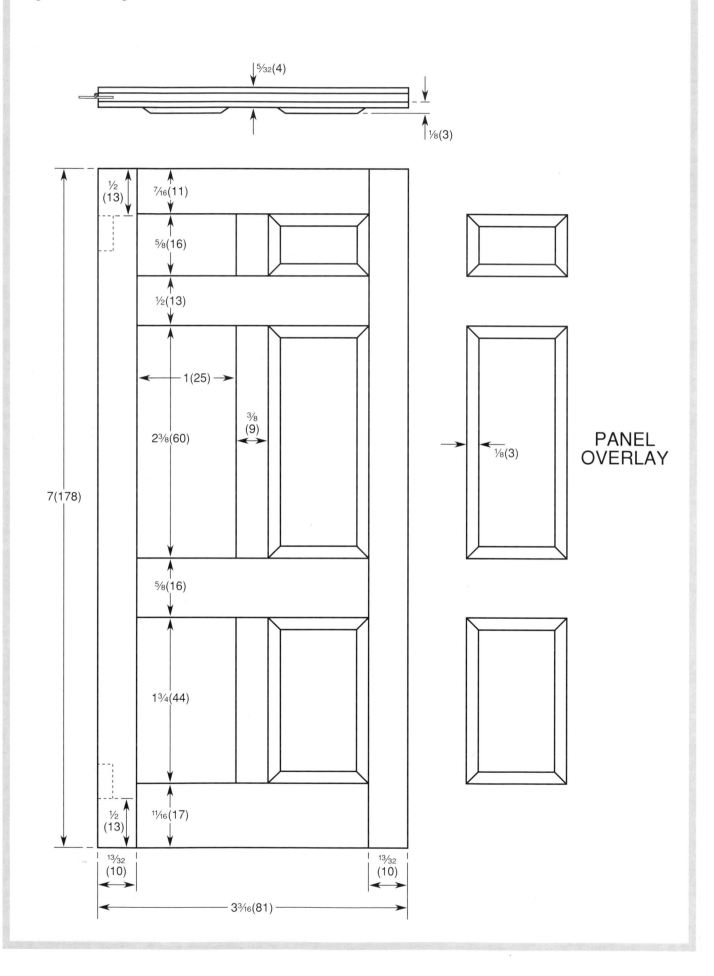

Fig 36 *Making the front door*

PANEL
OVERLAY

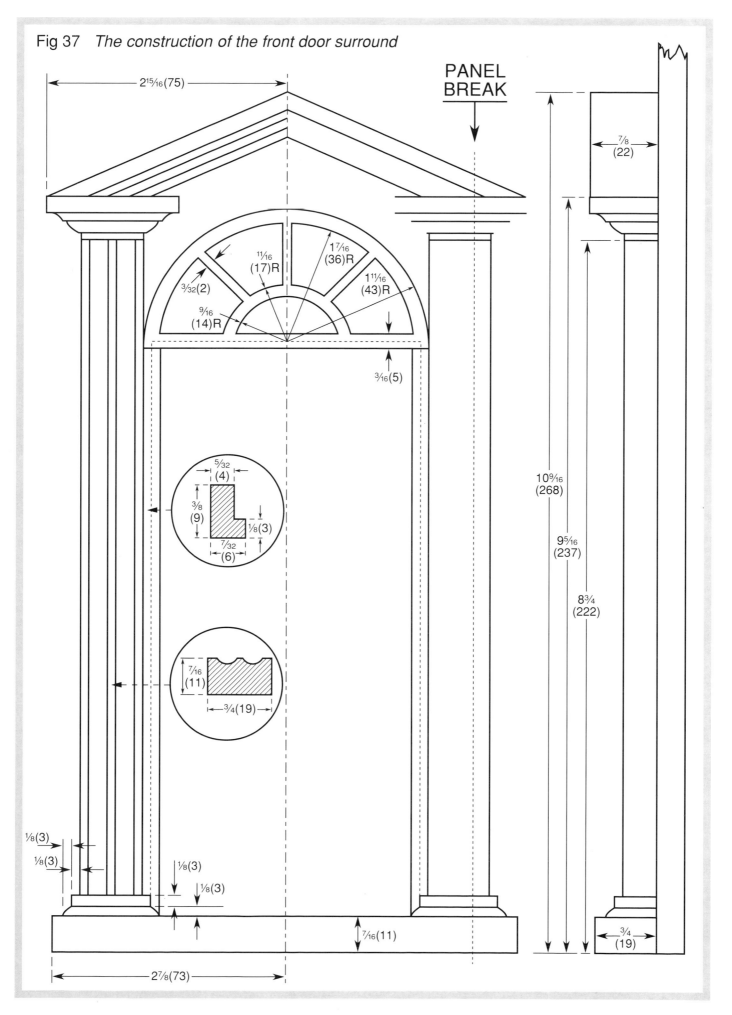

Fig 37   *The construction of the front door surround*

PANEL BREAK

2¹⁵⁄₁₆(75)

1⁷⁄₁₆ (36)R

¹¹⁄₁₆ (17)R

³⁄₃₂(2)

1¹¹⁄₁₆ (43)R

⁹⁄₁₆ (14)R

³⁄₁₆(5)

⁷⁄₈ (22)

5⁄₃₂ (4)

³⁄₈ (9)

⅛(3)

⁷⁄₃₂ (6)

10⁹⁄₁₆ (268)

9⁵⁄₁₆ (237)

8¾ (222)

⁷⁄₁₆ (11)

¾(19)

⅛(3)

⅛(3)

⅛(3)

⅛(3)

⁷⁄₁₆(11)

¾ (19)

2⅞(73)

STAIRCASE

Using the method described in Chapter 1 (p12), make the staircase in three sections to the dimensions shown in Figs 40 and 41. The main flight bearer is ¼in (6mm) plywood; all other parts are mahogany. To rise a total of 9¼in (235mm), from the top of the ground floor to the top of the first floor, in sixteen steps requires an individual step rise of ³⁷⁄₆₄in (15mm). As it is virtually impossible to maintain this tolerance over the length of the staircase, a rise of ⁹⁄₁₆in (14mm) has been adopted, ie, ½in (13mm) step plus ¹⁄₁₆in (2mm) tread. This will leave a ¼in (6mm) shortfall at the top, which will be corrected as construction proceeds. Start by making the main flight (steps 2 to 13 inclusive; no 1 is a bullnose step), but do not yet add the treads. Smooth both sides, so that the steps are flush with the plywood bearer. Place this assembly against the left-hand wall of the hall, with the bottom step (no 2) resting on the ground floor, and the back of no 13 (which is the quarter landing) against the back wall. Then measure the total rise needed to reach from step no 13 to the top of the first floor, deducting ¹⁄₁₆in (2mm) for each tread, to be fitted later. Divide this measurement between the four remaining steps required (nos 1,14,15,16). Although each of these should be nominally ⁹⁄₁₆in (14mm), these four can be adjusted by plus or minus ¹⁄₁₆in (2mm), to compensate for any shortfall, without it being noticeable. Before proceeding further, paint the open side of both steps and bearer with three coats of Humbrol white acrylic, and varnish the front faces of all steps (satin finish). Next make the bullnose step (no 1) and, using a fretsaw and then a needle file, cut the hole for the lower newel post. Glue and pin this step under no 2.

Cut the skirting from ¹⁄₁₆in (1·5mm) ply to the profile ABCDEFGH (Fig 40), and glue this to the wall side of the staircase, having first put a slight chamfer on the stair side of the top edge. The open side of the staircase can now be notched at steps nos 12 and 13, for the next newel post. Replace the stairs in the hall and mark a pencil line on the back wall below step no 13. Remove the stairs and glue and pin a 2½in (64mm) length of ¼in (6mm) square lime to the back wall below this line, to act as a bearer for the quarter landing (no 13). Following the plan in Fig 41, steps 14 to 16 can now be assembled. No 16 should be notched to receive the upper newel post, and the bottom front edge of no 14 cut to fit no 13, and its newel post. After painting and

Dining-room of the Georgian House

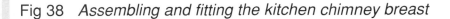

Fig 38 *Assembling and fitting the kitchen chimney breast*

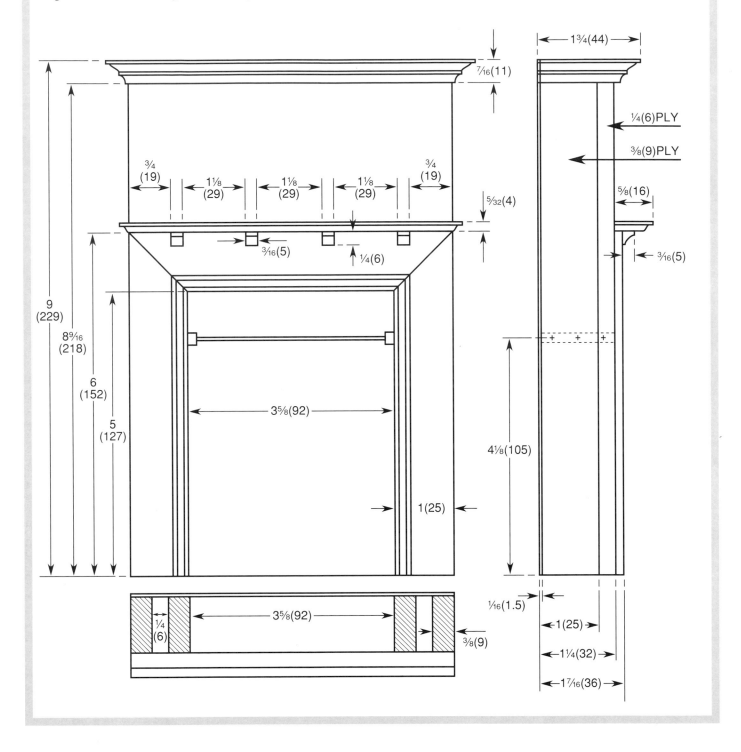

varnishing, a further 1·5mm skirting JKLMNOPQR (Fig 41) should be glued to the back, noting that it extends 2in (51mm) beyond step no 16 and 2½in (64mm) beyond no 14. Glue a ¹⁄₁₆in (1·5mm) mahogany tread, ¹³⁄₁₆in (21mm) wide and 2¹¹⁄₁₆in (69mm) long, to the top of each step *except* nos 1 and 13; the back edge of each tread should be recessed under the step above, with ¹⁄₁₆in (1·5mm) nosing projecting at both the front and open side. The tread for no 13 should be 2½in (64mm) wide and 2¹¹⁄₁₆in (68mm) deep. The tread for the bullnose

step is cut to the pattern in Fig 40, from a piece of ¹⁄₁₆in (1·5mm) mahogany, 3¹⁄₁₆in (78mm) long and 1¹⁄₁₆in (27mm) wide. Both are notched where the newel posts will fit. Make the newel posts ¼in (6mm) square. Glue and pin the newel posts to the stairs, and when set, varnish both the posts and the stair treads.

OVERLEAF *Drawing-room of the Georgian House*

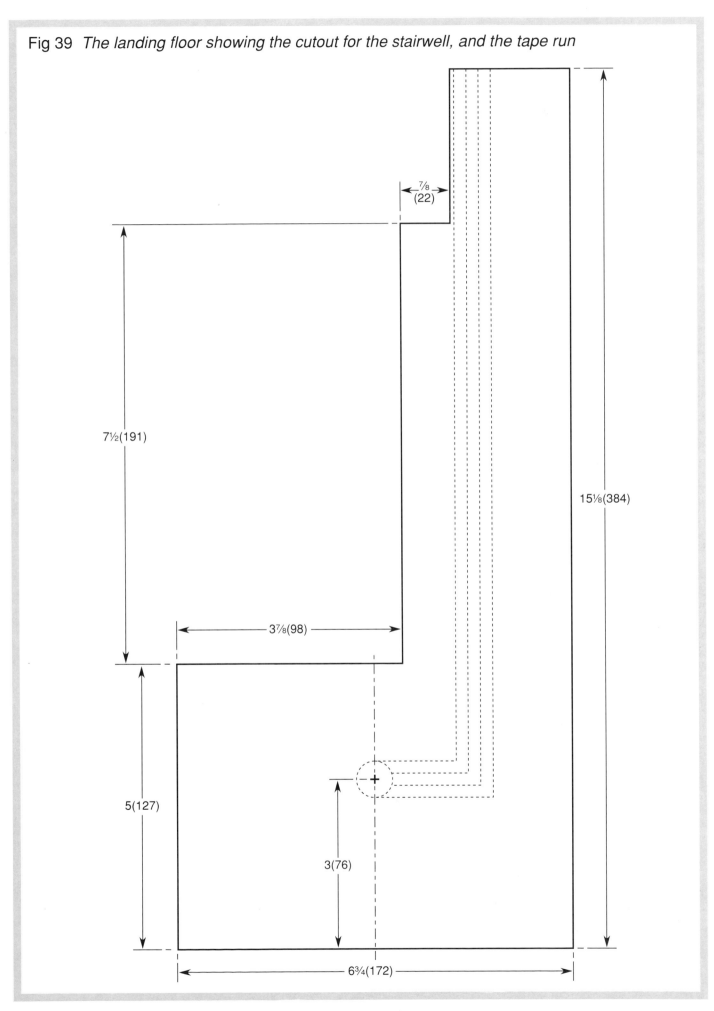

Fig 39 *The landing floor showing the cutout for the stairwell, and the tape run*

Fig 40 *Detailed plan for the lower staircase*

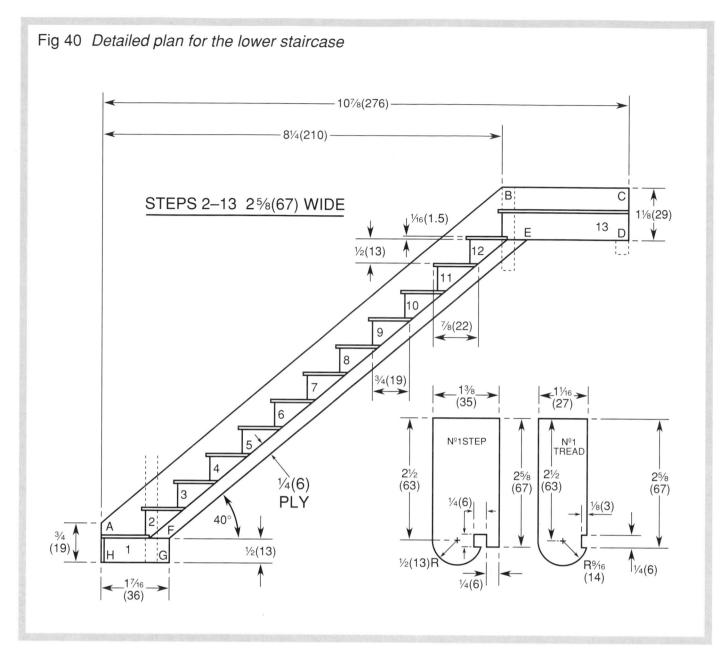

Handrail Each tread should now have two holes drilled at $^{11}/_{32}$in (9mm) centres to a depth of $^1/_8$in (3mm) as shown in Fig 42, $^3/_{16}$in (5mm) inside the edge of the side nosing, to receive the balusters. Make the handrail from three lengths of mahogany, one $^1/_8 \times ^1/_{16}$in (3×1.5mm) sandwiched between two further lengths $^3/_{16} \times ^3/_{32}$in (5×2.5mm) — see enlarged detail in Fig 42. Note that this leaves a channel on the underside of the handrail to receive the angled tops of the balusters. Once the handrail has been cut to fit between the newel posts, it should have a $^1/_4$in (6mm) length of $^1/_{16}$in (1.5mm) square mahogany glued into the channel at each end. The ends can then be drilled for $^1/_{16}$in (1.5mm) diameter dowel to make the joint between rail and post. The hole in the lower post should go right through so that the dowel can be inserted from the outside; however, do not glue yet. Assemble the top flight to the lower flight with glue, pinning through

the plywood bearer into the edge of step no 13, and also through the lower part of the upper skirting into the back of the same step. Referring to Fig 42, cut the balusters to length, with the tops angled to fit in the handrail channel. Round the bottom ends for a length of $^1/_8$in (3mm) either with a drawplate or a file to give a snug fit. Glue and peg the upper end of the lower handrail to the newel post at step. 13, and then glue the balusters into the handrail and the stair treads. Finally glue the lower end of the handrail and peg it in place with a dowel from the outside of the lower newel post. Repeat this for the upper flight. After varnishing both the handrails and balusters, the staircase is complete.

FLOORBOARDS

First glue wood fillets $^3/_8$in (9mm) wide and $^7/_{32}$in (6mm) thick into the grooves left in the ground-floor door openings. Cut approximately 125ft (38m)

Fig 41 *Detailed plan for the upper staircase*

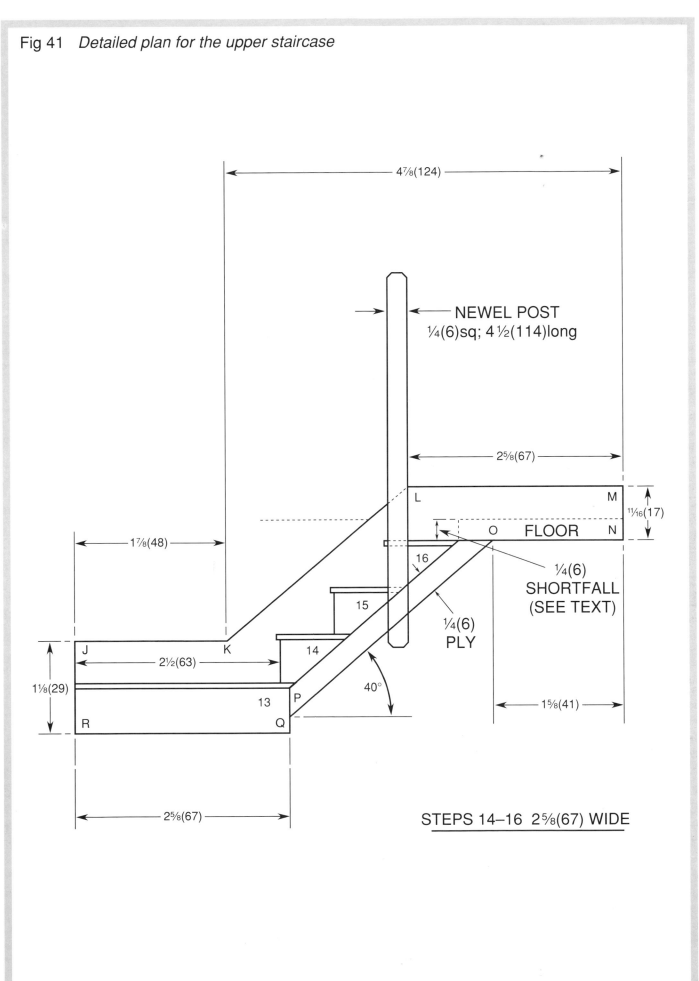

NEWEL POST
¼(6)sq; 4½(114)long

4⅞(124)

2⅝(67)

L   M

FLOOR

O   N

¹¹⁄₁₆(17)

¼(6)
SHORTFALL
(SEE TEXT)

1⅞(48)

16

15

14

¼(6)
PLY

40°

1⅝(41)

J   K

2½(63)

1⅛(29)

13   P

R   Q

2⅝(67)

STEPS 14–16 2⅝(67) WIDE

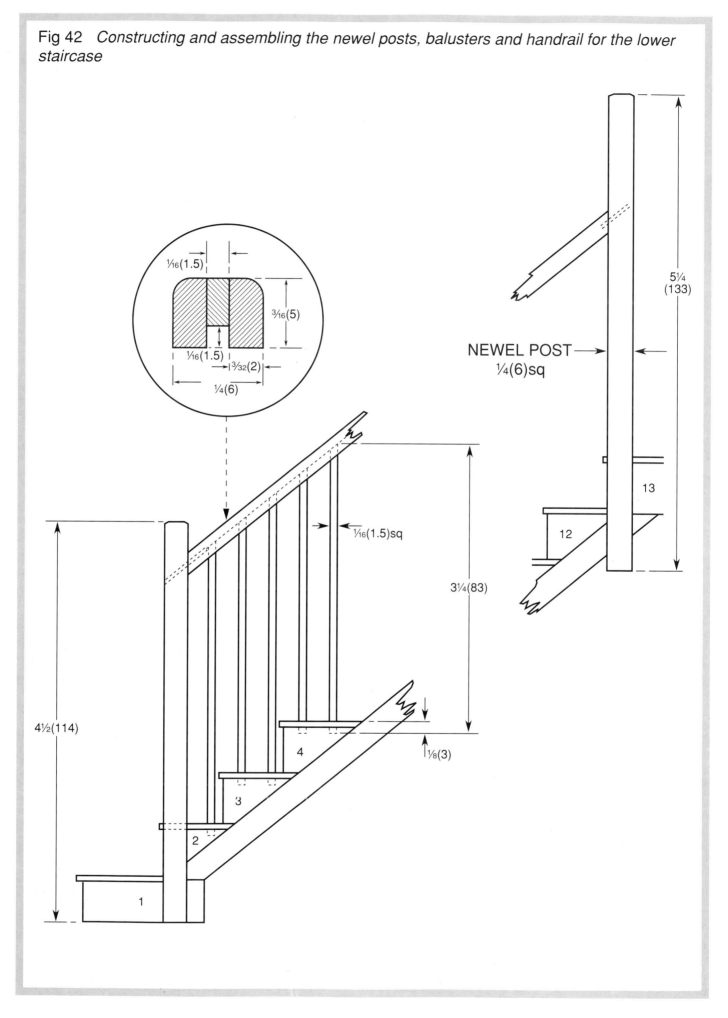

Fig 42 *Constructing and assembling the newel posts, balusters and handrail for the lower staircase*

of lime ½in (13mm) wide and 1⁄32in (0·8mm) thick. Of this total, about thirty-one pieces 15⅜in (391mm) long will be needed for the dining-room floor, and the remainder will be in pieces 14⅞in (378mm) long. A further three pieces, the same thickness but ¼in (6mm) wide, will be needed for the crossbanding at the front edge of each first-floor section. They will be 12⅜in (314mm), 6¾in (172mm) and 15⅜in (391mm) in length. Starting in the dining-room, reduce one 15⅜in (391mm) length to just over ⅛in (3mm) in width. Using contact adhesive, glue this across the floor from side to side, against the back wall. Now, with the ½in (13mm) wide boards, continue towards the front for four or five inches (100 – 127mm); then start again at the front edge and work back. This ensures that the final gap, if not exactly ½in (13mm), can be filled with a wider or narrower board where it will not show. A realistic effect can be achieved by cutting some boards into two or more sections and laying them with the ends butted. When doing this, bear in mind that floor joists in real houses are normally spaced at 15 – 16in centres (381 – 406mm) and that the butt between two lengths of floorboard occurs over the centre of a joist. You should cut the lengths of butted sections in multiples of 1¼in (32mm) to 1 5⁄16in (33mm) and not fit consecutive boards with the cut in the same place.

The first-floor sections all have a ¼in (6mm) wide crossbanding laid from side to side at the front edge, with the ½in (13mm) wide boards laid from front to back behind it. Start in the left-hand room (bedroom) and glue the 12⅜in (314mm) length of crossbanding across the front. Both this floor section and that in the right-hand room (drawing-room) have Cir-Kit tape laid in a groove. Note that the width across the conductor strips is just under ½in (13mm). Glue the first two boards to the floor, one on either side of the conductors leaving a ½in (13mm) gap in the centre. The slight lap over the grooves will not matter. Work outwards from each of these boards to the side walls where any adjustment in width will be made. Glue a further short board in the central gap from the front to ½in (13mm) in front of the brads in the tape. The remainder of the gap over the tape from here to the back wall will be filled with a loose board 1⁄16in (1·5mm) thick to provide access for soldering the light wires to the brass brads. The drawing-room floor can now be boarded in exactly the same way, using the 15⅜in (391mm) length of crossbanding.

The landing floor can be removed for ease of handling. First apply the 6¾in (172mm) long crossbanding, then glue the first board from front to back along the side of the stair-well. Work to the right first, and then fill the area to the left with shorter boards.

The staircase from the Georgian House

LANDING BALUSTRADE

Once the landing boards are laid, holes can be drilled into the floor for the landing balusters; these holes should be 1⁄16in (1·5mm) in diameter, and ⅛in (3mm) deep at ⅜in (10mm) centres (see Fig 43). The slots can be cut for the newel posts — note that the left-hand post in the front section is only ⅛in (3mm) wide, to allow the floor to slide past the bedroom door surround. A further half post ¼ × ⅛in (6 × 3mm) is glued to the side wall of the landing. The handrails are constructed and fitted in the same way as those on the stairs, but note that the inner end of the rail which meets the post at the top step is not fixed, leaving the floor free to slide outward.

Wiring A short length of twin wire should be soldered to the brads on the underside of the floor, with a Cir-Kit 1004 plug fitted at the end for connection to the socket under the stairs.

ROOF SLATES

These are simulated from strips of thin grey card ¾in (19mm) wide and 35in (889mm) long. They are

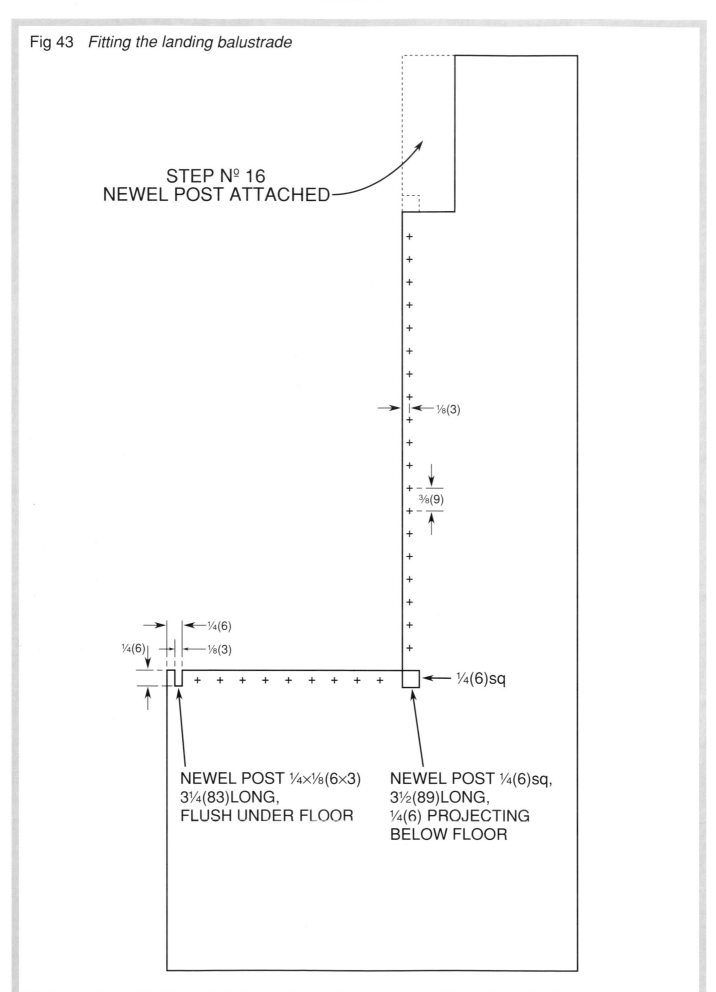

Fig 43   *Fitting the landing balustrade*

STEP Nº 16
NEWEL POST ATTACHED

¹⁄₈(3)

³⁄₈(9)

¹⁄₄(6)

¹⁄₄(6)

¹⁄₈(3)

¹⁄₄(6)sq

NEWEL POST ¹⁄₄×¹⁄₈(6×3)
3¹⁄₄(83)LONG,
FLUSH UNDER FLOOR

NEWEL POST ¹⁄₄(6)sq,
3¹⁄₂(89)LONG,
¹⁄₄(6) PROJECTING
BELOW FLOOR

cut through to a depth of ⅝in (16mm) at ⅞in (22mm) intervals from the lower edge, leaving an uncut top edge ⅛in (3mm) wide. Starting at the bottom of the roof, they are glued on with the cuts staggered, and each successive strip overlapping the one below it by ⅛in (3mm). The ends are then trimmed back to the roof edge. The top course will be narrower than the lower ones. The strips are cut to fit between the dormers on the front roof, and at the back they should stop at the lower edge of the hinge.

DECORATING AND FINAL ASSEMBLY

When dry, paint the roof and the dormer tops and sides with a slate grey undercoat, followed by one coat of matt varnish. The outside of this house is finished with three coats of matt varnish, rubbed down between coats. It is as well to do this before decorating the inside, to avoid splashes getting on the wallpaper. All the floors should have two coats of satin varnish except the hall and kitchen which are covered with a tile paper. Ceilings and walls which are not to be papered are given three coats of matt white emulsion; the internal doors and surrounds have two coats of Humbrol satin finish white acrylic. Paint the front door on the outside with Humbrol gloss, and on the inside with satin varnish. Both inside and outside faces of the front panels have three coats of satin varnish. When dry, glue the windows in place, flush with the front face of the panel, behind the surround. Cut 2mm glass or Glodex to fit in the opening behind the windows, and secure with a ⅛in (3mm) wide strip of white card or plastic glued to the inside edges of the opening. Fix and glaze the back windows in the same way.

The reverse order is used on the dormers. First fit the glazing into the front rebates, followed by the window, and finally glue a ⁵⁄₁₆in (8mm) wide mitred surround ¹⁄₃₂in (0·8mm) thick to the front edges of the dormer carcase. The surround is then given two coats of satin varnish.

Wiring   Some of the solder connections for the lighting can be made now, to avoid marking the wallpaper, but those for ceiling lights are made on the floors and are best left until later, as the ceiling lights will hinder the wallpapering. Thread the wire tails from the three attic lights (Peter Kennedy — List of Suppliers) through the holes in the ridge beam, connect them in parallel by twisting the bared ends together and solder to the brass brads behind the ridge beam. Drill a ³⁄₃₂in (2mm) diameter hole through the back wall of the carcase ½in (13mm) above floor level and just to the left of the vertical tape. Thread a 36in (1m) length of twin wire through the hole, and solder the ends to the brads

on the tape. This wire will be used for connection to the transformer. Make it into a small coil and attach it to the back wall with masking tape. A facing of card should be glued to the inside face of the back eaves support in the attic, to cover the cutouts used to connect the tape.

Interior fittings and decoration   Wallpaper can now be applied where required following the instructions given in Chapter 1; note that the side wall of the bedroom will require a card overlay to cover the connections for the wall lights. After trimming the wallpaper, fit the brass knobs (Hobby's) to the internal doors; to hang the doors, first glue the hinges into the door edge, and then into the slots in the jambs. It is better to do this in two stages, and check that the hinge still pivots freely before gluing it to the door jamb. Use a quick-setting epoxy, but take care to remove any excess while it is still slightly rubbery, particularly round the hinge barrel and on the door edges.

Apply the brass knob and lion knocker (Tony Hooper) to the front door, and then hang this on the front panel in the same way. Glue the semi-circular glazing in the opening above the door, followed by the fanlight bars and surround (from plastic sheet) which is overlaid on the outside. Re-hang the front panels, then drill into the top and bottom edges of the left-hand panel, about ¼in (6mm) in from the open end, to receive a small ball catch; these will engage under the parapet and on top of the base projection. The ideal ball catch is ³⁄₁₆in (5mm) in diameter, but these seem to be very difficult to obtain. The ¼in (6mm) diameter catch can be used, but the flange round the ball should be skimmed off on a lathe.

Referring to Fig 5 in Chapter 1, make 30ft (9m) of skirting. Pre-paint this with Humbrol satin acrylic before cutting and gluing to the walls with mitred corner joints.

The light fittings from Wood 'n' Wool for the kitchen and dining-room can now be glued to the ceiling, with the wires led upwards through the holes, and soldered to the brads in the tape on the first floor. The wall-mounted oil light in the kitchen is connected through a hole in the wall behind it, to the spare outlet on the Cir-Kit socket below the stairs. The remaining three ceiling lights (all from Cir-Kit Concepts — see Suppliers) have canopy connections.

Finally the chimney caps are made from lime 3¾ × 2⅛ × ⅛in (95 × 54 × 3mm); they have the pots fixed to them, and are then glued to the tops of the stacks. The pots can be either of turned wood or fired clay.

GEORGIAN HOUSE – LIST OF SUPPLIERS

The furniture and accessories used in the Georgian House are from the following suppliers; see Acknowledgements for addresses.

Acorn Crafts: Bath mat and roller towel.
Lucy Askew: Fireplaces in drawing-room, dining-room and nursery; drawing-room mirror.
Avon Miniatures: Kitchen crockery, washbasin, jug and chamber pot; piggy bank.
Gordon Blacklock: Silver ashtray, tankard, wine coaster and cruet set.
Blackwells: Picture frames.
Patricia Borwick: Tapestry foot-stool (kit).
Rohanna Bryan: Bunch of rhubarb.
Bryntor Pottery: Kitchen crockery, mixing bowls, and storage jars.
C & D Crafts: Cane baskets.
Irene Campbell: Blue and white tea set with tray, stoneware flagon and vases.
Malcolm Chandler: Towel rail.
Copycats: Green glassware, curio cabinet, sideboard and small mirror on stand.
Véronique Cornish: Beatrix Potter figurines.
Cir-Kit Concepts (Dijon): Lighting in hall, landing and drawing-room.
Dijon: Small chest of drawers, white bed, upholstered bedroom chair; (the canopied bed has been adapted from a Dijon base).
The Dolls' House (Covent Garden): Octagonal work table, pole screen, what-not, and wine cooler.
Dolphin Miniatures: Washstand, bedroom chair, chest of drawers, nursery desk and stool, dolls' house, blackboard, rocking horse, hobby horse, toybox, cheval mirror, bureau, circular pedestal table, bookcase, dining table and chairs, kitchen table and chair, plate rack, dresser, candle and salt boxes, hall tables, and ship model.
Dorking Dollshouse Gallery: Pair of slippers, toy brick trolley, 'Rupert', slate and chalk, parcel, spaniel.

David Edwards: Shaving brush and silver hairbrush.
Marie Theresa Endean: Dolls — cook, lady in blue, and children.
Escutcheon: Dressing table and corner what-not.
From Kitchen to Garret: Suitcase, brass bed and small doll.
Isobel Hockey: Nursery sampler.
Tony Hooper: Fire-baskets, fire-irons, fenders, coffee mill, water-carrier, door porter, coal scuttle and kitchen brassware.
Peter Kennedy: Attic and main bedroom lighting.
Carol Lodder: Delft and spongeware pottery, and Devon Harvest jug.
Stuart McCabe: Silver chamber candlestick.
Pauline and John Meredith: 'Staffordshire' figurines.
Miniature Curios: Wine bottles.
Miniature Model Imports: Long-case clock and small tilt table.
Anita Oliver: Teddy bear (Benjamin).
Petite Porcelain Miniatures: Bathroom suite.
Phoenix Model Developments: Bedroom fireplace, kitchen range, mincer and train set (kits).
Quality Dollshouse Miniatures: Kettle, cleaver and knife.
Smallholdings: Boxed set of huntsmen.
Sunday Dolls: Pleater for making curtains.
Sussex Crafts: Housemaid's box.
Thames Valley Crafts: Bag of flour, Sunlight Soap, cotton wool, pill bottle and cough mixture.
The Singing Tree: Wall and floor papers.
Bernardo Traettino: Mahogany tilt table.
Warwick Miniatures: Noah's Ark, pushalong horse, and aeroplane.
Wentways Miniatures: Small brass keys.
Wood 'n' Wool Miniatures: Lighting for kitchen and dining-room.

The dolphin table, silver coffee service, and upholstered chairs in the drawing-room are from the author's own collection.

PREVIOUS PAGE *The Georgian House, fully furnished*

4
THE
THATCHED
COTTAGE

*The lack of symmetry and flowing roof lines of a
Westcountry thatched cottage are in complete contrast
to the formality of the Georgian house. Thatch can be represented
in several ways, though it is worth mentioning that if materials like
coconut fibre or raffia are used, they become a dust trap.
The teak veneer used here may lack something in texture but
it has proved to be very durable. Careful selection of the grain patterns and
a dead matt finish help to further the illusion.*

The basic carcase of this cottage is much simpler than that of the Georgian House, and there are fewer components such as doors, windows, and mouldings; however, it is nonetheless rather more difficult to make, largely owing to the complexity of the combined front panel and roof, which slides in a groove. The swept dormer windows are built up on the surface of the roof with wood blocks, which are carved and sanded to the correct contour before being veneered with teak.

The illustrations show a white roughcast or cob finish, but the stonework described in Chapter 5 can be used if you wish.

CUTTING
Referring to Fig 44, cut one base, one back, and three walls — two end and one partition — from ⅜in (9mm) plywood. A further panel 24 × 12in

(610 × 305mm) will be needed later for the front, but this will be described after the main carcase is completed.

BASE
Rebate the top surface of the base along the full length of the back edge, ⅜in (9mm) wide, and ⅛in (3mm) deep, and on each side from the back for 12¼in (311mm). A groove of similar dimensions is cut 8in (203mm) from the left-hand side, again extending 12¼in (311mm) forward from the back edge. A further groove is cut along the full length of the panel, with its inside edge 12¼in (311mm) from the back.

BACK PANEL
Cut ⅜in (9mm) wide rebates, ⅛in (3mm) deep, at both ends of the back panel, and a similar sized groove 8in (203mm) in from the left-hand end. Cut out the two back window openings as shown in Fig 44.

END WALLS/PARTITIONS
Glue a ⅜ × ⅛in (10 × 3mm) elm edging strip to one vertical edge of each wall — this will be the front or

The Thatched Cottage — view of the exterior and garden

TIMBER REQUIREMENTS

WOOD	THICKNESS		WIDTH		LENGTH	
	in	mm	in	mm	ft/in	m
Lime	1/16	1.6	1/2	13	6in	0.16
	1/8	3	1/4	6	2ft	0.61
			3/8	10	12in	0.31
			7/16	11	5ft	1.53
	5/32	4	3 1/2	89	12in	0.31
	3/16	5	5/16	8	12in	0.31
Pine	5/8	16	2 1/2	64	16ft	4.87
	3/4	19	2 1/8	54	12in	0.31
			3 3/8	86	12in	0.31
	7/8	22	3 5/8	93	12in	0.31
	1	25	1 1/2	38	18in	0.46
	1 1/16	27	1 3/8	35	6in	0.16
Elm	1/32	1	3/8	10	2ft	0.61
			1/2	13	20ft	6.1
	1/16	1.6	3/16	5	18in	0.46
			1/4	6	12in	0.31
	1/8	3	1/4	6	9ft	2.75
			5/16	8	12in	0.31
			3/8	10	5ft	1.53
			5/8	16	14ft	4.27

WOOD	THICKNESS		WIDTH		LENGTH	
	in	mm	in	mm	ft/in	m
Elm	3/16	5	3/16	5	12in	0.31
	1/4	6	1/4	6	28ft	8.53
			1/2	13	5ft	1.53
			3 1/4	83	2ft	0.61
	1/2	13	2	51	12in	0.31
			3 1/2	89	12in	0.31
	5/8	16	5/8	16	3ft	0.92
			7/8	22	12in	0.31
	7/8	22	6	152	18in	0.46
	1	25	1	25	2ft	0.61
			3 1/4	83	9in	0.23

WOOD	THICKNESS		AREA	
	in	mm	sq ft	sq m
Birch Plywood	3/8	9	15	1.4
	1/4	6	5	0.5
	1/8	3	3	0.3
	1/16	1.5	1	0.09
Teak Veneer			6	0.6
Formica or similar laminate			2	0.18

open edge. This increases the width of the walls to 12in (305mm) which, with the lap of the back panel, makes the full 12¼in (311mm) needed to fill the rebates in the base, behind the transverse groove. Follow these dimensions carefully, as the end and partition walls must not project into the transverse groove; this must be clear for the sliding front panel.

RIGHT-HAND END WALL
Mark the fireplace opening on the right-hand wall, 5¼in (133mm) wide and 4½in (114mm) high (Fig 44). When cutting this out, keep fractionally on the waste side of the marks, so that the sides of the opening can be smoothed back flush with the inside face of the chimney assembly, which will later be fastened to the outside.

PARTITION WALL
Mark both faces with the upper and lower limits of the upper floor, 7⅛in (181mm) and 7⅜in (187mm) respectively from the bottom. Cut out the two door openings and note that the upper opening is inset a further 1½in (38mm) and is ¼in (6mm) shorter than the one below. The bottom of the upper door opening should lie on the upper floor line; its top outer corner is cut parallel to and ⅝in (16mm) in from the sloping front edge.

LEFT-HAND END WALL
The roof over this end has a half hip. Mark across the wall 14¼in (362mm) up from the bottom, and

Fig 44 *Patterns and measurements for the walls, base and back panel*

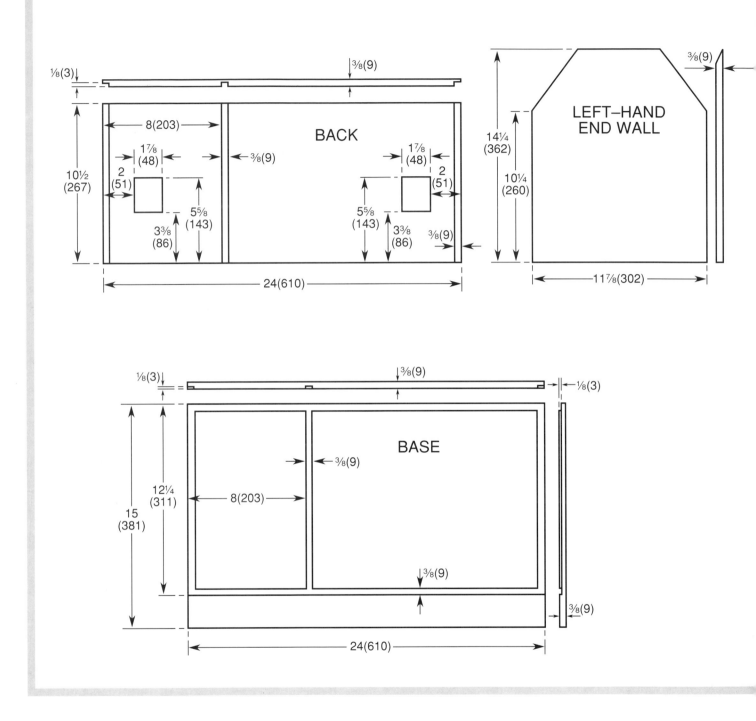

cut off the triangular section above this line. This new top edge should be bevelled to 25° (Fig 44).

TRIAL ASSEMBLY

Assemble the carcase without glue, using two or three ¾in (19mm) no 6 screws in each joint line. Several other jobs will need to be done before final assembly, but having a basic structure will make the marking out and fitting of some components easier. Individual sections can be removed as required for more detailed attention.

FLOOR BEARERS

Using a 7in (178mm) high plywood spacer, mark a line on all inside faces of the carcase. Additionally mark each inside face of the end walls, and both faces of the partition vertically, where they enter the rebates or groove at the back, at the same level. Remove the end walls and partition. Prepare a 5ft (1·5m) length of ½ × ¼in (13 × 6mm) elm, for the

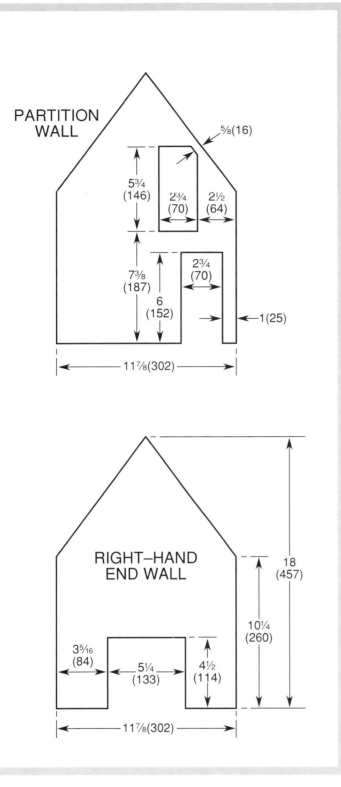

PARTITION WALL

⁵⁄₈(16)

5¾ (146)

2¾ (70)   2½ (64)

7⅜ (187)

2¾ (70)

6 (152)

1(25)

11⅞(302)

RIGHT–HAND END WALL

18 (457)

10¼ (260)

3⁵⁄₁₆ (84)

5¼ (133)   4½ (114)

11⅞(302)

back to allow entry into the back panel. The inside of the right-hand wall does not have a bearer as the fireplace surround performs this function.

Now glue a 7⅛in (181mm) length to the short back wall section, with an equal space of ¼in (6 mm) at each end, between it and the rebate to the left and the groove to the right. A 14¼in (362mm) length is glued to the right-hand section of the back wall, spaced ¼in (6mm) from the groove at the left and ¾in (19mm) from the rebate at the right.

INTERNAL FRAMING

A border and collar of ⁵⁄₈ × ⅛in (16 × 3mm) elm framing is glued to both faces of the partition wall, and the inside face of each end wall (Fig 45). The vertical sections should be inset ⅛in (3mm) at the back of the walls, and also at the bottom, to allow the walls to engage in both the back panel and the base. These sections are omitted below upper-floor level at the back of the right-hand face of the partition, and at both back and front on the right-hand end wall. Spaces for the upper floor can be left by fitting the vertical frames in two sections, or they can be cut out afterwards. A total length of framing around 14ft (4·3m) will be needed. Using a Dremel drum sander, form one waney edge, and scrape the top surface with an old razor-saw-blade to accentuate the grain.

CHIMNEY

Referring to Fig 46, cut two pieces of ⅜in (9mm) ply 2in (51mm) wide, and two pieces 1¼in (32mm) wide, all 16in (406mm) long. Glue and pin these, with the 1¼in (32mm) widths sandwiched between the 2in (51mm) widths, to form a box section A 2in (51mm) square. Cut two further 2in (51mm) side spacers B, each 5¼in (133mm) long, with the top edge bevelled to 45°. Glue and pin one of these to each side of the stack A, with all bottom edges flush. Cut one outer facing C and bevel the top edge to 45°. Glue and pin this to the outside face of the stack A, so that it overlaps the edges of the side spacers B, and the bevelled edges of B and C are level at the top. Cut two further spacers D from ⅜in (9mm) ply, 2in (51mm) wide and 5¼in (133mm) long. These are glued and pinned behind the lower part of the outer facing C with their top edges bevelled to conform with the slope. A 6 × 2⅜ × ⅜in (152 × 60 × 9mm) plywood floor F is rebated to fit between D and C.

Stand the right-hand end wall in position on the base, with its bottom edge resting in the rebate. Place the chimney assembly centrally outside it, so that the lower spacers D fit either side of the fireplace opening, and the bases of both house and chimney are level. Hold the chimney and wall together with G-cramps, and then fasten them with

floor bearers. Following Fig 45, cut two pieces 11⅞in (302mm) long, and glue these with contact adhesive to the inside of the left-hand wall, and to the left-hand side of the partition, with their top edges butting the line previously marked. Cut a further 11⅞in (302mm) length and glue this to the right-hand side of the partition at the same level. Note that the outer ends of these bearers should be flush with the outer edges of the left-hand end wall and partition, leaving a gap of ⅛in (3mm) at the

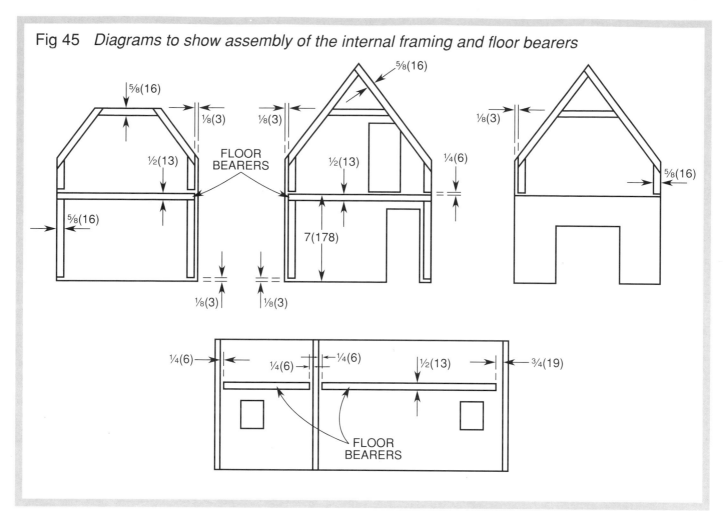

Fig 45 *Diagrams to show assembly of the internal framing and floor bearers*

two screws inserted through the wall from the inside into the stack. The upper one should be just below the border framing and the lower one about 1in (25mm) above the fireplace opening. With a pencil, mark round the chimney assembly on to the outside face of the wall. Separate the wall and chimney, and re-mark the wall with a further line inset 3⁄16in (5mm). Drill pilot holes 1⁄32in (0·8mm) in diameter through the wall on this line at 2in (51mm) centres. This will ensure that the pins, when driven from the blind side (inside of right-hand wall) will enter the centre of the 3⁄8in (9mm) plywood edges on the chimney assembly.

Re-assemble with glue and panel pins using the two screws to hold the correct location. When the glue has set, smooth the sides of the fireplace opening back to the inside faces of the lower spacers D.

Now make the two side roof sections E from 1⁄8in (3mm) plywood and glue them in place.

PREVIOUS PAGE *Fully furnished Thatched Cottage, showing small bedroom*

INTERNAL FIRE SURROUND

Referring to Fig 47, prepare a 9in (229mm) length of lime, or knot-free softwood, 3⅜in (86mm) wide and ¾in (19mm) thick. Cut this into two 4¼in (108mm) lengths, and reduce the width of one piece to 3¼in (83mm). Temporarily refasten the right-hand end wall and chimney to the base and back panel. Using contact adhesive, glue the narrower piece to the inside of the end wall so that it fits between the back wall and the inner edge of the fireplace opening; the wider piece is glued on the other side of the opening and should finish flush with the outside edge of the right-hand wall. Cut a piece of elm for the lintel 11⅞in (302mm) long, ⅞in (22mm) wide and ⅝in (16mm) thick. Lay this across the tops of the side blocks just fitted, resting on its side so that it projects ⅛in (3mm) over the side support blocks, but do not glue it in place. Now cut a further length of softwood or lime 11⅞ × 2⅛ × ¾in (302 × 54 × 19mm) and lay this on edge across the top of the lintel. The upper edge should coincide with the line marking the underside of the floor. Adjust if necessary and then glue to the wall with contact adhesive, and back up the joint by screwing through the wall into the softwood blocks, on either side of the chimney.

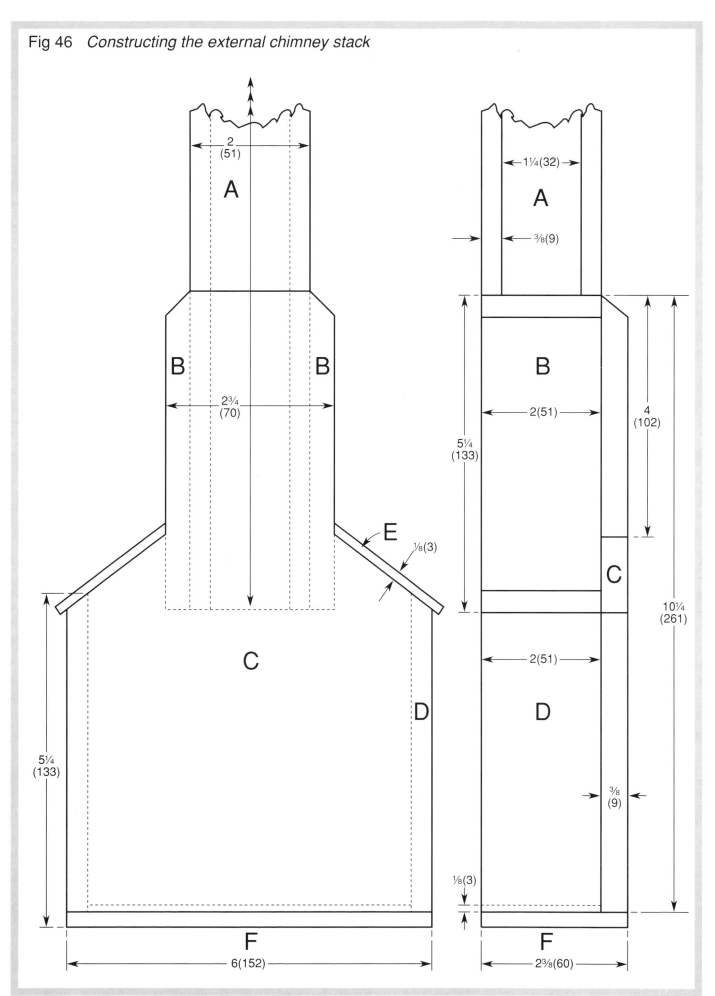

Fig 46 *Constructing the external chimney stack*

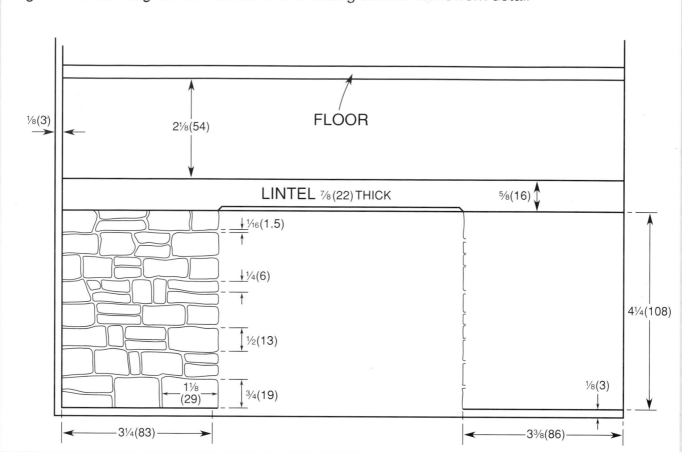

Fig 47   *Assembling the fire surround and cutting out the stonework detail*

LINTEL

Mark the lintel where it crosses each side of the fireplace opening, then remove. Chamfer the bottom outer edge between the marks, and with a saw-blade, accentuate the grain on the surface throughout its length. Lightly wane all the sharp edges at the front. Do not replace until stonework has been completed.

STONEWORK

Remove the wall/chimney assembly from the carcase, and lightly pencil lines across the upright blocks below the lintel, and on their return edges surrounding the fireplace opening. Start ¾in (19mm) from the bottom, and continue upwards at approximately ½in (13mm) intervals. Using Fig 47 as a guide, outline the stone pattern with a small chisel or gouge, cutting the joints between the stones about 1⁄16in (2mm) deep. Do not be too precise or the effect will be spoiled. Round over the edges of the stones and clean out the 'joints' with coarse sandpaper. Apply one coat of textured masonry paint to the stonework, and to the plain surface above the lintel slot. This will give greater contrast to the stonework pattern, and show where additional cutting or sanding is required. Lightly

sand the surfaces, then apply one coat of matt white emulsion (a further coat of texture paint will make the surface too gritty and obliterate some of the stonework detail).

UPPER FLOORS

Cut the two upper-floor sections from ¼in (6mm) birch plywood, to the patterns in Fig 48. Note that the grain should run from front to back on the right-hand section, and from left to right on the other. Lay them in position, and check that they rest evenly on all the floor bearers, as adjustments can be made more easily now, before the carcase is finally glued. Put the floors aside for more detailed attention later, and dismantle the carcase.

INTERNAL DOORS

Referring to Fig 49, and following the method described in Chapter 1, make and fit the two internal doors and frames. The planking is elm,

Scullery of the Thatched Cottage

$\frac{1}{32}$in (1mm) thick, and cut in random widths around $\frac{1}{2}$in (13mm), sufficient to cover the surface of the core. No core is required for the dummy back door, as the planking is glued directly on to the plywood back panel, with a frame of $\frac{3}{16} \times \frac{1}{16}$in (5 × 1·5mm) elm fitted round it. If you wish to further the illusion, the other side of this door can be applied to the outside of the back panel in the same manner. When fitting the header to the upper door, the angled section at the top outer corner can be ignored as it is hidden on the finished model.

WINDOWS

Construction of windows is explained in Chapter 1. Make five small and two large windows from lime, to the dimensions given in Fig 50. The large windows should be glued together in the centre, to form one unit, ensuring that the faces and edges are level. This can best be done by clamping to a small square of glass with spring paper-clips. When dry, lightly sand all the windows and apply two coats of matt varnish, leaving the outer edges bare.

BACK WINDOW LINING

Prepare a 5ft (1·5m) length of lime $\frac{7}{16}$in (11mm) wide and $\frac{1}{8}$in (3mm) thick. This is enough for all the windows, and after lining the back windows the remainder should be put aside for later use on the front panel.

Cut four $1\frac{7}{8}$in (48mm) lengths, and four more 2in (51mm) long. Start by gluing the shorter lengths into the openings in the back panel at top and bottom, and follow with the longer uprights glued between them, allowing an overlap of about $\frac{1}{32}$in (1mm) on each side of the panel. When the glue has set, plane the overlaps flush on both faces of the panel.

BACK WINDOWS

Glue a small window into each opening in the back panel, flush with the back face, so that glazing can later be fitted from the inside. The window face showing continuous upright bars should be towards the inside of the house.

DECORATING

Much of the inside can now be painted while the carcase is separated. First apply two coats of matt varnish to all surfaces which are to have a natural wood finish; this includes the internal doors and fireplace lintel, though the latter should have one coat only to leave a dull, rough finish. When the varnish has dried, apply two coats of matt white emulsion to all wall surfaces, cutting in carefully when coming against a varnished section. Do not paint either the back and bottom edges, or the rebates which will later be glued. Some touching up

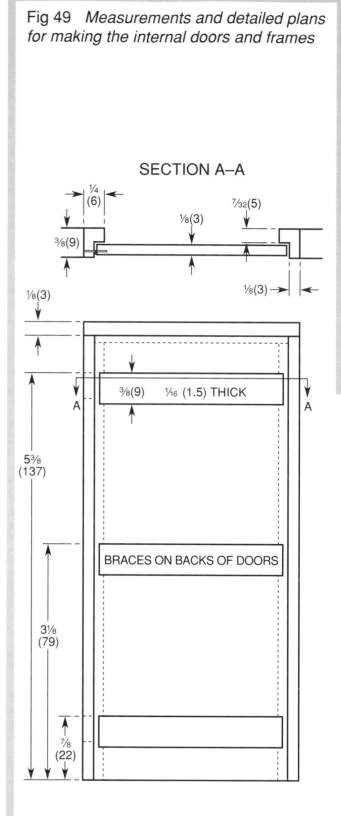

Fig 49 *Measurements and detailed plans for making the internal doors and frames*

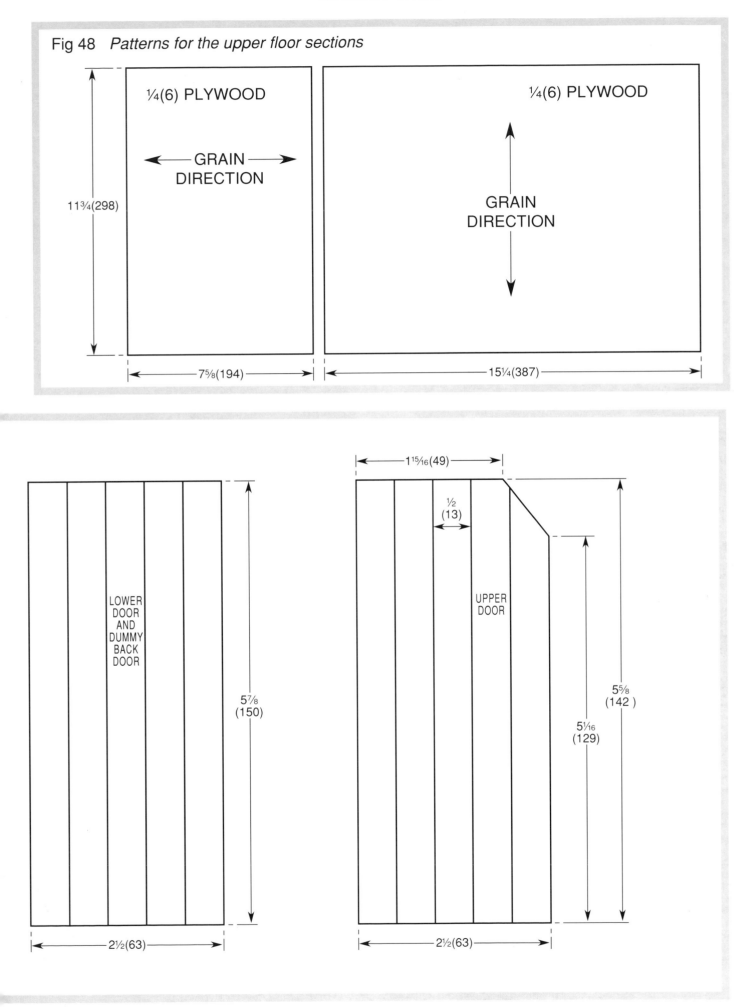

Fig 48   *Patterns for the upper floor sections*

¼(6) PLYWOOD

← GRAIN → DIRECTION

11¾(298)

7⅝(194)

¼(6) PLYWOOD

GRAIN DIRECTION

15¼(387)

LOWER DOOR AND DUMMY BACK DOOR

5⅞ (150)

2½(63)

1¹⁵⁄₁₆(49)

½ (13)

UPPER DOOR

5⅝ (142)

5¹⁄₁₆ (129)

2½(63)

will be required but this can wait until the floor and stairs are fitted.

FINAL ASSEMBLY

The carcase can now be re-assembled with glue. It is helpful to drill 1/32in (1mm) pilot holes through the back panel and base on the centreline of the grooves and rebates, at about 2in (51mm) centres between the existing screw holes, for ease of pinning. Start by fastening the end walls and the partition to the back panel with screws and glue while all are standing in their correct location on the base, and then glue and screw the base to this assembly from underneath. Finally hammer panel pins into the joints through the pilot holes, in the spaces between the screws. Clean off all surplus glue and when dry, plane off any irregularities on the outside of the carcase. Nail and screw holes should be filled with Brummer stopping. Fill the groove on the base in the lower doorway with a strip of 3/8 × 1/8in (10 × 3mm) lime.

STAIRS

Prepare a piece of elm 6in (152mm) wide, 15in (381mm) long, and 7/8in (22mm) thick. Following the diagram in Figs 51 and 52, cut ten steps 2 1/8in (54mm) wide, noting that with the exception of no 7, the grain runs across the steps. Now that the width has been reduced, they can be re-sawn and planed to the finished thickness of 23/32in (18mm) — though step no 10 should remain 7/8in (22mm) thick as this will be used for fine adjustment.

Stack the ten blocks against the right-hand side of the partition wall, and adjust the thickness of no 10 so that it is level with the pencil line representing the top of the floor. Form a nosing on the front and open side of steps 1 to 4, and then on the front only of 5 to 10, by cutting away the lower part of the step front (riser) with the router, to leave a 1/8in (3mm) square projection at the top. Steps 6 and 7 should first be cut to the required angle.

Assemble steps 1 to 5 with glue and pins — these should be at least 1 1/8in (28mm) from the front edge of each step, so that the following step will cover the nail holes. Keep all the edges flush on both the plain side and the back. When the glue has set, draw a line connecting steps 1 to 4, at the junction of the treads and risers (see Fig 52), and cut away all the side nosings behind this line, to leave a flat

Unfurnished interior of the Thatched Cottage, separated from its garden base, and showing the removable stairs and floors

area; the side of step no 5 will overhang the top by ⅛in (3mm).

Cut two newel posts from elm ¼in (6mm) square, one 3¾in (95mm) long, and the other 10in (254mm). Carefully cut away ¼in (6mm) of the side nosing on step no 1, to locate the lower newel post (Fig 52).

Cut ⅛in (3mm) from the side nosing at the back of step no 4, and the front of step no 5, for the upper newel post. Glue and pin the posts to the stair edge, making sure that they are upright. Glue a ⁵⁄₁₆ × ⅛in (8 × 3mm) elm stringer to the stair sides, between the posts, with its top edge against the angled backs of the side nosings. Cut a triangle of ¹⁄₁₆in (1·5mm) plywood to fit the area A B C , and glue this to the stair side between the stringer and the back newel-post.

Allow the glue to dry thoroughly, and then add steps 6 and 7. The front nosing on both steps must be cut away to fit against the upper newel post, and because of their shape they must be pinned to each other, and to step no 5, through an exposed part of the tread. Fill the nail holes with Brummer stopping.

A side support wall of ⅜in (9mm) plywood, 2⅛in (54mm) wide and 7in (178mm) long is now glued and screwed to the edge of step no 7, flush with that step at front and back, and notched at the back to fit the floor bearer.

You should now check that the stairs so far assembled fit evenly against the partition and back walls of the carcase, and adjust where necessary.

Steps 8 and 9 are now fixed to no 7, flush at the back and butted against the support wall at the sides. Step no 10 is rebated on two edges (Fig 53), to fit over both the side support and the floor bearer on the back wall of the carcase, before being glued and pinned in place. Remove the stair assembly.

STAIR CUPBOARD
Referring to Fig 53, glue a ⁵⁄₁₆ × ⅛in (8 × 3mm) elm door frame to the front edge of the side wall, and the lower part of step no 7, leaving a ¹⁄₁₆in (1·5mm) ledge at the top and right-hand side of the opening, for use as a door stop. Cut a square of ¹⁄₁₆in (1·5mm) plywood DEFG and glue this to the edges of steps 7, 8, 9, 10 above the door frame and to the right of the newel post.

Make the door from ¹⁄₁₆in (1·5mm) plywood planked on the outside only with ¹⁄₃₂in (0·8mm) thick elm. The planks are of random widths, approximately ½in (13mm) to cover the surface of the plywood. Triangular strap hinges are glued and pinned on the outside face of the door, inset ¼in (6mm) at the top and bottom. The pins used here are those sold for laying model railway track. They should be driven right through the door, then cut off and filed smooth on the back. With the loose

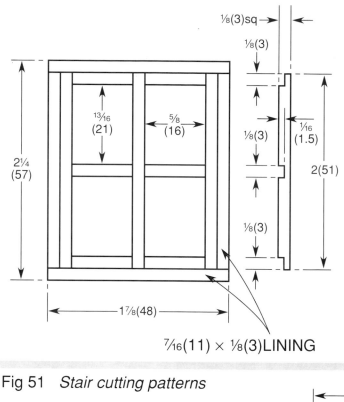

Fig 50 *Detailed plans for constructing the windows and linings*

⁷⁄₁₆(11) × ⅛(3)LINING

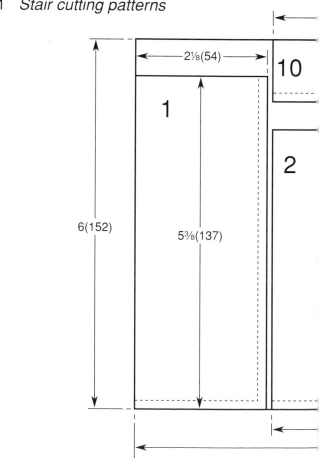

Fig 51 *Stair cutting patterns*

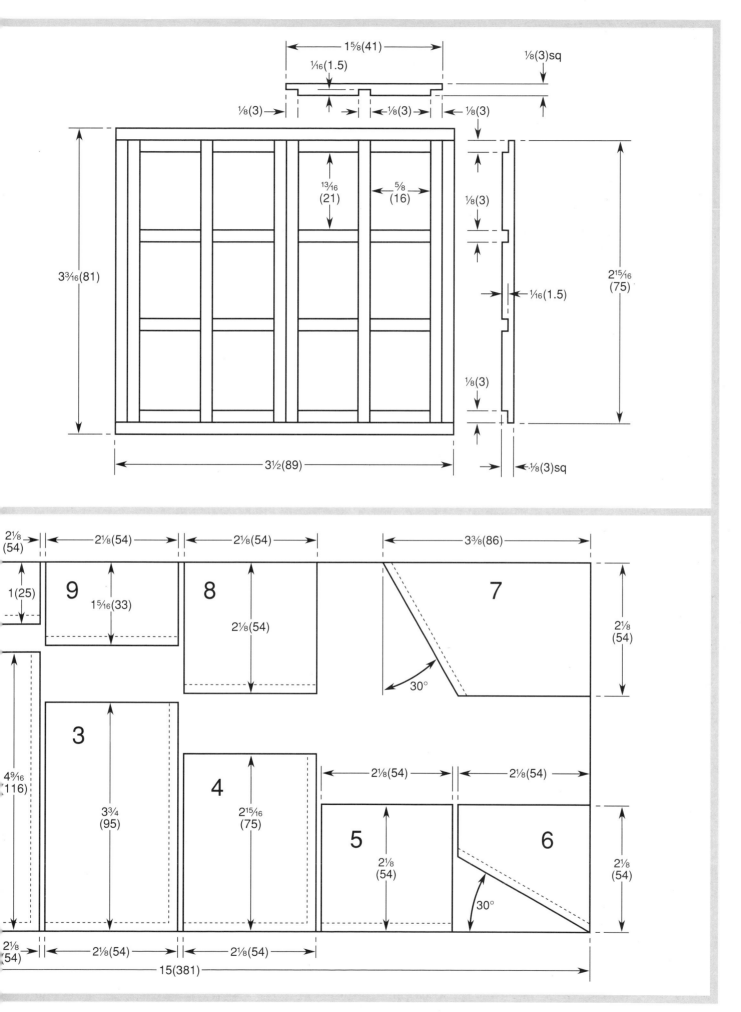

hinge flaps bent outwards, set the door in place and mark their positions on the newel post, which will be slotted to receive them. Cut the slots by drilling a line of ¹⁄₃₂in (1mm) diameter holes with a pin chuck, and then connecting these with a knife or small chisel. Final cleaning out is done with the narrow end of a small sandplate. Once fitted, the door can be removed and put aside for varnishing.

LOWER HANDRAIL

A 4in (102mm) length of elm, ¹⁄₄in (6mm) square should be cut with its ends angled to fit between the two newel posts, parallel to the stringer. Round over the top edge and fasten it to the newel posts with glue and ¹⁄₁₆in (2mm) diameter dowels (Fig 52). The lower edge should be 2¾in (70mm) above the floor on the front post.

WIRING

Drill a ³⁄₃₂in (2mm) hole through the back panel, ½in (13mm) above the floor, and a similar distance to the right of the partition. Apply Cir-Kit twin tape from here — run it along the bottom edge of the back wall for 7½in (191mm) to the right, then turn it upwards to finish 1in (25mm) above the floor bearer; a section, ⅝in (16mm) wide must be cut

away from this bearer, to allow the tape to pass. It need not be replaced, as the cutout will be hidden by a beam. Fit a Cir-Kit 1003 socket at the top of the tape, and brad the conductor strips close to the hole through the back panel.

A further tape is applied to the scullery side of the partition wall, to run from the ground floor to 1in (25mm) above the bearer of the upper floor, close alongside the vertical elm framing at the back. Cut away ⅝in (16mm) of the floor bearer to let the tape pass. Brad the bottom of the tape ¼in (6mm) above the ground floor, and fix two Cir-Kit sockets, one ½in (13mm) above the brads, and the other at the top of the tape. Cut off the tape immediately below the brads at the bottom, and then drill a ³⁄₃₂in (2mm) diameter hole below the tape, obliquely through the partition wall to emerge close to the bradded tape on the other side.

A short length of twin wire — about 1in (25mm) — is threaded through this hole and soldered to the brads on either side. A 36in (915mm) length of twin wire is threaded through the hole in the back panel and soldered to the brads inside, taking care not to disconnect the short wires from the scullery. This wire will later connect to the transformer, and should be coiled up and taped to the outside of the back wall until required.

UPPER FLOORS

These have already been cut to size. On the right-hand section a groove ½in (13mm) wide and ¹⁄₁₆in (2mm) deep is cut on the top surface, from the back edge to the centre of the floor, in line with the vertical tape on the back wall. This should have a further shallow groove ¹⁄₁₆ × ¹⁄₁₆in (1·5 × 1·5mm) cut centrally within it. Working outwards from the ½in (13mm) wide groove, scribe ½in (13mm) wide floorboards from front to back, over the full width of the floor. Starting from the front edge, scribe similar boards from left to right across the smaller floor section. Both floors can now have an edging strip of ¼ × ⅛in (6 × 3mm) lime glued to the front edges.

Replace the stairs, cutting away the lower inside corner at the back, to fit over the wires from the scullery, and cut out the stairwell to the dimensions shown in Fig 54. Now re-fit the floors, trimming as necessary to give enough clearance at the sides for easy removal. The front edges should be flush with the outer edges of both the partition and end walls. Glue a strip of lime ⅜ × ⅛in (10 × 3mm) and 10½in (267mm) long, to the back wall, above the floor.

Main bedroom of the Thatched Cottage

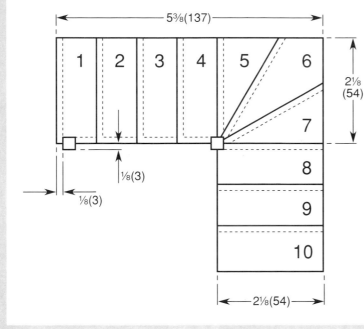

Fig 52 *Assembling the cottage stairs*

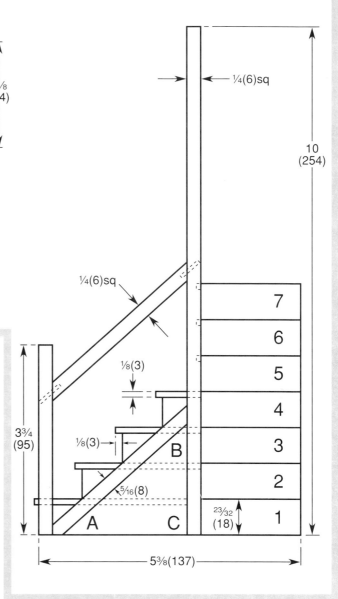

This will hold down the back edge of the floor which is free to slide under it. A similar strip can be glued to the side walls if you wish, but should not be necessary if the floor is truly flat.

UPPER HANDRAIL

The back newel post on the stair assembly rises 2¾in (70mm) above the floor. Three more pieces of ¼in (6mm) square elm should be cut to this length to support the upper handrail. One will be glued to the partition wall but the other two will only be pegged into the top surface of the floor (Fig 54) — they will not be glued, nor will the rail of ³⁄₁₆in (5mm) square elm pegged between them, with its top edge 2½in (64mm) above the floor. Assembled in this way, they can then be dismantled whenever the floor or stairs need to be removed.

The exposed top surfaces of the floor bearers in the stairwell should have ¼in (6mm) square elm glued on top to bring them level with the top of the floor.

Cut a loose floorboard of lime ½ × ¹⁄₁₆in (13 × 1·5mm) to fill the lighting groove on the floor. Apply two coats of satin varnish to the top surface of both floors, and the front edges.

CEILING BEAMS

The five joists in the scullery are of ¼in (6mm) square elm, each 11⅝in (295mm) long; they should be glued to the underside of the floor at approximately 1¼in (32mm) centres, flush at the front, and ¼in (6mm) in from the back edge where

they will butt against the floor bearer.

The larger room has three main beams running from front to back with the smaller joists slotted into them. Only the main beams will be glued, allowing the joists to slide into position *after* the ceiling has been painted.

Prepare the main beams by cutting a piece of elm 2in (51mm) wide, ½in (13mm) thick, and 11⅝in (295mm) long. Nine slots, ¼in (6mm) wide and ¼in (6mm) deep are routed across the 2in (51mm) face, at 1¼in (32mm) centres starting ¼in (6mm) in from one end. This should be marked as the outer end (see Fig 55).

Re-saw the 2in (51mm) face to give one length ½in (13mm) wide and two more each ⅜in (10mm) wide. Chamfer both lower edges of the ½in (13mm) width, then one edge only of each ⅜in (10mm)

Fig 53 *Fitting the top stairs and the stair cupboard*

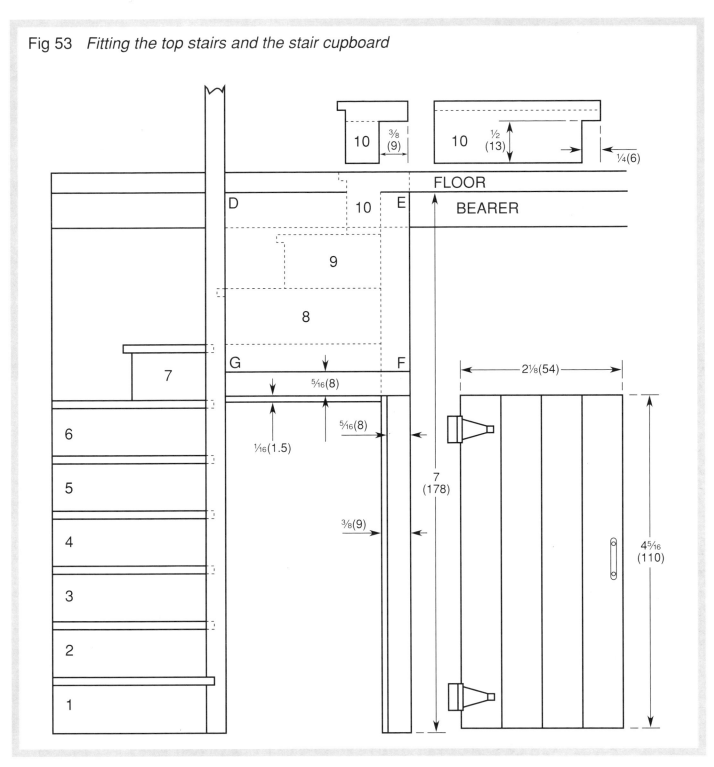

width, as a handed pair. With the marked ends at the front, fix the beams to the underside of the floor as follows (see Fig 55).

The ½in (13mm) beam is glued directly beneath the scribed plank that has been grooved for lighting. One ⅜in (10mm) beam is glued under the right-hand side of the floor, inset ¾in (19mm) so that its plain face slides against the upper part of the fireplace wall.

The other ⅜in (10mm) beam is glued to the underside of the floor at the left-hand side, inset ¼in (6mm) to fit outside the floor bearer, and cut off

at the back where it reaches the stairwell. A ⅝in (16mm) length of elm, ½in (13mm) deep and ³⁄₃₂in (2·5mm) thick, is glued to the sliding face of this beam at the front, to make up the difference in thickness between the floor bearer and the vertical frame.

Following Fig 55, glue ¼ × ¼in (6 × 6mm) elm trimmers to the underside of the floor, round the stairwell. Now, for this same section of ceiling, cut nine joists from ¼ × ¼in (6 × 6mm) elm. The first six are each 14¼in (362mm) long, followed by one of 12in (305mm) and two of 9⅜in (238mm). Slide these

Fig 54 *To show details of floors, stairwell and upper handrail*

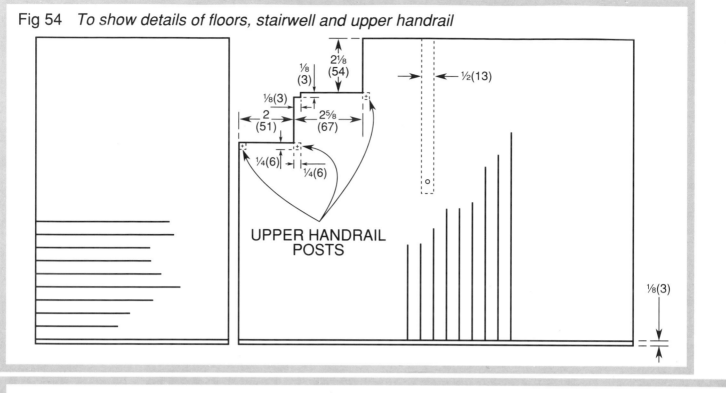

UPPER HANDRAIL
POSTS

Fig 55 *The construction and fitting of the ceiling beams and joists*

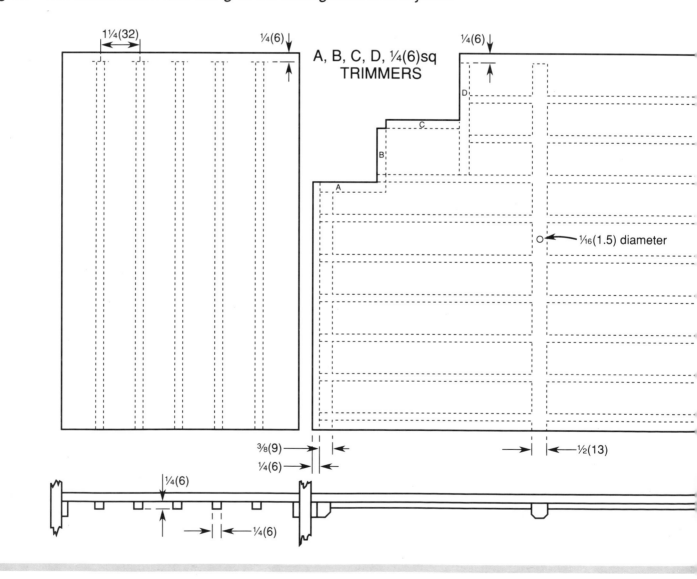

A, B, C, D, ¼(6)sq
TRIMMERS

¹⁄₁₆(1.5) diameter

Fig 56 Pattern for the sliding front panel

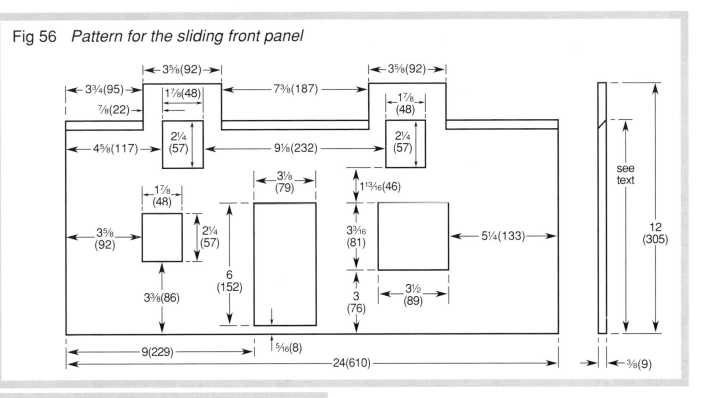

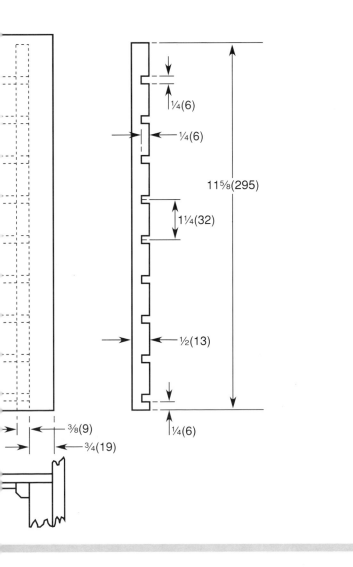

into position, and trim the ends if required so that there is no projection on the sliding faces of the side beams.

Drill a ¹⁄₁₆in (2mm) diameter hole from the groove in the floor through the centre beam for lighting.

With a small disc fitted to the Minicraft drill, sand a waney edge on all the scullery joists, and also those in the main room where they are exposed between the beams. Apply one coat of matt varnish to all the beams and joists, and before sliding the joists into position, paint the ceilings.

FRONT PANEL AND ROOF

Cut the front panel from ³⁄₈in (9mm) birch plywood 24in (610mm) long and 12in (304mm) high. From the dimensions in Fig 56, mark and cut out the door and window openings. A minimum of ⁵⁄₁₆in (8mm) must be left below the door opening for adequate strength. Before cutting out the stepped top profile, rest the panel in the groove at the front of the carcase. From the angle of the end walls use the adjustable bevel to transfer the line of the anticipated roof slope on to each outside edge. Draw a line from each point right across the full length of the panel. These give the upper and lower limits of the bevel which will be required on the panel's top edge, to fit the roof (see Fig 58). Now draw vertical lines from the top edge, ⁷⁄₈in (22mm) either side of the upper window openings, to meet the upper bevel line. Cut out the three sections to leave two tongues, each 3⁵⁄₈in (92mm) wide. With a sharp chisel, cut the bevel on the outside down to the lower line (approx 38° — see Fig 58).

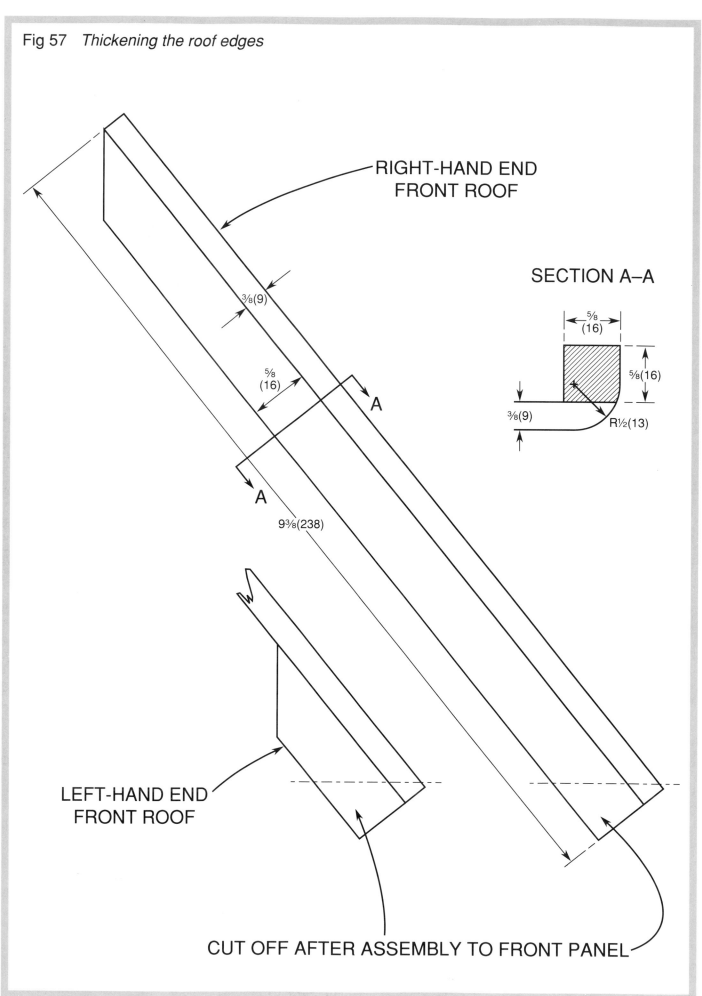

Fig 57 *Thickening the roof edges*

RIGHT-HAND END
FRONT ROOF

SECTION A–A

⅜(9)

⅝
(16)

A

A

9⅜(238)

⅝
(16)

⅝(16)

⅜(9)

R½(13)

LEFT-HAND END
FRONT ROOF

CUT OFF AFTER ASSEMBLY TO FRONT PANEL

Fig 58   *Fitting the roof to the front panel*

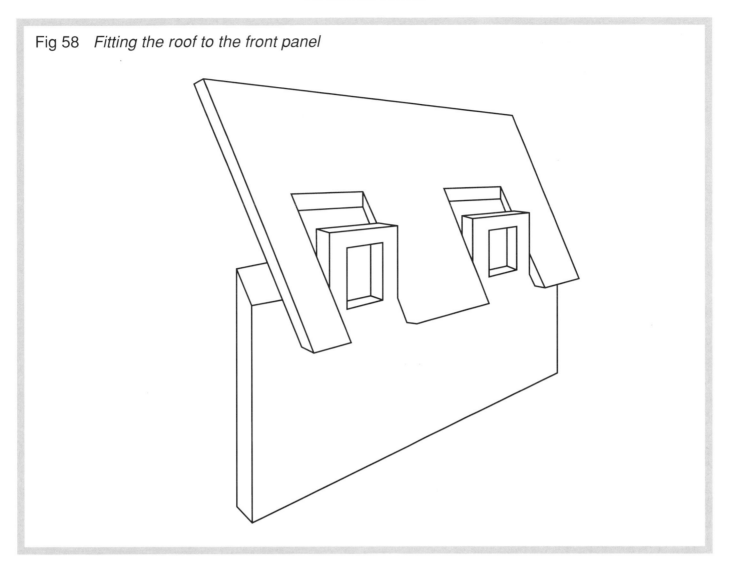

Cut two roof panels from ¼in (6mm) birch plywood, both 25¼in (641mm) long, the front panel 9⅜in (238mm) deep and the back 12in (305mm). Prepare a 36in (915mm) length of elm, ⅝in (16mm) square; this will be used to thicken the ends of the roof at the gables. Cut off one piece 9⅜in (238mm) long, and angle its top edge to about 38° so that when fitted under the roof this cut edge is vertical. Glue it under the right-hand end of the roof panel (Fig 57) with contact adhesive, and apply pressure to the joint in a vice. No pins should be used, as at a later stage this edge will be rounded and they will impede the router.

Replace the front panel in the groove, and temporarily hold it in position against the front of the house with masking tape. Lay the front roof in place behind the dormer tongues so that the elm thickening piece is tight against the outside of the right-hand wall, and with a ⅝in (16mm) overlap at the left-hand wall. Mark the lower edge of the roof each side of the dormer tongues and then cut two slots in the roof edge, each 3⅝in (92mm) wide and 2¼in (57mm) deep, to fit round the tongues. The edges of the slots which bear against the backs of

the tongues must be bevelled to give a close fit (Fig 58). Temporarily tack the roof in place with three or four panel pins driven through the roof into the bevelled top edge of the front panel, leaving the heads slightly proud so that they can be removed later.

Check that the underside of the roof bears evenly on both end wall and partition slopes, and adjust the bevel on the front panel if necessary, until a good fit is achieved. Carefully drill through the roof into the top edge of the front panel in three places: midway between the tongues, and 2in (51mm) in at each end, and insert a ¾in (19mm) no 6 screw at each point.

Now make the eaves fillet: a 2ft (610mm) length of 1 x 1in (25 × 25mm) elm is cut diagonally along its length to produce two pieces, triangular in section, so that the faces including the right angle

---

OVERLEAF *'Rest after jam-making', in the living-room of the Thatched Cottage*

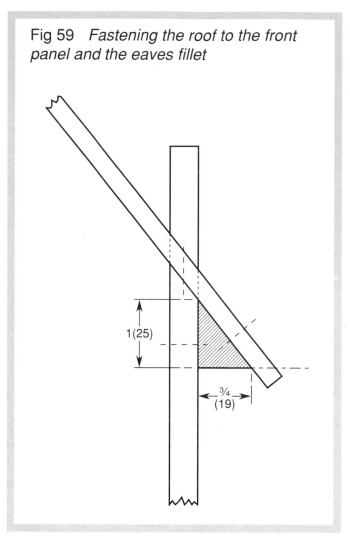

Fig 59 *Fastening the roof to the front panel and the eaves fillet*

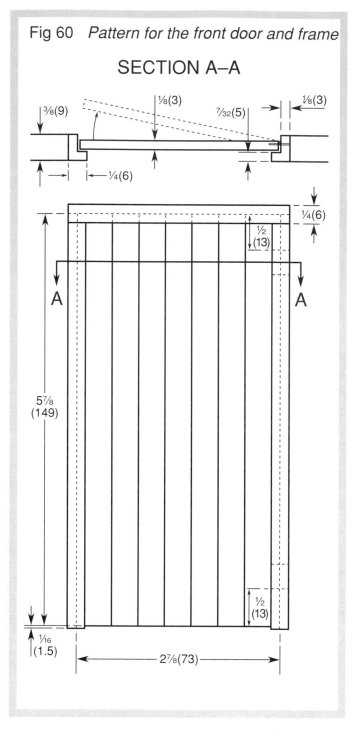

Fig 60 *Pattern for the front door and frame*

SECTION A–A

are 1in (25mm) and ¾in(19mm) wide respectively, and the third face conforms to the roof angle (Fig 59). Fit one length under the roof overhang on the outside of the front panel, from the inside face of the edge thickener at the right-hand end to finish flush at the left-hand end. (The other length will go under the back roof.) Fasten with screws, both through the roof, and through the front panel from the back (Fig 59), and check again that the roof angle has not altered.

For the whole front and front roof section to slide out freely there must be a clearance of about ⅟₃₂in (0·8mm) between the underside of the roof and the sloping tops of the end walls and partition; to achieve this a strip of elm ⅜in (9mm) wide and ⅟₃₂in (0·8mm) thick should be glued to the bottom edge of the front panel. Glue a further short edge thickener of ⅝ × ⅝in (16 × 16mm) elm (Fig 57) under the left-hand side of the roof, with the angled end in line with the inner face of the front panel. Cut off the lower edge of both this, and the section to the right of the roof, flush with the underside of the triangular eaves fillet.

Separate the wall and roof, and either with a router or by hand, round over the right-hand roof

edge and thickener to a ½in (13mm) radius (see Fig 57). The left-hand end is best left square for now.

Glue a ⅜ × ⅛in (9 × 3mm) elm edge strip to the top of the roof. This serves as both an edge veneer for the plywood, and a rubbing surface (see Fig 61).

FRONT WINDOW LINING AND FRONT DOOR

Before re-assembly, the front window openings should be lined with the ⁷⁄₁₆ × ⅛in (11 × 3mm) lime left over when lining the back windows, and the front door and framing made (Fig 60). The framing should be glued in place, and the door removed and put aside for varnishing.

Re-assemble the wall and roof with glue, and leave to set thoroughly, preferably overnight. The

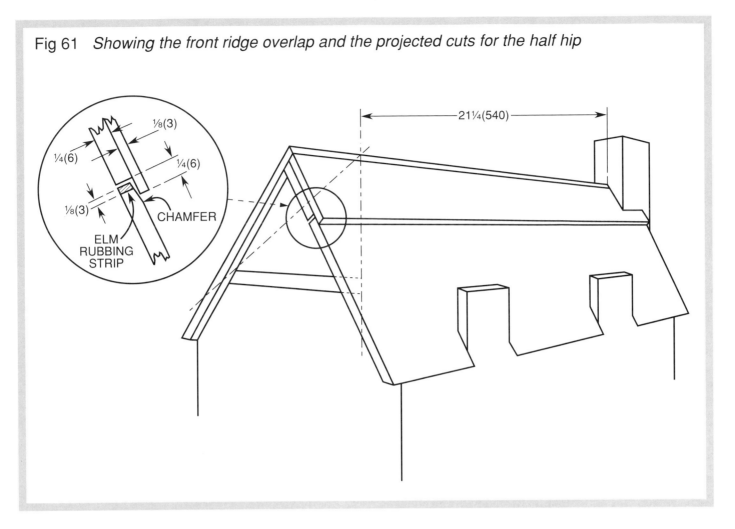

Fig 61 *Showing the front ridge overlap and the projected cuts for the half hip*

triangular eaves fillet must not be glued where it passes in front of the dormer windows as these sections will be removed later. Cut off and plane the lower edge of the front roof panel flush with the underside of the eaves fillet.

FRONT RIDGE

Cut one 24½in (622mm) length of ¼in (6mm) plywood, 2¾in (70mm) wide, and a similar length of ⅛in (3mm) plywood, 3in (76mm) wide. Glue the ⅛in (3mm) plywood on top of the ¼in (6mm) plywood, flush at the top, and projecting ¼in (6mm) at the bottom. Contact adhesive should be used here as pressure can be applied in a vice, and work can continue without waiting for glue to dry. With the combined front panel in position at the front of the house, lay the ridge along the top edge of the front roof with the ¼in (6mm) projection overlapping (see Fig 61). Mark and then cut out the notch required to fit round the chimney, so that the right-hand end of the ridge is flush with that of the roof.

Temporarily screw the ridge to the slopes of both the partition and right-hand end wall. Now plane the top edge of the ridge to the angle of the back roof slope. Mark the top of the ridge 21¼in (540mm) from the inside face of the chimney, and with the

adjustable bevel set at 115°, draw a line from here across the corners of both the ridge and roof, to meet the bevel on the top edge of the left-hand end wall (also Fig 61).

Remove the ridge and cut off the corner ¹⁄₁₆in (1·5mm) on the waste side of the pencil line. Repeat this cut on the roof. The ridge can now be permanently fastened with glue and screws. The top of the roof is now planed, both on the edge and for about ⅜in (10mm) on its face, to give ¹⁄₁₆in (1·5mm) clearance where it slides under the lip of the ridge (see Fig 61). The slight bevel on the top surface should be faired to give a smooth transition from the flat.

BACK ROOF

Plane a bevel along the top edge of the back wall to conform with the roof slope. Cut the back roof panel to fit round the chimney at the upper left-hand corner, with its top edge overlapping the ridge. It should also overhang the end walls by ⅝in (16mm) at each side.

Cut a length of elm ⅝in (16mm) square to fit under the left-hand overhang, with its upper end angled at 38° to butt against the chimney, and the lower end square with the bottom edge of the roof. Glue this in place with contact adhesive, and round over the edge as on the front roof, for the lower 9in (229mm) only.

Cut a 24½in (622mm) length of ⅛in (3mm) plywood, 3in (76mm) wide for the ridge. Cut this to fit the chimney at the left-hand end, with the right-hand end cut at 115° as on the front ridge. Cut the top right-hand end of the roof at a similar angle.

Glue and pin the back roof in position, and then fix the ridge over it. The remaining 2ft (610mm) length of triangular eaves fillet can now be glued and pinned under the roof overhang at the top of the back wall.

HALF HIP

With the front panel firmly taped in position, plane the angled ends of both the front and back roof sections, and the ridges, fair with the bevel at the top of the end wall. Measuring from the underside of the base, draw a horizontal line across the end wall at a height of 13⅛in (333mm). A length of elm ⅝in (16mm) square is glued under the side overhang of the back roof with its upper end angled to conform with this line, and the lower end cut at a similar angle to be flush with the underside of the eaves fillet. A further length is glued to the wall only under the side overhang of the front roof, cut as before at the top, but with the lower end angled downward flush with the front edge of the end wall (see colour illus.), where it butts against the short piece already fitted to the sliding roof (Fig 62).

Cut a triangle of ⅜in (9mm) plywood to cover the hipped end, including the face of the horizontal ⅝in (16mm) square section, and step the sloping sides so that they are flush with the upper faces of both the roof and ridge. Slide the front panel out of the way, and then glue and pin the plywood triangle to the remaining surfaces, with the heads of the pins left proud for later removal.

When the glue has set, remove the pins and glue a further triangle of ⅛in (3mm) plywood at the top to continue the ridge across the hip.

A short section of elm ⅝in (16mm) square should now be glued under the ridge overhang at the right-hand end of the front roof, angled at the top to fit against the chimney, and at the bottom to butt against the section already fitted to the sliding roof.

When the glue has set, trim the lower edges of the roof panels, including any ⅝in (16mm) square that is still projecting, flush with the underside of the eaves fillets, and then round over the remaining side edges of the roof, ridge, and hip. However, take care not to lose the sharp edge on the underside of the hip, where the sliding roof will fit. The bottom edge of the hip should be planed back in line with the lower part of the roof ends, and rounded over (Fig 63).

DORMER STRUCTURE

Cut away the two sections of triangular eaves fillet immediately in front of the dormer tongues. Prepare two blocks of elm 3⅝ × 3¼in (92 × 83mm) and 1in (25mm) thick, with their lower edges shaped to the pattern in Fig 64. Glue and clamp these to the outer faces of the dormer tongues, so that the top edges are flush, and the arched lower profiles just clip the upper corners of the window openings (see Fig 65). When the glue has set, remove the clamps.

Now cut two pieces of knot-free pine or lime 3⅝in (92mm) wide, 5in (127mm) long, and ⅞in (22mm) thick. Bevel one end of each to fit behind the dormer tongues, and plane the top surfaces so that they taper in thickness from ⅞in (22mm) at the front to ⅜in (10mm) at the back. Glue and screw these to the roof, and then similarly fasten a triangular section 7½in (191mm) long on either side (see Fig 65). Leave the joints to harden overnight, and then remove all the screws.

DORMER SHAPING

Remove the front panel from the house; clamp the wall section to the bench with the roof overhanging. A larger electric drill fitted with a 4in or 5in (100 – 125mm) sanding disc will now be needed. First sand the front edges of the triangular pieces on either side of the dormer flush with the elm facing blocks; then with a sharp chisel, and referring to Figs 64 and 65, cut the bottom edges of the facing blocks to the curved profile shown, and sand smooth.

Remove the front panel from the bench, and re-clamp it with the roof section flat, and the wall overhanging. Using the disc sander, shape the tops of both the tongues and facing blocks, to leave an edge about ⅛in (3mm) thick at the front, with the same profile as the underside. Carefully sand the whole top surface to form an ellipse with the edges feathered out all round, and the contours of the front profile becoming progressively shallower as they reach the feather edge at the back. The front edges are best reduced with a spokeshave (preferably with a curved sole) to avoid cutting away too much of the top surface, and thereby altering the front profile.

Fill the screw holes with stopping, and also any imperfections in the feathered edges, and finish by hand sanding. Try to keep surface filling to a minimum, as large areas can adversely affect the adhesion of the surface veneer.

On the inside of the front panel, the lower edge of the roof projects into the window opening where it joins the wall. This is removed by cutting a bevelled slot in the roof, extending to ¼in (6mm) on either side of the window opening.

Fig 62   *To illustrate the roof edge thickening under the half hip*

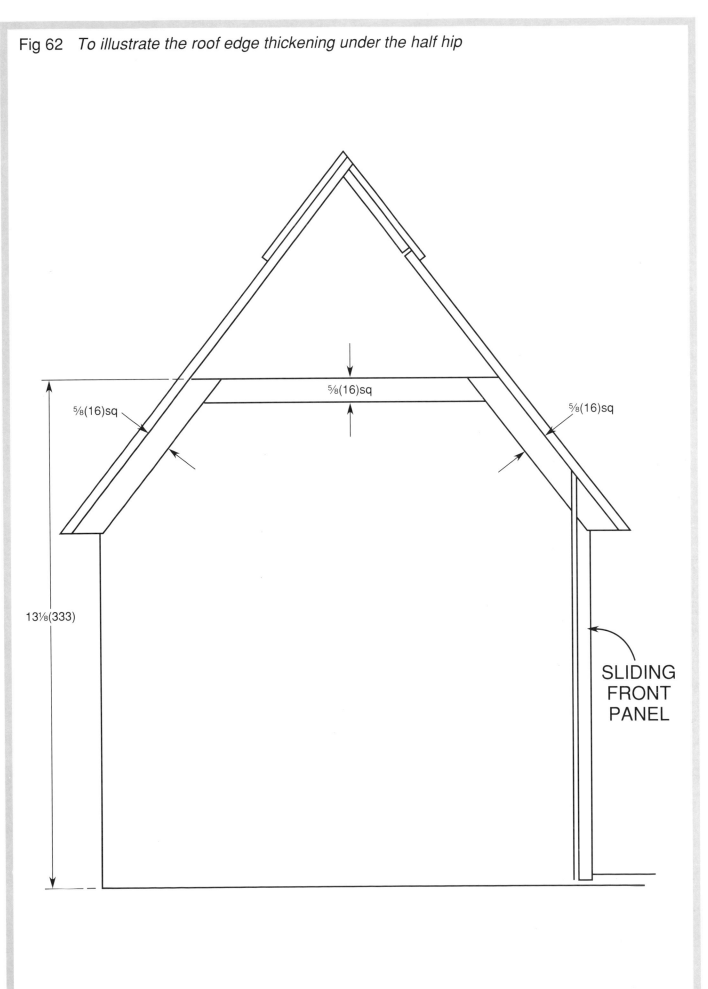

⁵⁄₈(16)sq

⁵⁄₈(16)sq

⁵⁄₈(16)sq

13⅛(333)

SLIDING
FRONT
PANEL

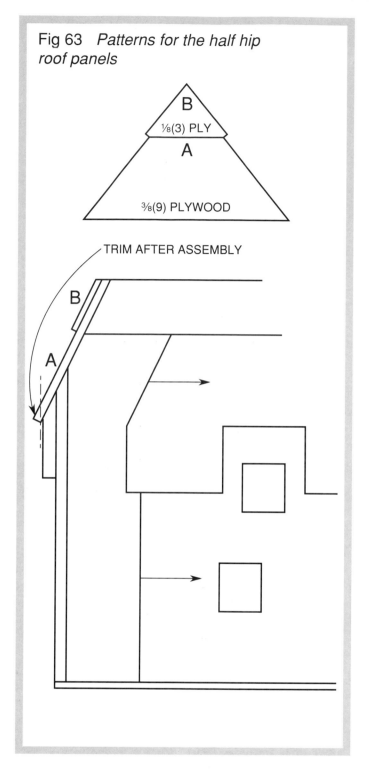

Fig 63 *Patterns for the half hip roof panels*

B
⅛(3) PLY
A
⅜(9) PLYWOOD

TRIM AFTER ASSEMBLY

B

A

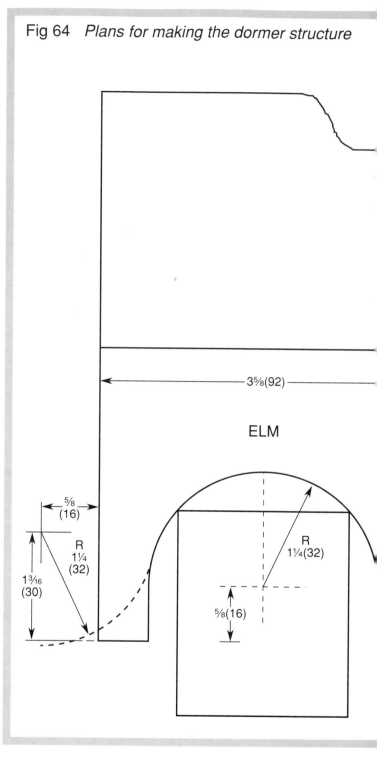

Fig 64 *Plans for making the dormer structure*

3⅝(92)

ELM

⅝
(16)

R
1¼
(32)

1³⁄₁₆
(30)

R
1¼(32)

⅝(16)

ROOF VENEER

Method Teak veneer is applied to the roof surface with contact adhesive. Particular care should be taken to line up the veneer sections correctly before they come in contact with the roof, as the instant adhesion will make them impossible to move without being spoiled. Chalk marks across adjoining pieces before they are glued will make the positioning easier. Masking tape applied to the top face of the veneer where cuts or bends are to be made, will lessen the risk of splitting, particularly when turning over a rounded roof edge, or cutting

to fit round the chimney. Try to use sections of veneer with a reasonably straight grain, and match adjoining sheets. Areas with a wild grain pattern should be discarded if possible, or used on the back roof. Having first pressed the glued veneer down on to the roof with the finger tips, more pressure can be applied by rubbing over the surface with a softwood block.

Application Remove the front panel, and glue a strip of veneer just over ⅛in (3mm) wide along the lower edges of the ridge at the front and back of the

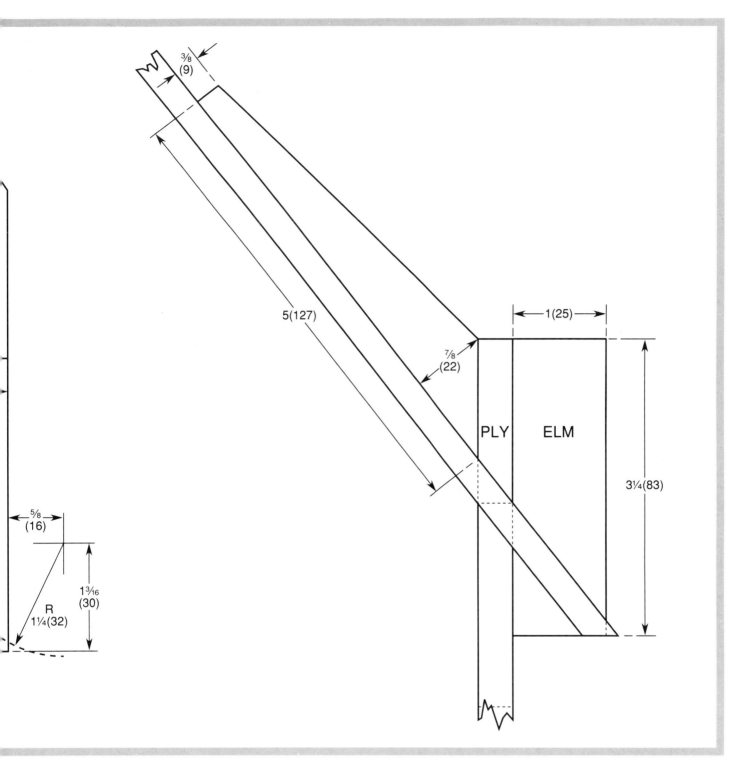

roof, followed by a short strip under the ridge at the hip. Using a sandplate, smooth away any overlap on the outer faces of the ridge, and also under the lip at the front. Replace the front panel and check that there is sufficient clearance under the lip by testing with a small piece of veneer between the lip and the roof. If necessary plane or sand off a little more under the lip or on the top of the roof. The faces of the ridge will be left until last, as short ends can be used to veneer them.

Front Starting at the right-hand end of the front

panel, mark a line down the roof where the dormer contour starts to rise. Cut the first piece of veneer wide enough to reach from here to the right-hand edge, and turn down over the elm thickener. The length should be about ⅛in (3mm) longer than the depth of the roof. Spread the adhesive evenly over this area, and on the back of the veneer, taking particular care that the extreme edges of both are covered.

Bring the left-hand edge of the veneer into contact with the roof at the pencil line, smoothing away from here to the right-hand edge and down

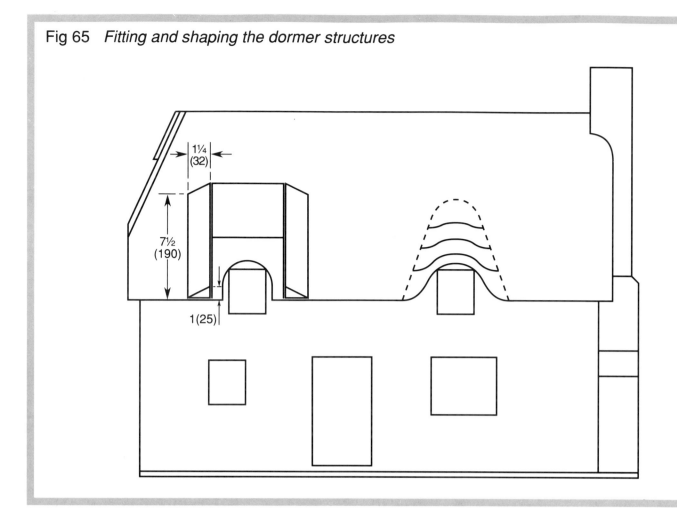

Fig 65 *Fitting and shaping the dormer structures*

over the thickener. Mark a second line down the roof on the other side of the dormer, and cut the next piece of veneer wide enough to reach this line from the edge of the piece just placed. When measuring this width ignore the rise of the dormer. After gluing, butt the right-hand edge of the veneer against that already placed, and smooth out to the left along the top edge while keeping the remainder of the veneer out of contact. Then smooth downwards over the crown of the hump, and from there out towards each side. The veneer should be allowed to split naturally as it tries to stretch over the contours of the dormer. These splits will form darts which can later be straightened with a knife, and filled with a tapered sliver of veneer (Fig 66). Continue in this way over the second dormer to the left-hand end of the roof, turning down over the short thickening piece, and finishing flush with the roof edge above this. Use the round handle of a screwdriver to rub down the concave sides of the dormers, and carefully trim off the veneer round all the edges with a sharp knife and a sandplate.

BACK
The back roof should be veneered next, starting at the chimney end; as there are no dormers to cover,

the sheets can be wider. The last sheet A should turn down over the gable edge at the bottom, and extend over the rounded corner on to the hip face for ¼in (6·4mm) at the top (Fig 67). The lower hip section B is now glued under the ridge from the edge of A to the front where it is trimmed to meet the sliding roof. A further section C is now glued to the side of the front gable thickener.

Ridge Veneer the back face of the ridge first, starting at the chimney and finishing ¼in (6mm) over the hipped end. Trim the top edge, and veneer the front in the same way, finishing with the triangular section D on the hipped end.

VARNISHING
Leave the roof for at least twenty-four hours before removing any traces of glue from the surface with nail varnish remover. The roof can now be sanded, taking care not to rub right through the veneer at the edges, and finished with two coats of Humbrol matt varnish.

INTERIOR GROUND FLOOR
Both ground-floor areas are covered with flagstones. These are made from Formica or other plastic laminate cut into pieces 2 × 2in (51 × 51mm)

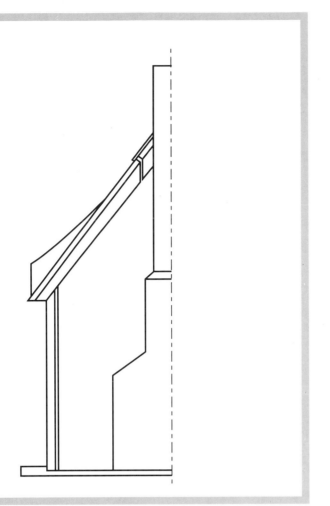

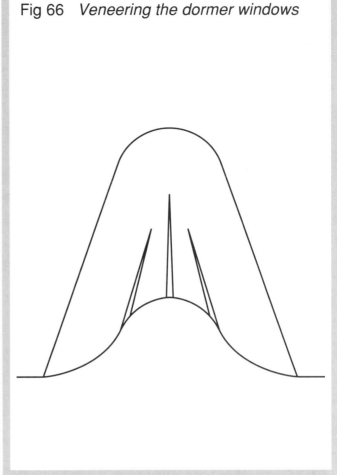

Fig 66   *Veneering the dormer windows*

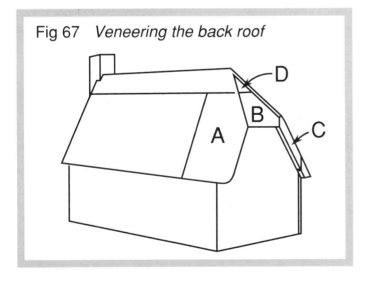

Fig 67   *Veneering the back roof*

and 2 × 1in (51 × 25mm). They are first cut square, and then the irregular edges are shaped with a small sanding disc. You should wear a mask for this. Following the pattern in Fig 68, they are fixed to the floor using contact adhesive with the reverse face of the laminate upwards, and leaving a gap of ⅟₁₆in (1·5mm) between each piece. The edges of pieces that butt against walls, or behind the front groove, should be left straight. Start at the back of a room and work forward, cutting as necessary to fit

round the stairs and into the fireplace. Grout the gaps with Polyfilla or a similar powder filler that has been tinted with black poster paint to a medium grey colour.

When dry, sand the surface and apply two coats of satin varnish. Greater realism can be achieved by mixing blue and green Humbrol paint with the varnish to give each stone varying colour tones.

RANGE

The range used is from Blockhouse Models (see Acknowledgements). To look convincing in a large open fireplace, it needs to be bricked in at the back and sides:

Cut a backboard of ⅛in (3mm) plywood 4½in (114mm) high and 5¼in (133mm) wide, and glue to this two hardwood blocks each 1⅟₁₆in (27mm) wide, 1⅜in (35mm) deep and 2⅜in (60mm) high (see Fig 69). The fronts of the blocks, and the backboard above them, are faced with Houseworks clay bricks available from Blackwells (see Acknowledgements), the mortar joints are grouted with Polyfilla.

LIGHTING

All the lights used in this cottage are from Wood 'n' Wool. The candlesticks in the bedrooms, and the oil lamp in the scullery, need only to be fitted with a

Fig 68 *The flagstones for the ground floors*

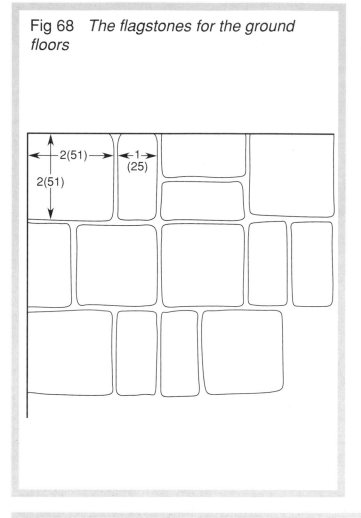

Cir-Kit 1004 plug. The hanging oil lamp in the living-room is fitted by threading the wire tails up through the 1/16in (2mm) hole in the main beam and along the groove in the floor above and finished with a Cir-Kit plug to connect to the socket. The inner end of the loose floorboard should be slotted to let the wire come up outside the skirting.

INTERIOR COMPLETION

To complete the interior, paint or varnish all the remaining surfaces, and hang the doors.

EXTERIOR

Cut one piece of Glodex to the dimensions of each size of front window. Using these as spacers from the back, glue the windows into the linings on the front panel. When finally glazed there must be no projection behind the front panel to impede its movement. When the glue round the windows has set, cut 2mm Glodex or glass to fit the openings; fix behind the windows by lightly gluing the edges.

WINDOW SILLS

Prepare a 12in (305mm) length of lime 5/16in (8mm) wide, and tapering in thickness from 3/16in (5mm) at the back to 1/8in (3mm) at the front. Cut off three pieces 2 3/8in (60mm) long for the small windows and one piece 3 7/8in (98mm) long for the double window. Glue these to the front panel with their

Fig 69 *The brick surround for the range*

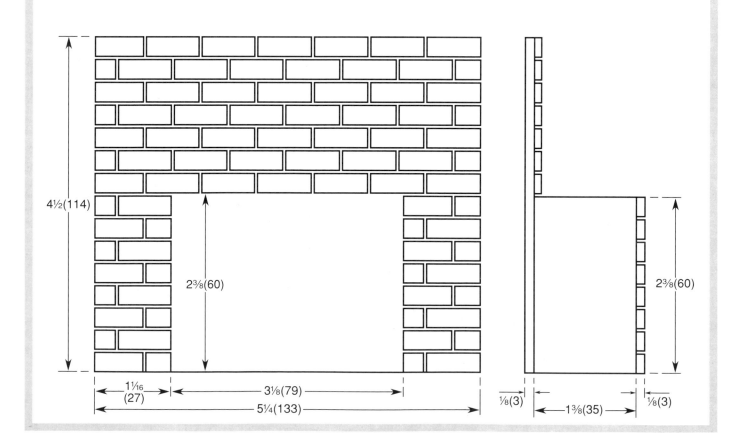

top edges level with the top of the lower lining, and an equal overlap at each end.

LINTELS
Glue lintels above the upper lining on the two ground-floor windows, and above the door frame. They are made from ¼ × 1⁄16in (6 × 1·5mm) elm, with the edges sanded to an irregular rough-hewn shape, and extend ¼in (6mm) either side of the door and window openings.

PAINTING
All the outside walls have two coats of white textured masonry paint, followed by a 1in (25mm) high band of matt black paint at the bottom. The base projection in front of the groove should be painted with grey undercoat only. The window sills, lintels, door frame and roof soffits have two coats of matt varnish.

LOWER CHIMNEY ROOF
The two roof sections on either side of the chimney base should have four courses of slates glued to them. These are made from formica or card, and painted matt grey. Finally, hang the front door.

GARDEN
Base Frame Following the plan in Fig 70, make the frame from 2½ × 5⁄8in (64 × 16mm) pine. The top surface of 1⁄8in (3mm) plywood is glued and pinned to it, working in the order shown in Fig 71. It is easier to fix sections 1 and 2 and then stand the house on the frame so that sections 3 and 4 can be fitted round it. Pads of 1⁄16in (1·5mm) plywood are glued under the joins at both ends of section 4.

Plane smooth all the outer edges of the frame and then drill nine 1⁄8in (3mm) diameter holes, each 3⁄8in (10mm) deep, for the fence post dowels (Fig 71).

Fence Posts and Rails Using the method described in Chapter 1 for window bars, make nine elm posts to the dimensions given in Fig 72, and put two aside for later use on the gate. Of the remaining seven, six should have their bases cut at 15° towards the back, and one is left square. Drill a 1⁄8in (3mm) diameter hole, 3⁄8in (10mm) deep, centrally in the bottom of each, and glue in a ¾in (19mm) length of dowel. Cut ¼ × 1⁄8in (6 × 3mm) elm rails in the following lengths : four pieces 14in (356mm) long for the front, and six pieces 7in (178mm) long for the sides. Stand six posts in the holes along the front of the garden, and one in the back hole at the left-hand side, with the slots facing outwards. Now cut two further posts with plain faces, 3⁄8in (10mm) square and 3¼in (83mm) long. After drilling, cut the bases at 12°. Insert the dowels and stand these posts in the two remaining holes.

Starting at the left-hand side, temporarily fit two short rails in the back post, and mark the centre post where they cross it. From here mark the angle required to project forward and downward to meet the rails in the front of the corner post. This post should now have angled slots cut in the side face. The middle post requires compound slots, the forward half being angled downward, and the back half horizontal. The plain post and the corner post at the right-hand side of the garden should both have angled slots cut into their side faces. Glue the long rails into the slots on the front posts, inset 1⁄8in (3mm) at each end to allow the side rails to be fitted later. Assemble the side sections (see Fig 72), but do not yet glue them to the corner posts at the front, as the four sections will be separated until the palings have been fitted.

Palings About 100 of these will be needed; they are cut 1⁄16in (1·5mm) thick, from a pre-shaped block (Fig 73). They are glued and fastened to the rails with model railway track pins, which are then cut off and filed smooth at the back.

Gate Referring to Fig 74, reduce the dimensions of the two remaining fence posts, and make the gate to fit the space between the two front sections.

Painting Remove the fencing and gate. Paint the top and side surfaces with green undercoat, one coat on the top, and two on the sides. When dry, apply two coats of satin varnish over the undercoat at the sides and to all the under surfaces of the framework.

Grass With the cottage in place, mark the path from front door to gate. Now remove the cottage and apply, first, an even coat of PVA glue to this top surface, then, using a fine sieve, scatter grass and gravel powder on to it; allow to dry thoroughly. The powders used are stocked by most model shops. Several shades of green should be loosely mixed together to give a better effect.

The fence and gate can now be replaced and the side rails glued into the corner posts.

Apply gravel-coloured powder in the same manner over the grey paint at the front of the house base. When dry, the cottage can be replaced.

The plants and flowers used are a combination of the dried variety and those that are modelled by hand (see List of Suppliers, p120).

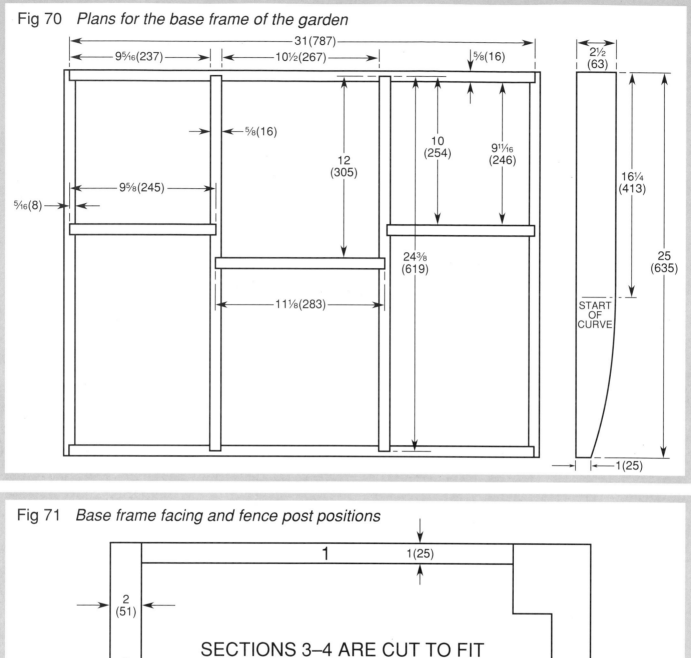

Fig 70 *Plans for the base frame of the garden*

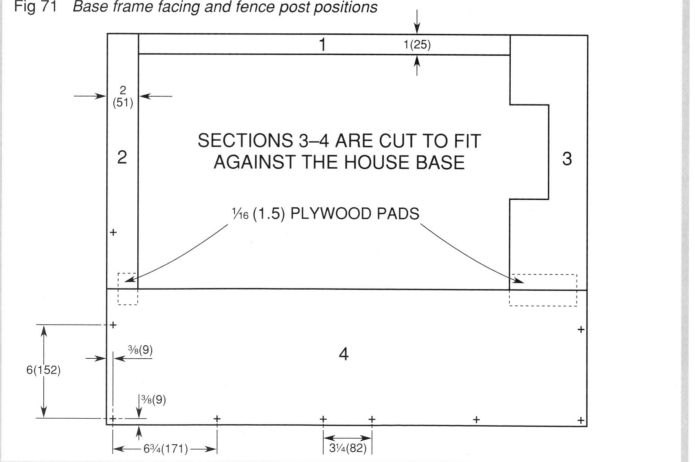

Fig 71 *Base frame facing and fence post positions*

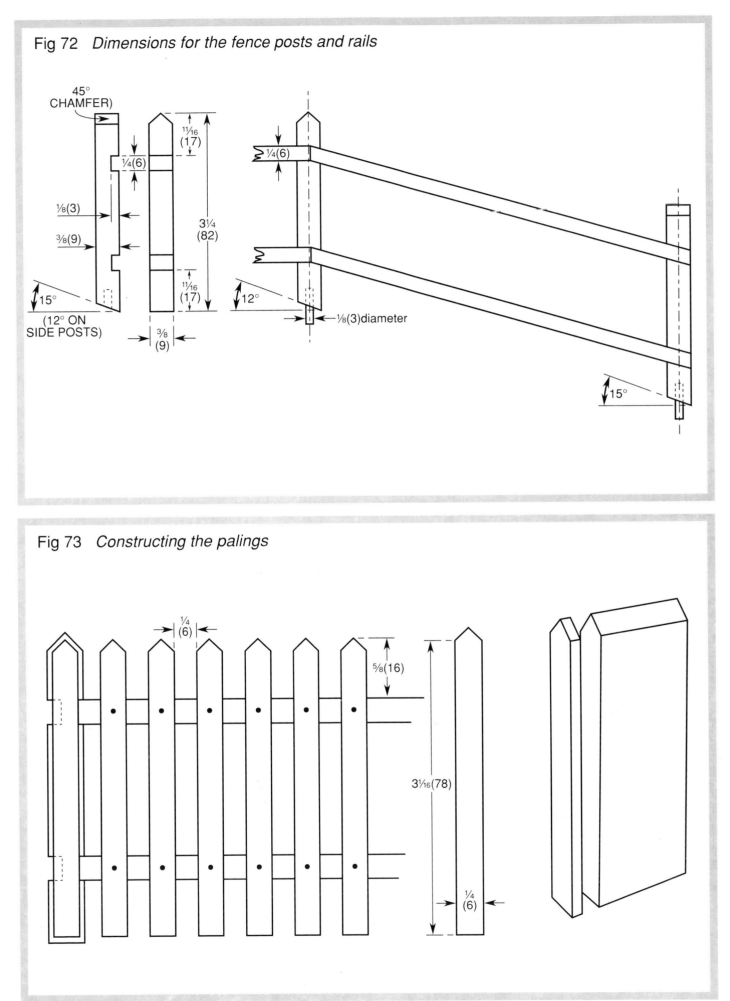

Fig 72   *Dimensions for the fence posts and rails*

45°
CHAMFER)

¹¹/₁₆
(17)

¼(6)

⅛(3)

⅜(9)

3¼
(82)

¼(6)

12°

15°
(12° ON
SIDE POSTS)

⅜
(9)

¹¹/₁₆
(17)

⅛(3)diameter

15°

Fig 73   *Constructing the palings*

¼
(6)

⅝(16)

3¹/₁₆(78)

¼
(6)

Fig 74 *Making the garden gate*

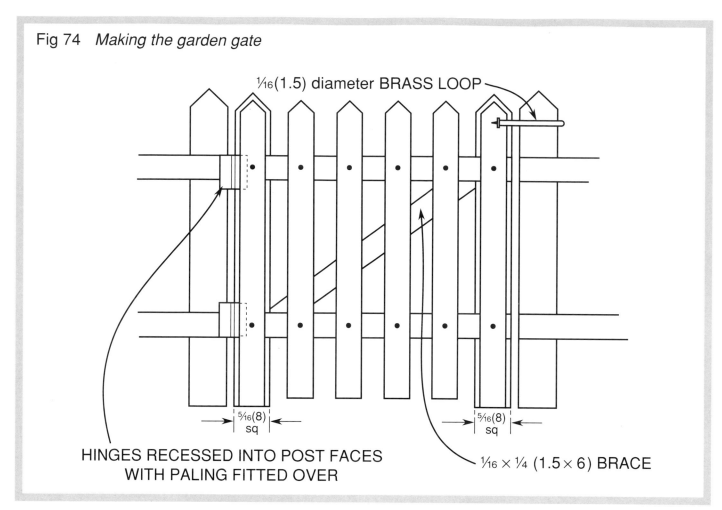

¹⁄₁₆(1.5) diameter BRASS LOOP

⁵⁄₁₆(8) sq

⁵⁄₁₆(8) sq

HINGES RECESSED INTO POST FACES
WITH PALING FITTED OVER

¹⁄₁₆ × ¼ (1.5 × 6) BRACE

THE THATCHED COTTAGE – LIST OF SUPPLIERS

The furniture and accessories used in the Thatched Cottage are from the following suppliers; see Acknowledgements for addresses.

Blackwells: Houseworks clay bricks.
Blockhouse Models: Cooking range.
Rohanna Bryan: Pheasants, potted geranium and primula, vegetables.
Bryntor: Flower pots, hot water bottle, storage jars, sink and draining board.
Irene Campbell: Flower pots and stoneware flagons.
C & D Crafts: Laundry basket.
Malcolm Chandler: Towel rail.
Country Treasures: Warming pan.
Dijon: Tin bath.
Dolphin Miniatures: Barrel, flower tubs, rake, axe, wheelbarrow, yoke, cradle, toy doll, chest of drawers, wheelback chair, spinning wheel, washstand, slop-pail, swing mirror, toybox, tables, dresser, ladderback chairs, settle, corner cupboard, salt box, candle box, bellows.

Tony Hooper: Brass kettle, and copperware.
From Kitchen to Garret: Brass bed.
Lesley Anne Dolls: Lady with laundry basket.
Carol Lodder: Flagons, storage jars, spongeware, washbasin and jug; teapots, mugs, milk jugs, plate and candlestick.
Mainly Men Minis: Sleeping granny doll.
John and Pauline Meredith: 'Staffordshire' figurines.
Leo Pilley: Baby bottle, demi-john, yard of ale, and milk bottle.
Quality Dolls' House Miniatures: Spade, fork and trowel; flat iron.
Secret Garden: Rose bushes.
June Stowe: Miniature knitting.
Sussex Crafts: Jam-making set, jars, preserving pan and spoon.
Thames Valley Crafts: Sunlight Soap.
Wood 'n' Wool Miniatures: Lighting.

The watering can, trug, clock, bargeware plate and large bed are from the author's own collection.

5
THE FISHERMAN'S COTTAGE

*This design is a collation of features from harbourside
cottages all around Cornwall.
The roof should really be slated, but as the stonework is
fairly dark the lighter colour of the shingles helps to give a little warmth.
Although the loft is shown here as a fisherman's store, it
would make a superb art gallery or pottery showroom.*

The carcase is constructed in the same manner as that for the Thatched Cottage, with the base and back panel rebated and grooved for the end and dividing walls. The front wall, with part of the front roof attached to it, also slides in a groove, though the break line occurs lower down the roof, beneath a course of shingles. Access to the loft is through a removable front panel. Three further techniques are introduced — stonework, roof trusses, and shingles. These are all time-consuming, but are well worth the effort, and having just a simple ladder to the bedroom in place of stairs compensates to some degree. The fireplace, chimney, flagstone floor, windows and front door are all identical to those in the Thatched Cottage, and reference should be made to that chapter for details.

End view of the Fisherman's Cottage, showing loft doors and hoist

---

CARCASE

From the patterns in Figs 75a and 75b, cut out the base A, back panel B, left-hand wall C, and the two walls with loft extension D and E, all from ⅜in (9mm) plywood. Cut the grooves and rebates to the dimensions shown.

For simplicity, the grooves on the base for the extended walls continue right across the panel; those sections that remain exposed under the covered passage can be filled with a wood strip later. Note that the rebates on the extended walls D and E are on the inner faces only, to house the cross walls under the loft. Both inner rebates are ⅜in (9mm) wide and extend for 6in (152mm) only above the bottom edge; while the rebate at the outer edge is only ¼in (6mm) wide but extends for the full height of the wall.

Cut the window opening in the back panel B, and the two door openings in the right-hand wall E only, together with the ½ × ⅜in (13 × 10mm) slot for the hoist beam. The passage opening under the loft extension should be cut out on both D and E. The fireplace opening should be cut out on the left-hand wall C (see Fig 75b).

Temporarily fasten the three walls and the back panel to the base with screws. Now fit the three

TIMBER REQUIREMENTS

WOOD	THICKNESS in	mm	WIDTH in	mm	LENGTH ft/in	m	WOOD	THICKNESS in	mm	WIDTH in	mm	LENGTH ft/in	m
Lime	1/16	1.5	3/8	10	9in	0.23	Elm	5/32	4	1/2	13	18in	0.46
	1/8	3	1/4	6	18in	0.46		3/16	5	5/16	8	5ft	1.53
			7/16	11	4ft	1.22				1/2	13	11ft	3.35
	5/32	4	3½	89	12in	0.31		1/4	6	3/8	10	4ft	1.22
	3/16	5	5/16	8	9in	0.23				7/16	11	6in	0.16
	1/4	6	1/2	13	12in	0.31				5/8	16	15in	0.38
Pine	5/8	16	3	76	22ft	6.70		3/8	10	1/2	13	2ft	0.61
	3/4	19	2⅛	54	12in	0.31		1/2	13	1/2	13	39in	1.0
			2¼	57	7ft	2.14		5/8	16	5/8	16	39in	1.0
			3⅜	86	9in	0.23				7/8	22	12in	0.31
Elm	1/32	1	1/2	13	20ft	6.1							

WOOD	THICKNESS in	mm	AREA sq ft	sq m
Birch Plywood	3/8	9.0	16	1.5
	1/4	6.0	3	0.3
	1/8	3.0	8	0.75
	1/16	1.5	1	0.09
Formica or similar laminate			2	0.18

(Continuation of Elm left-hand column: 1/16 | 1.5 | 1/4 | 6 | 6in | 0.16 · 7/16 | 11 | 18in | 0.46 · 1/8 | 3 | 3/16 | 5 | 18in | 0.46 · 1/4 | 6 | 9in | 0.23 · 3/8 | 10 | 3ft | 0.92 · 3/4 | 19 | 2ft | 0.61 · 1 | 25 | 8ft | 2.44)

cross walls between the rebates of D and E. All three are cut 8½in (216mm) wide and 6in (152 mm) high, two from ⅜in (9mm) plywood and one from ¼in (6mm) plywood (Fig 75b). Mark the inside faces of D and E, and also that part of the back panel which lies between them, with a horizontal line level with the top edges of the cross walls. The floor bearers for the loft will be glued below this line. Now draw a similar line inside the remaining section of the carcase, this time 6¾in (172mm) above the top of the base, for the floor bearers in that section.

INTERNAL TIMBER FRAME AND FLOOR BEARERS

Cottage Prepare 11ft (3·4m) of ½ × ³⁄₁₆in (13 × 5mm) elm, and, following Fig 76, cut and glue this as a border on the inside face of the end wall C down to upper-floor level. On the opposing wall D it should continue to base level, with a ¼in (6mm) gap at each side for the floor, and a further section fitted horizontally, as a floor bearer. It is important to leave ⅛in (3mm) clear at the bottom and back edges of both walls, for location in the back panel and base. The area below upper-floor level on the end wall C must be left clear for the fireplace surround which will also form the floor bearer on that wall.

Loft The cross walls support the floor at the front. Three further sections of bearer should be glued to walls D and E behind the inner cross wall, and across the back panel, with their top edges on the pencil line. All the faces, and the inner or lower edges of the framing and bearers, should now be shaped and textured with a small sanding disc or drum, fitted in a Minicraft drill, to give the rough-hewn finish as in the Thatched Cottage.

Chimney and Fire Surround Following the instructions in Chapter 4 and Figs 46 and 47, the

Fig 75a *Patterns for the base and the back panel*

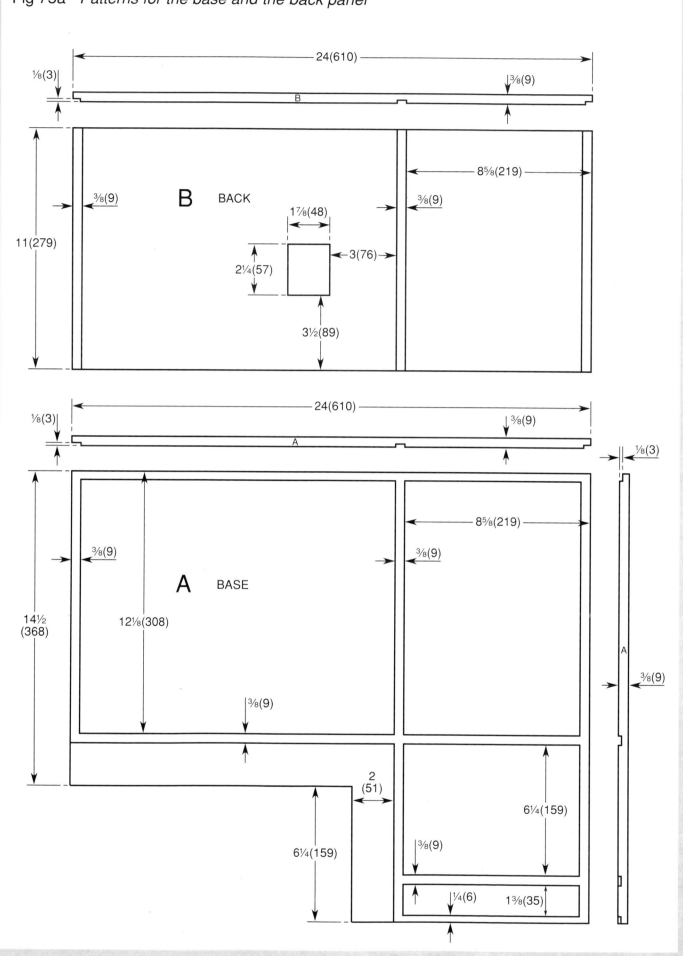

Fig 75b *Patterns for the carcase walls*

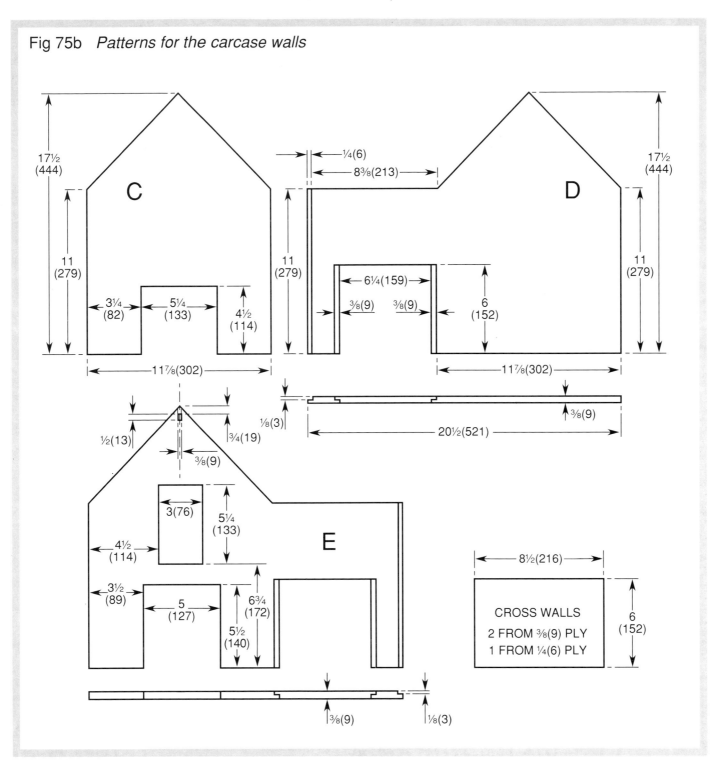

chimney can now be made; it is then fastened to the outside of the end wall C, and the internal stonework and lintel built on the inside. The upper part of the stack should be 1in (25mm) shorter than that on the Thatched Cottage, giving an overall height of 20in (508mm).

WINDOWS AND LININGS
The windows are made to the same dimensions as those in the Thatched Cottage (see Fig 50). Three small windows and one larger double window will be needed. The linings are made and fitted as before, but the wood used is left ¹⁄₁₆in (1·5mm) wider (⁷⁄₁₆ × ⅛in (11 × 3mm) lime), to allow a projection at the outside of the front and back panels. This will be flush with the finished surface of the stonework.

Varnish all the windows, and line the opening in the back panel. When dry the back window can be glued in place using a Glodex or glass spacer to set

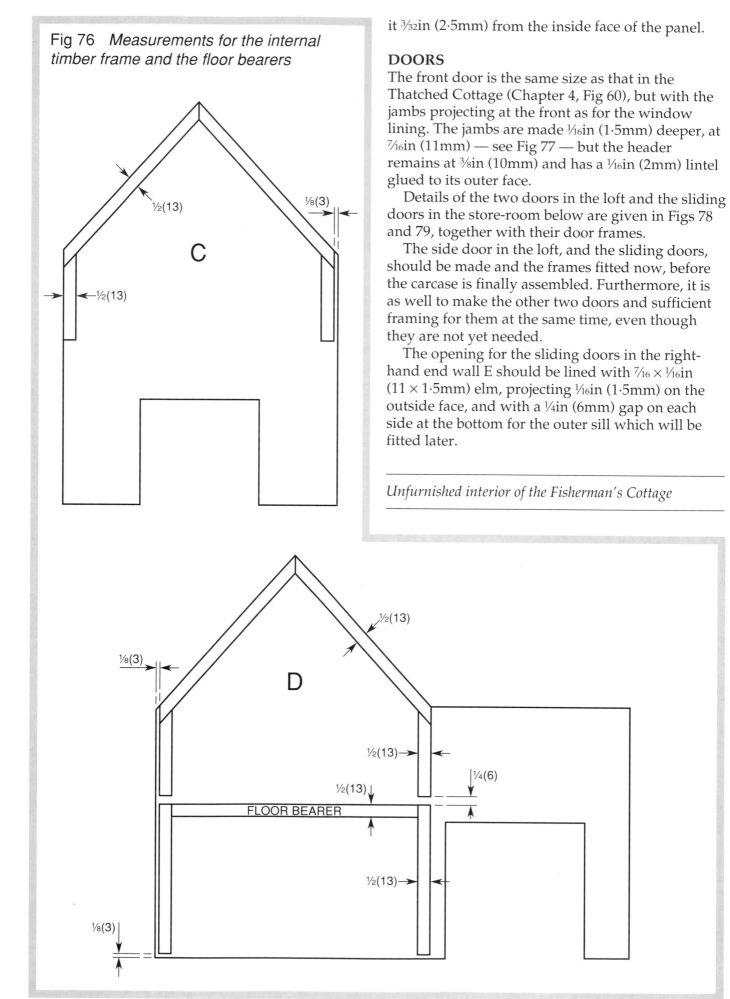

Fig 76 *Measurements for the internal timber frame and the floor bearers*

it ³⁄₃₂in (2·5mm) from the inside face of the panel.

DOORS

The front door is the same size as that in the Thatched Cottage (Chapter 4, Fig 60), but with the jambs projecting at the front as for the window lining. The jambs are made ¹⁄₁₆in (1·5mm) deeper, at ⁷⁄₁₆in (11mm) — see Fig 77 — but the header remains at ³⁄₈in (10mm) and has a ¹⁄₁₆in (2mm) lintel glued to its outer face.

Details of the two doors in the loft and the sliding doors in the store-room below are given in Figs 78 and 79, together with their door frames.

The side door in the loft, and the sliding doors, should be made and the frames fitted now, before the carcase is finally assembled. Furthermore, it is as well to make the other two doors and sufficient framing for them at the same time, even though they are not yet needed.

The opening for the sliding doors in the right-hand end wall E should be lined with ⁷⁄₁₆ × ¹⁄₁₆in (11 × 1·5mm) elm, projecting ¹⁄₁₆in (1·5mm) on the outside face, and with a ¼in (6mm) gap on each side at the bottom for the outer sill which will be fitted later.

Unfurnished interior of the Fisherman's Cottage

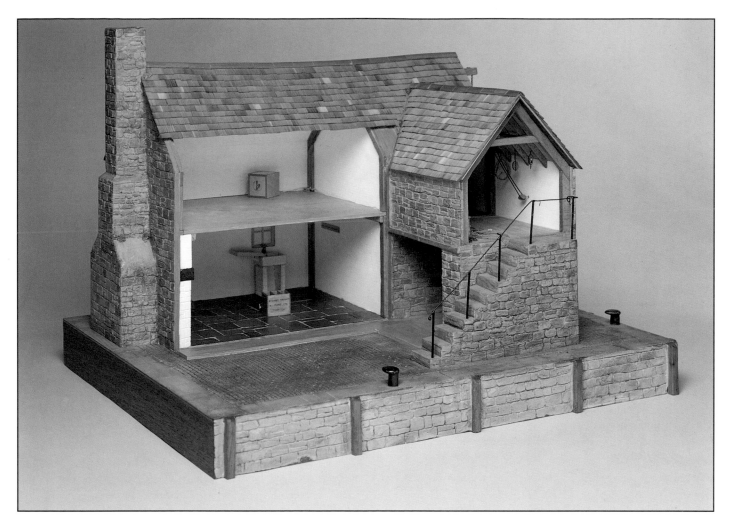

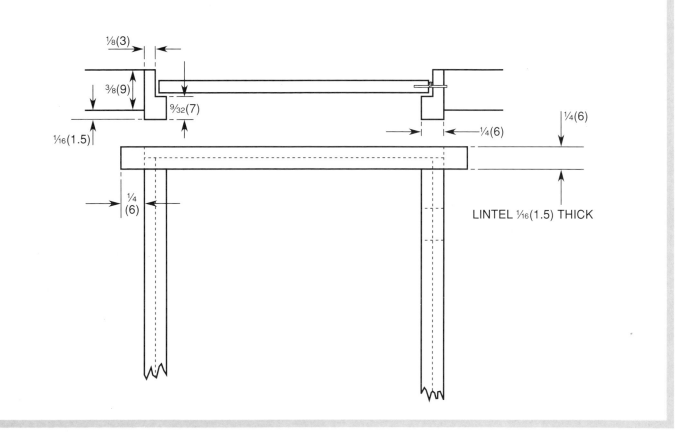

Fig 77 *Making the front door jambs and header*

⅛(3)

⅜(9)

9/32(7)

1/16(1.5)

¼(6)

¼(6)

¼(6)

LINTEL 1/16(1.5) THICK

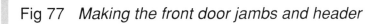

The top guide for the sliding doors is made from ½ × ¼in (13 × 6mm) lime, 11¾in (299mm) long; it should be rebated as shown in Fig 79, and glued to the inside of E (Fig 79).

ASSEMBLY

The carcase can now be finally assembled with glue and screws.

UPPER FLOORS

Cut the floors F and G from ¼in (6mm) birch plywood to the dimensions shown in Fig 80, noting that the grain should run from side to side on F, and from front to back on G. Cut out the trap-door opening on F. Scribe the floorboards ½in (13mm) wide, except for the two margin boards on G which are ⅝in (16mm) wide. F has an edging strip of lime, ¼ × ⅛in (6 × 3mm) glued to the front.

Two ½ × ⅜in (13 × 10mm) elm beams are glued under F where shown in Fig 80, with their inner faces chamfered and textured. They are spaced to fit outside the fire surround on the left and the floor bearer on the right. The floors can now be fitted to the cottage but should not be glued.

LOFT TRUSSES

Following Fig 81, cut out two loft roof trusses from ⅜in (9mm) plywood. Veneer the inner edges and faces with ¹⁄₃₂in (1mm) elm. Using contact adhesive, apply the edge veneers first, and allow the face veneers to overlap them. Trim and sand to a rough-hewn textured finish. Cut a slot in the apex of each truss ¼in (6mm) wide and ⁵⁄₁₆in (8mm) deep, for the ridge beam. With their bases resting on the floor, glue and screw the trusses to the inside of the loft walls D and E. The inner truss should be directly above the inner cross wall, and the outer truss set back ¼in (6mm) from the outer edges of the loft walls, flush with the rebates. Do not glue under the truss bases, as the loft floor needs to remain portable.

WIRING

Remove the loft floor and drill a ⅛in (3mm) diameter hole through the back panel ½in (13mm) to the right of wall D, and ½in (13mm) above the base. Cut away ⅝in (16mm) of the floor bearer on the back panel, where it butts D. Now apply Cir-Kit tape upwards from the hole to 1¼in (32mm) above the floor bearer, and from here run a further length along the inside face of the wall D, at the same level, to finish just behind the inner truss. Brad the tape at the connection, and also at the bottom. Fit a Cir-Kit 1003 socket behind the truss. Another tape is applied to the cottage side of D to reach from the back panel forward for 6in (152mm). Brad the inner end, and fix a similar socket at the outer end. Now

drill a ¹⁄₁₆in (2mm) diameter hole through D, close to the back edge, and thread through a length of twin wire, which is soldered to the brads on each side of the wall. A further 36in (915mm) of twin wire is soldered to the brads at the start of the tape above ground-floor level, and threaded through the hole to the outside. Coil this and tape it to the back wall.

INTERIOR PAINTING

Most of the interior painting should be done now while still accessible. The elm framing, bearers, and fireplace lintel should have one coat of matt varnish, and the upper floor surfaces two coats. Walls and ceilings have two coats of white emulsion. The ground floor in the cottage will be covered by flagstones, but the small floor area in the store-room under the back of the loft is painted matt grey.

SLIDING DOORS

Cut a notch ⅜ × ³⁄₃₂in (10 × 2·5mm) in each door where they meet over the central stop (Fig 79). Apply two coats of matt varnish, and when dry fit the handles (Houseworks no 1123).

Position the doors inside the store-room with their top edges under the guide, and trim as necessary so that they slide freely. A strip of elm ⅜ × ⅛in (10 × 3mm), and 11¾in (299mm) long, is glued and pinned to the floor behind them, and a sill of ⁷⁄₁₆ × ¼in (11 × 6mm) elm fastened into the base rebate on the outside (Fig 79). The door stop — made of ⅛ × ³⁄₃₂ × ¾in (3 × 2 × 19mm) elm — is now glued centrally in the channel between the inner and outer sills.

FRONT PANELS

Referring to Fig 82, cut out the two front panels; note that the cottage front is from ⅜in (9mm) plywood, and the loft front from ¼in (6mm) plywood. The door frames can now be cut to length, slotted for the hinges, and glued into the panel openings (see Figs 77 and 78).

The window openings are lined next, remembering to leave a projection of ¹⁄₁₆in (1·5mm) at the front. Varnish the doors and put them aside. Glue and pin the loft floor in position, and then glue a strip of lime, ¼ × ¼in (6 × 6mm), outside it and on top of the outer cross wall. The loft floor should now be varnished.

A ¼ × ⅛in (6 × 3mm) elm strip is glued right across the bottom edge of the loft front, as a stiffener. When dry, position the loft front above the floor and between the rebates on the side walls. Trim the top edges in line with the upper edges of the truss behind it. There should be clearance at each side of the panel of a little under ¹⁄₃₂in (1mm) to allow for easy removal. A small magnet should

Fig 78   Constructing the two loft doors

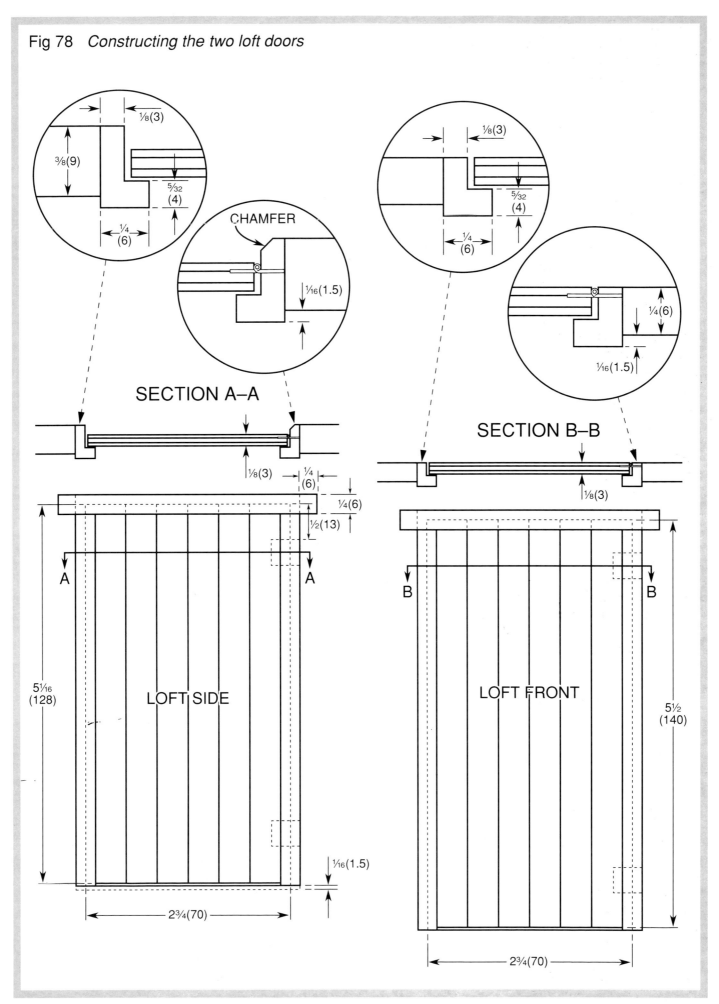

⅛(3)

⅜(9)

5/32 (4)

¼ (6)

CHAMFER

1/16(1.5)

⅛(3)

5/32 (4)

¼ (6)

¼(6)

1/16(1.5)

SECTION A–A

SECTION B–B

⅛(3)   ¼ (6)

¼(6)

½(13)

⅛(3)

A   A

B   B

5 1/16 (128)

LOFT SIDE

LOFT FRONT

5½ (140)

1/16(1.5)

2¾(70)

2¾(70)

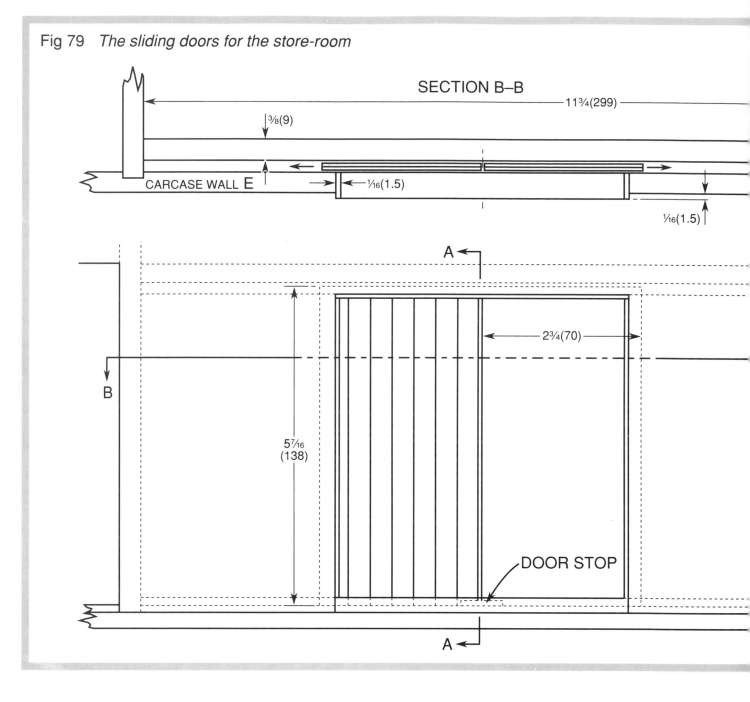

Fig 79   *The sliding doors for the store-room*

SECTION B–B

11¾(299)

⅜(9)

CARCASE WALL E

1⁄16(1.5)

1⁄16(1.5)

A

2¾(70)

B

5⁷⁄16
(138)

DOOR STOP

A

be sunk into the face of the outer truss, near the top, with its contact plate fitted to the inside of the loft front.

FITTING THE ROOF
Bevel the top edges of the back panel and the sliding front to conform with the slope of the main roof, and then cut a similar bevel on the side walls of the loft. From ⅛in (3mm) birch plywood, cut the two main roof panels, both 25in (635mm) long; one is 9⅞in (251mm) deep for the front, and the other 10in (254mm) deep for the back. Two loft roof panels are also required, both from ⅛in (3mm) plywood 12½in (318mm) long, and 7in (178mm) deep.

Referring to Fig 83, prepare 8ft (2·5m) of elm tiltboard, 1in (25mm) wide, and tapering in thickness from ⅛in (3mm) to a feathered edge. Cut and glue this to the four roof panels, flush at the lower edges.

Lay the front roof in place with an equal overhang of ½in (13mm) at each end. Mark where it rests on top of the bevelled loft walls, and cut away both here and round the chimney to allow the panel to drop over the bevels until its top edge is flush at the apex of the three main walls. Temporarily pin the roof in position.

Loft Ridgeboard   Cut a 12¼in (311mm) length of ⅝ × ¼in (16 × 6mm) elm, and halve this into the

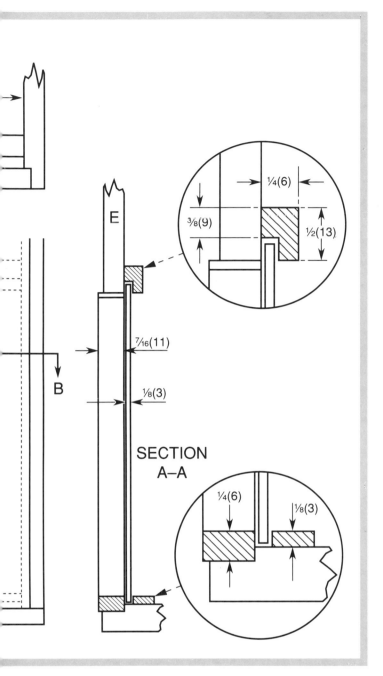

E

¼(6)

⅜(9)

½(13)

⁷⁄₁₆(11)

⅛(3)

B

SECTION
A–A

¼(6)

⅛(3)

it to the top edge of the sliding front panel with three screws, in the centre and 1½in (38mm) from each end.

Marking the break line Draw a provisional line across the roof, 3⅝in (92mm) above the lower edge, from the left-hand end to the guide line for the loft roof cutout. This will be the break line, and should lie ¼in (6mm) above what will be the exposed section of the sixth shingle (see Fig 87).

The position of this line should be checked as follows: cut three Greenleaf shingles (see page 141) in half to leave six pieces, each ¾in (19mm) long. Tack these to the lower left-hand side of the roof with a small blob of hot-melt glue, starting as shown in Fig 88 with the first shingle flush with the lower edge of the tiltboard, and each successive shingle overlapping by ³⁄₁₆in (5mm) to leave an exposed area ⁹⁄₁₆in (14mm) deep. Then *cut* the sixth shingle to ⁹⁄₁₆in (14mm) — this should leave its top edge ¼in (6mm) below the pencil line previously marked. Adjust the position of this break line if necessary, and then remove both the shingles and the roof.

Cut out the truncated triangular area to locate the loft roof, and then cut along the break line from the left-hand end, to meet it (Fig 87). Cut a rebate ¼in (6mm) wide and ¹⁄₁₆in (1·5mm) deep along the top edge of the lower section just separated, and into this glue a strip of elm ³⁄₆₄in (1mm) thick to provide a rubbing surface and clearance under the overlap of the top section (see Fig 88). The lower section can now be glued and screwed to the top of the front panel, and a triangular section fillet glued under the overhang at the outside.

A slight sag in the ridge line improves the appearance of this cottage, but this must be done without distorting the front surfaces which slide against each other. Plane the back roof slope of wall D from ⅛in (3mm) at the top, to nothing at the lower edge. This will achieve the desired effect by creating a slight hollow in the roof and therefore altering the ridge profile when viewed from the front. The front roof surfaces remain flat.

UPPER FRONT ROOF
Glue a further length of elm tiltboard along the lower edge of the upper roof section, allowing it to overlap ¼in (6mm) at the bottom (Fig 88).Then replace the combined front roof and front panel in the base panel groove. Glue and pin the upper roof to the gable slopes of the three walls C, D and E. The front panel is now free to slide with the upper ¼in (6mm) of its roof section running under the overlap of the upper tiltboard.

Referring to Fig 89, cut two triangular pads of ¼in (6mm) plywood and glue them under the roof,

truss notches, with its inner end angled to butt the roof (Fig 84). Glue it in place on the trusses, but not where it butts the roof; when dry, trim off flush with the face of the outer truss. Plane the top of the ridgeboard to the slope of the truss on each side. Angle the inner ends of the two loft roof panels to fit against the main roof. Using these as a guide, mark the main roof so that it can be cut out to allow the loft roof to fit inside it. A line should also be marked on the main roof directly below the loft roof ridgeboard (Fig 85).

Slide the front panel into position and secure it with tape. Following Fig 86, remove the main roof and plane the eaves bevel across its lower edge. Now replace the main roof and temporarily fasten against the inner faces of walls D and E, and extending ⅛in (3mm) into the cutout for the loft roof. These will provide a land for the inner edges of the loft roof panels, and the left-hand pad will also fill the void exposed by the sliding roof.

BACK ROOF

With a spokeshave, shape the top edge of the front roof to a fair curve, dipping to meet the lowered back slope of wall D. The back roof can now be cut to fit round the chimney. Bevel the bottom edge and tiltboard as for the front, and then glue and pin

it in position with a triangular section fillet under the overhang at the outside of the wall. When dry trim the overlap at the ridge.

LOFT ROOF

Drill a ¹⁄₁₆in (2mm) diameter hole up through the centre of the collar on the inner truss, for the light which will be fitted later.

Bevel the lower edges of the loft roof panels. Temporarily pin the left-hand panel in position, with its lower edge level with that of the main roof. The inner end of the panel will need to be notched at the top to fit into the cutout. Trim the top edge flush, then fit the right-hand panel so that it overlaps it at the ridge.

LOFT RAFTERS

Cut six rafters from ⁵⁄₁₆ × ³⁄₁₆in (8 × 5mm) elm, each with its ends angled, one to fit against the ridgeboard, and the other against the inside face of the loft wall. Mark a pencil line on the underside of both roof panels behind the outer truss and in front of the inner truss. Lines should also be drawn along both sides of the ridgeboard and where the roof meets the bevelled tops of the side walls. Remove the panels, and using the pencil lines as a guide, space three rafters equally in each roof section.

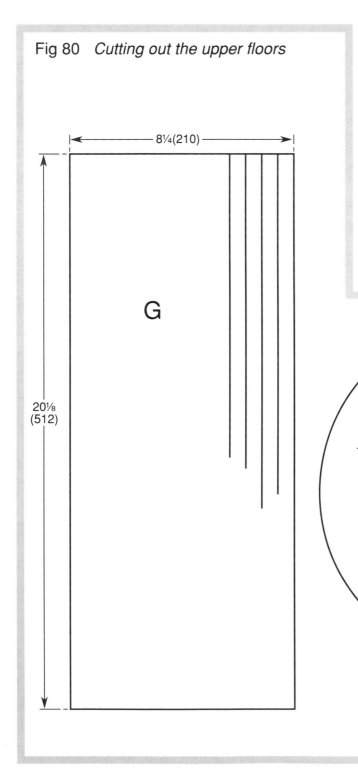

Fig 80 *Cutting out the upper floors*

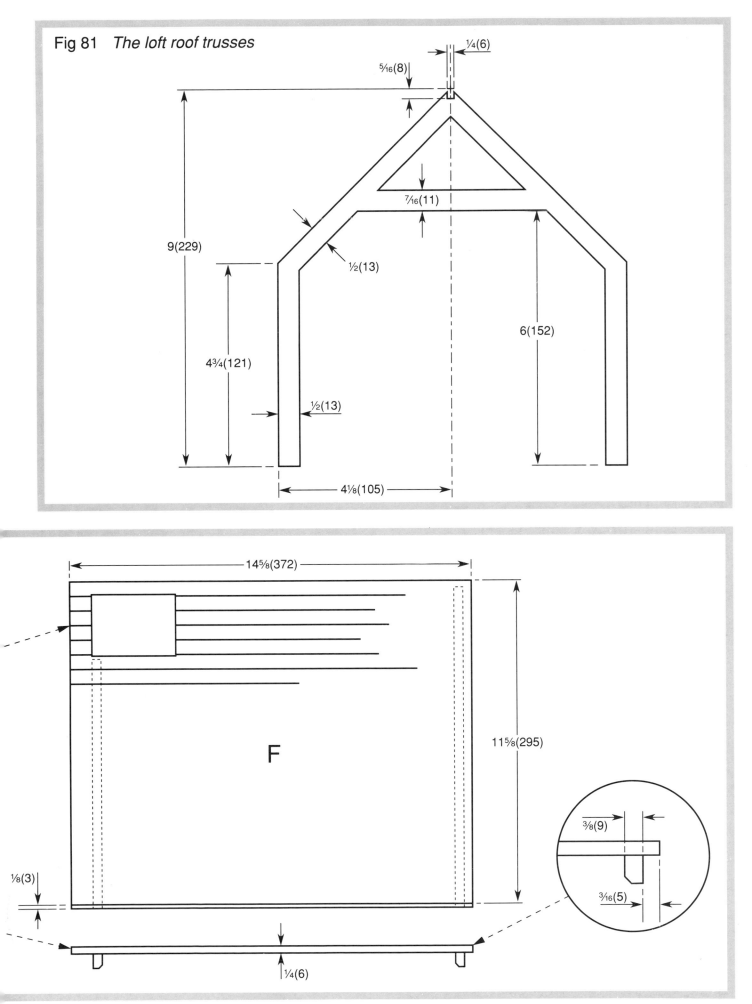

Fig 81 *The loft roof trusses*

¼(6)

⁵⁄₁₆(8)

9(229)

⁷⁄₁₆(11)

½(13)

6(152)

4¾(121)

½(13)

4⅛(105)

14⅝(372)

F

11⅝(295)

⅛(3)

¼(6)

⅜(9)

³⁄₁₆(5)

Fig 82 *Patterns for the front panels*

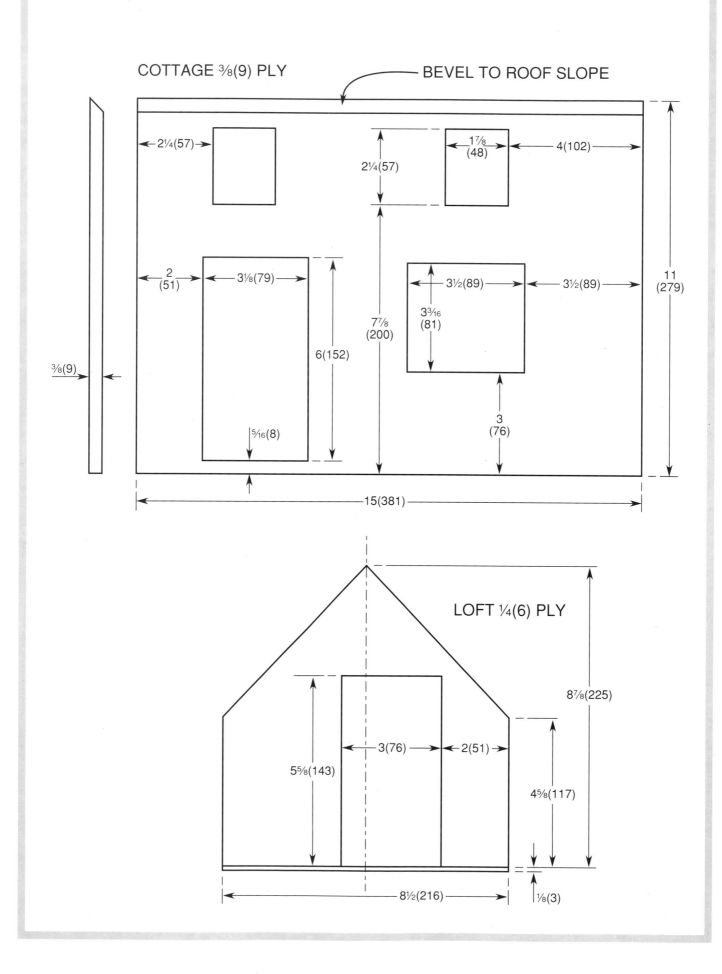

COTTAGE ⅜(9) PLY

BEVEL TO ROOF SLOPE

LOFT ¼(6) PLY

Inside the loft

Mark their outlines and apply contact adhesive to both roof and rafters; first re-assemble the roof, and then press the rafters in place.

Now cut two purlins from ³⁄₁₆ × ⅛in (5 × 3mm) elm and fit them one on each side, between the trusses in line with the centre collar beams; mark their position on the rafters. Once again remove the roof panels and apply pressure to the rafters in a vice, taking care not to alter their position. The purlins are now glued and pinned across the rafters. Leave for twenty-four hours to allow the adhesive to cure, and then apply two coats of matt varnish to both roof and rafters, avoiding those areas which are to be glued. When the varnish is dry, re-assemble the roof with glue and pins.

LADDER AND TRAP-DOOR
Following the dimensions in Fig 90, make the ladder from elm. The slots for the treads can either be cut with a small chisel, or on the router table

using a scrap of ¼in (6mm) plywood, cut at 65°, as a guide.

Smooth the edges of the trap-door opening in the floor F, and glue in the ³⁄₁₆ × ⁵⁄₃₂in (5 × 4mm) lime facings (see Fig 91). These should be flush with the underside of the floor, leaving a rebate at the top ¹⁄₁₆in (1·5mm) deep for the trap-door. Cut the trap-door from ¹⁄₁₆in (1·5mm) plywood to the dimensions of the opening, and then trim it to give a clearance of ¹⁄₆₄in (0·5mm) all round. Scribe the top surface to match the floor, and add the ⅜ × ¹⁄₁₆in (10 × 1·5mm) lime braces underneath. The hinges are Houseworks no 1130 (see Acknowledgements), glued and pinned on the surface, with a ring handle made from brass wire.

FLAGSTONES
These are made from plastic laminate as in the Thatched Cottage (Chapter 4, Fig 68). Those stones which lie under the base of the ladder should be notched to fit round the stringers before being glued to the floor.

FIREPLACE
The range used in this cottage is made up from a Phoenix kit (see List of Suppliers), and as in the Thatched Cottage, it needs to be bricked in for realism. Follow the instructions given in Chapter 4, Fig 69, varying the width of the wood blocks to suit the range.

If you wish to fit the range from Blockhouse Models (see Acknowledgements), which was used in the Thatched Cottage, the measurements for the brick infill will be identical.

The interior is now complete, apart from touching up the paintwork and connecting the lights.

OUTSIDE STAIRWAY
The steps are made from ten stacked lengths of softwood each 2¼in (57mm) wide and ²¹/₃₂in (17mm) thick. Each length is ¾in (19mm) shorter than the one below it, starting 11in (279mm) long at the bottom, and finishing 4¼in (108mm) long at the top (Fig 92). Glue and pin the steps together, and

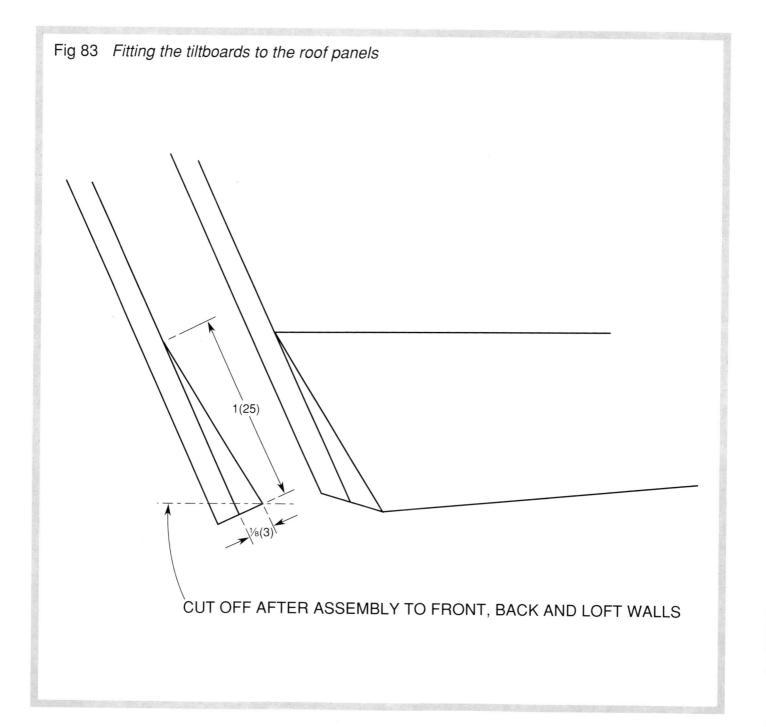

Fig 83   *Fitting the tiltboards to the roof panels*

1(25)

⅛(3)

CUT OFF AFTER ASSEMBLY TO FRONT, BACK AND LOFT WALLS

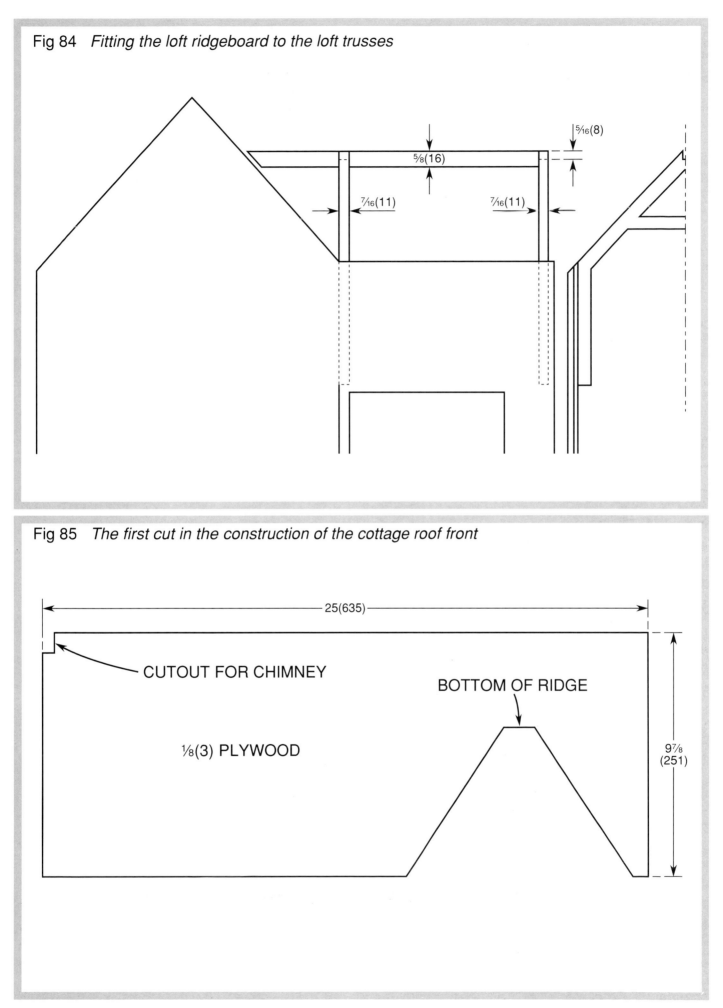

Fig 84   *Fitting the loft ridgeboard to the loft trusses*

Fig 85   *The first cut in the construction of the cottage roof front*

when dry plane the back face to fit evenly against the cross wall.

The stairway should now be glued and screwed to the cross wall at the front of the loft, with its bottom edge flush with the underside of the cottage base and the top step centred below the loft doorway. The screws will need to be 2½in (64mm) long, countersunk into the outer face of steps 4 and 7. There is no need to plane the outer face of the stairway, as stonework will be applied over it.

The handrail can be made now, but should not be fitted to the steps until the stonework is completed. Cut five 3in (76mm) lengths of ⅛in (3mm) diameter brass rod, and file the tops of three of them to 40°. Each post should now have a ³⁄₁₆in (5mm) length of brass tube (inside diameter ¹⁄₁₆in (1·5mm)) soldered to the top (see Fig 92). The ¹⁄₁₆in (1·5mm) diameter wire rail will be threaded through after the posts have been fitted to the stairway.

HOIST BEAM
This is made from elm as shown in Fig 93. If you have a lathe, the sheave can be turned from brass rod; alternatively, drill two ⅛in (3mm) diameter holes where shown, and connect them by cutting a groove ⅛in (3mm) deep in the top and bottom edges.

When the stonework is finished, the beam will be glued into the hole at the top of the right-hand wall E, with 2in (51mm) projecting.

WINDOW SILLS AND LINTELS
Referring to Chapter 4, the window sills are made to the same dimensions as those for the Thatched Cottage, but this time they should be made from elm instead of lime. Lintels will be required over the sliding doors, and on each side of the covered passage under the loft. These are cut from ⅜ × ⅛in (10 × 3mm) elm with a rough-hewn finish, and extend for ½in (13mm) beyond the openings at each end, except on the cottage side of the passage where the inner end butts the outside of the sliding front panel.

A further lintel ¼in (6mm) wide and ¹⁄₁₆in (1·5mm) thick should be glued above the double window on the front panel. (The lintels over the doorways were fitted earlier as part of the door frames.)

STONEWORK
The application and scribing of the stonework will take around eight hours to complete, and once started, it must be finished in one session. After this time the mixture becomes too hard to scribe successfully. The work can be split by plastering the ends and front on one day, and the back on the following day, but care will be needed to ensure

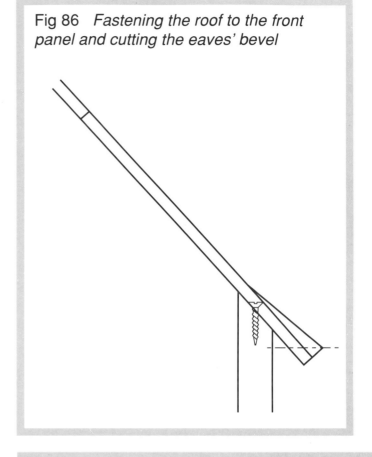

Fig 86 *Fastening the roof to the front panel and cutting the eaves' bevel*

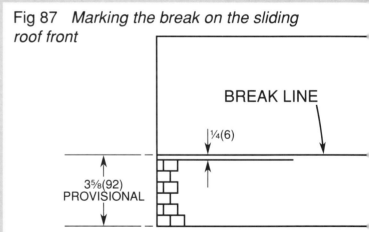

Fig 87 *Marking the break on the sliding roof front*

BREAK LINE

¼(6)

3⅝(92)
PROVISIONAL

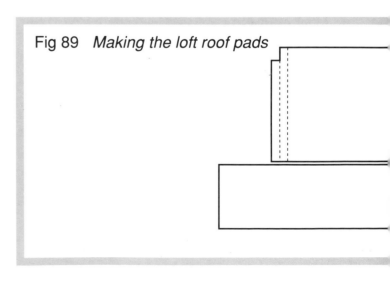

Fig 89 *Making the loft roof pads*

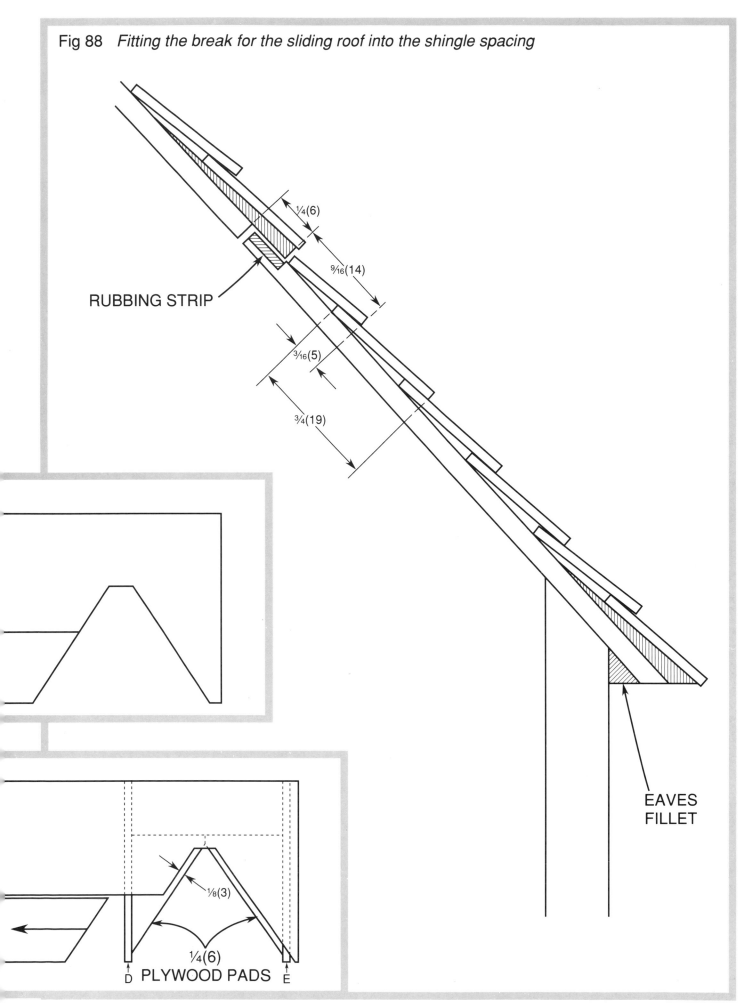

Fig 88 *Fitting the break for the sliding roof into the shingle spacing*

RUBBING STRIP

¼(6)

⁹⁄₁₆(14)

³⁄₁₆(5)

¾(19)

EAVES FILLET

⅛(3)

¼(6)

D   PLYWOOD PADS   E

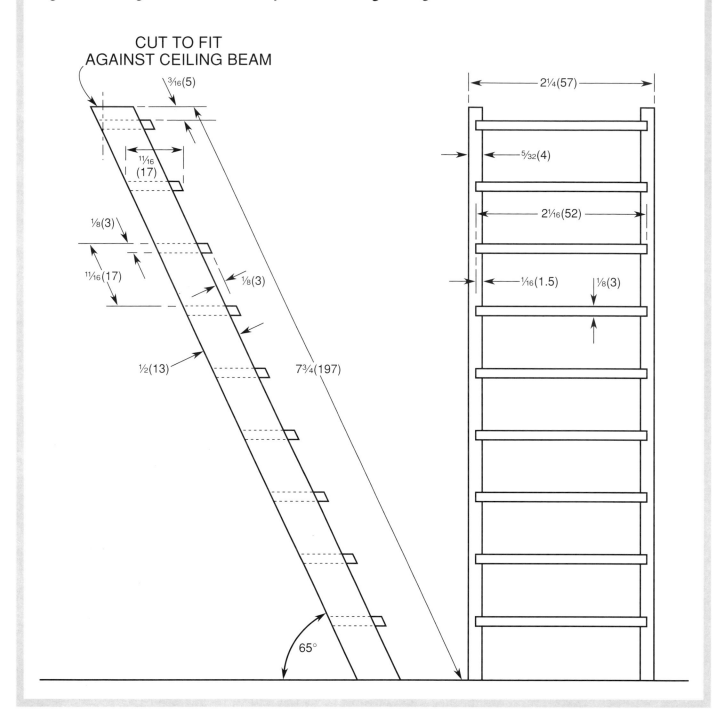

Fig 90 *Making the ladder stairway for the cottage living-room*

that the colouring of the mixture is consistent. Before tackling the cottage, you should have a trial run on a plywood offcut, to familiarise yourself with the various stages involved.

The ideal tool for scribing is a dental scraper with a round cutting edge about 1/16in (2mm) in diameter. Alternatively an old round needle file can be ground to shape. Start by masking all the areas which must not be plastered, particularly the roof soffits and the lower and right-hand edges of the sliding front panel. The masking should extend for

1/8in (3mm) up the front face of this panel, to allow it to fit in the groove.

Powder filler, such as Polyfilla, should be mixed with water to a stiff paste, sufficient to cover the walls to a depth of 1/16–3/32in (1.5–2.5mm). As a guide, half a packet will be needed. It is better to have too much, than to have to stop and prepare another mix. Add a tablespoon of PVA glue, and tone the mixture to a light grey brown with poster paint. Remember that the colour will be considerably lighter when the filler has dried.

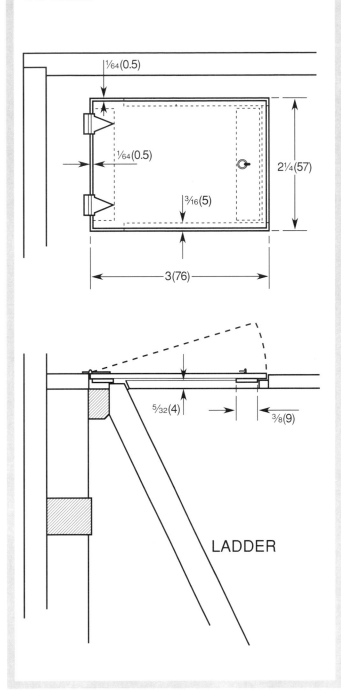

Fig 91 *Fitting the trap-door at the head of the ladder*

LADDER

(13mm) to ⅝in (16mm) apart, using a graduated batten with a panel pin driven through the end. Take care not to cut right through the coating, and if it shows any sign of lifting off or clinging to the panel pin, let it dry a little longer. Do not scribe the lines too precisely. Following the pattern in Fig 94, lightly pencil the outline of the stones on to the surface and cut the joints with the scraper. The cuts should not mark the plywood underneath.

Leave to harden overnight, and then remove any high spots with a chisel and sandpaper. Use a coarse paper very lightly to retain the same surface texture as the remainder. With the Skarsten scraper, clean off all the faces of window sills, linings, door frames and lintels.

COLOURWASH
Mix a little green, brown and yellow poster paint in about one pint (½ltr) of water to give the basic stone colour required, and brush this liberally over all the stonework. While the surface is still moist, mix a more concentrated combination of these colours in a saucer and with a ⅜in (9mm) chisel-edged brush, vary the tones of random stones — some with rather more yellow, others with more green, and so on until the desired overall effect is achieved. Allow to dry thoroughly before sealing with two coats of matt varnish. If the stonework is not completely dry, the varnish will bloom.

The inside faces of both the portable front panels should be painted next before finishing the roof.

ROOF SHINGLES
Three bags of Greenleaf rectangular shingles will be needed. These are available from Hobby's (see List of Suppliers). Each bag contains about three hundred shingles 1½in (38mm) long and ¾in (19mm) wide. Make a simple jig from a strip of plywood ¾in (19mm) wide, with a shingle glued across it ¾in (19mm) from the end, and using a sharp knife cut 800 shingles in half, to produce 1,600 pieces ¾in(19mm) square. There are sometimes marked colour variations between the shingles from different bags, so they should be well shuffled. A grid must be drawn on the roof as a guide when fixing the shingles. Starting at the left-hand end of each, draw a series of vertical lines down both the front and back roof panels ⅜in (10mm) apart. Now draw the horizontal guide lines starting ¾in (19mm) above the lower edge of the tiltboard, and then continuing parallel to it at 9⁄16in (14mm) intervals to the top of the roof.

All the shingles are placed with a 3⁄16in (5mm) overlap, leaving an exposed face of 9⁄16in (14mm) (see Fig 88). Using a hot-melt glue gun, and starting at the lower left-hand corner of the sliding roof, fix the first row of shingles with their top edges on the

Prime the walls with diluted PVA glue (+ 10% water) and then spread the paste, levelling it out. With a damp paintbrush, smooth the surface to remove any ridges, taking care to avoid excessive build-up against the sides of the door frames and window linings. When smoothing, work from side to side so that any residual brush marks are horizontal.

When the filler has dried sufficiently to be reasonably firm (usually half- to three-quarters of an hour), lightly scribe the stone courses ½in

The Fisherman's Cottage, fully furnished

first horizontal guide line, and their bottom edges flush with the tiltboard. Continue across the roof to the right of the loft roof projection, finishing with a half-width shingle.

Mathematically on a roof length of 25in (635mm) the last shingle should be only one-third of its full width, but in practice, errors in placing and slight variations in the width of individual shingles can alter this. If necessary, the width of the penultimate shingle can be reduced by up to ⅛in (3mm). Continue up the roof with each course staggered by half a shingle width, cutting the shingles as required to fit against the loft roof. When applying the sixth course take care to keep the sliding surfaces clear of glue.

On reaching the right-hand end of the sliding section, cut off the sharp top corner in line with the last shingle joint, and glue the small triangle of plywood to the main roof in the position it would occupy if still attached to the sliding section. Shingle with the main roof (see Fig 95.)

Leave a ½in (13mm) gap between the last (top)

course of shingles and the ridge to accommodate the ridge tiles (Fig 96). To maintain an even gap above the top course, where the roof sags, the shingles below this area must be closed up (otherwise the ridge tiles will be difficult to fit). Increase the overlap by ¹⁄₆₄in (0·5mm) on the upper eight courses below the dip, and arrange so that their top edges follow the concave curve of the ridge.

The loft roof should be shingled next, keeping the courses level with those on the main roof. A clearance of ¹⁄₃₂in (1mm) should be left where the first five courses of the loft roof shingles butt against those on the sliding roof. Complete the back roof in the same manner and then scrape any surplus glue from the ½in (13mm) space above the top courses, and plane the overlapping shingles at the roof edges level with the plywood.

RIDGE TILES

Prepare 39in (1m) of elm ⅝in (16mm) square, and cut this to the right-angled section shown in Fig 96. Now cut again into 1½in (38mm) lengths, and glue these along the ridge with a gap of ¹⁄₃₂in (1mm) between each. These gaps should be grouted with wood stopping of a slightly lighter colour. With a sharp chisel carefully remove any glue that has run

Fisherman's Cottage living-room

on to the shingle faces, and lightly sand the roof, following the vertical grain of the shingles. Finish with two coats of Humbrol matt varnish.

BASE FRAME
Following Fig 97, make the base frame from 3 × ⅝in (76 × 16mm) softwood. Then place the cottage on top in the position shown in Fig 98, and use it as a guide when fixing the ⅛in (3mm) plywood surface sections — these are best fitted in the order indicated 1–4. Plane all the edges smooth. Next glue and pin the ½in (13mm) square elm piles to the sides and front (see colour photograph). These will look more convincing if they are distressed with the sander and saw-blade.

Stonework Remove the cottage and apply plaster mixture to the front, sides and top surface of the base. The sides are scribed with stones following the pattern used for the cottage walls (Fig 94). The top surface is scribed with cobbles, surrounded by a border of 1¾–2in (45–51mm) square slabs (Fig 99).

Colouring Colour the stonework as before but use rather more green to simulate weed and slime. Paint the cottage base front projection and the floor in the covered passage to match. Finish with two

coats of matt varnish, including the plain back edge and the underside of the frame.

COMPLETION
Following the instructions in Chapter 1, hang the doors and glue in the front windows, followed by the glazing. Drill the outside steps where shown in Fig 92 and fix the handrail.

A 16in (406mm) length of chain will be needed for the hoist. This should have a wire hook at one end and a 'rope' tail at the other. Alternatively, the elm blocks from Dolphin Miniatures (see List of Suppliers) can be used.

A small screw eye should be fitted on the outside wall E, a little to the left of the upper door sill, and a cleat made from wire fixed at the left-hand side of the sliding doors.

Cover the small roof sections at the chimney base with slates, as on the Thatched Cottage.

The wire tails from the loft light (Peter Kennedy) should be threaded up through the collar on the inner truss and fitted with a Cir-Kit plug to suit the

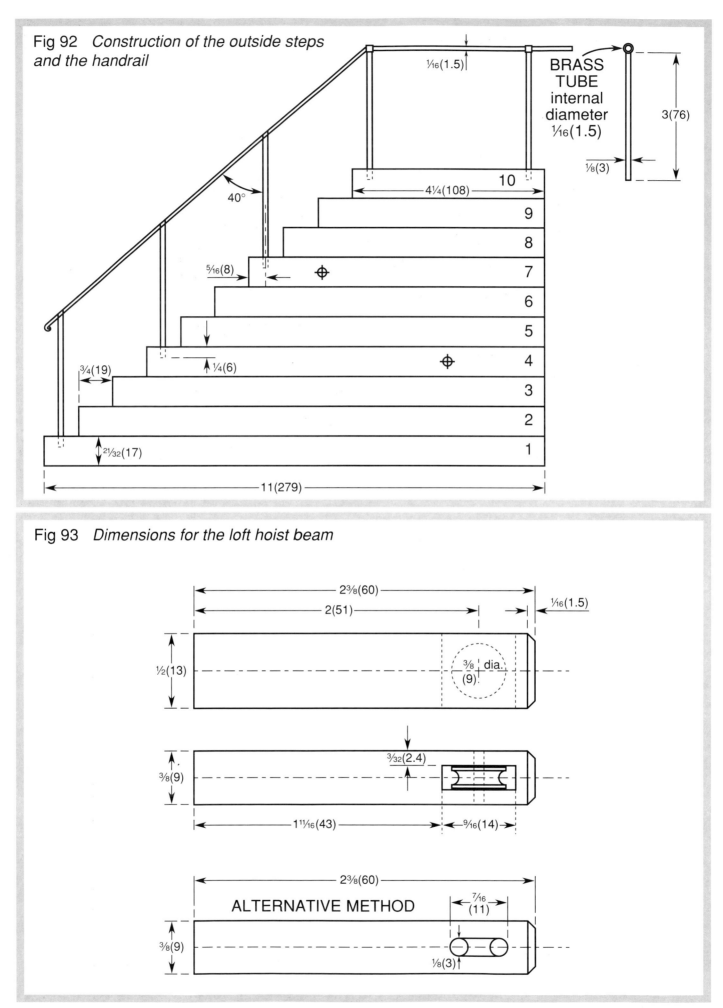

Fig 92 *Construction of the outside steps and the handrail*

1/16(1.5)

BRASS TUBE internal diameter 1/16(1.5)

3(76)

1/8(3)

40°

4 1/4(108)

10
9
8
7
6
5
4
3
2
1

5/16(8)

3/4(19)

1/4(6)

21/32(17)

11(279)

Fig 93 *Dimensions for the loft hoist beam*

2 3/8(60)

2(51)

1/16(1.5)

1/2(13)

3/8 dia. (9)

3/8(9)

3/32(2.4)

1 11/16(43)

9/16(14)

2 3/8(60)

ALTERNATIVE METHOD

7/16 (11)

3/8(9)

1/8(3)

Fig 94   *Pattern for the outside stonework*

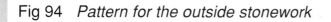

Fig 95   *Removing the corner from the sliding roof*

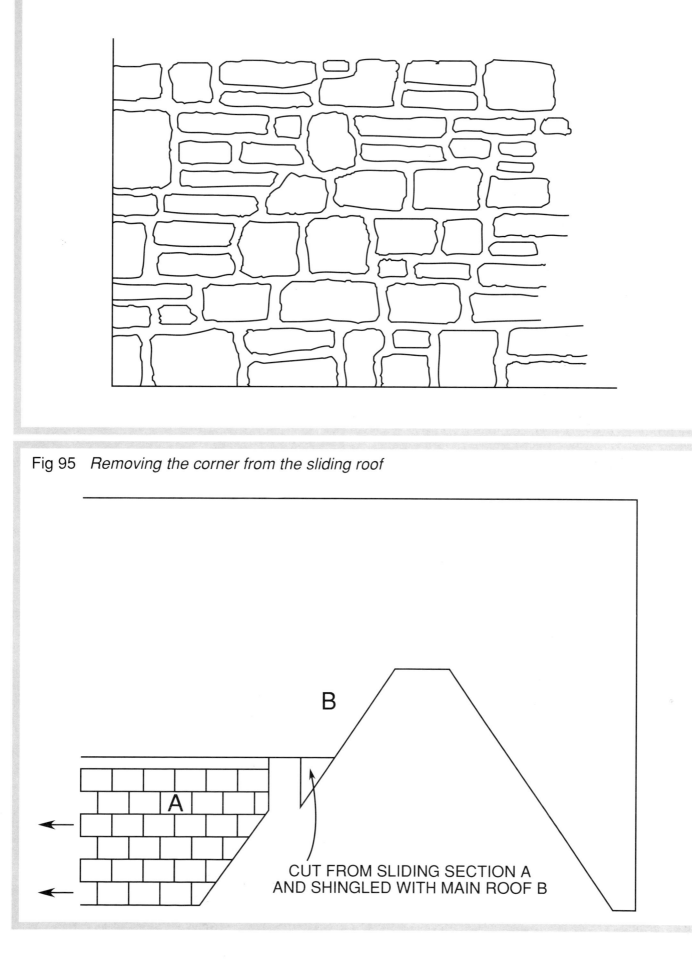

B

A

CUT FROM SLIDING SECTION A
AND SHINGLED WITH MAIN ROOF B

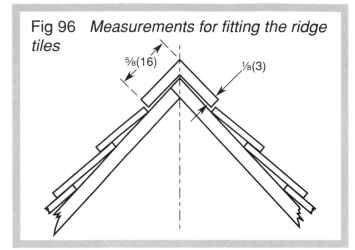

Fig 96 *Measurements for fitting the ridge tiles*

⅝(16)   ⅛(3)

socket already placed. The bedroom candlestick (Wood 'n' Wool) needs only a Cir-Kit plug. The oil lamp on the living-room table (Wood 'n' Wool) is wired through a hole in the flagstone floor.

Screw a small terminal block to the top of the base frame at the back, close to the transformer feed wire. This wire should be cut and reconnected through the terminal block. The wire tails from the oil lamp should be extended by about 12in (305mm), passing under the cottage in notches cut in the base frame to a similar connection.

Front of the Fisherman's Cottage and loft

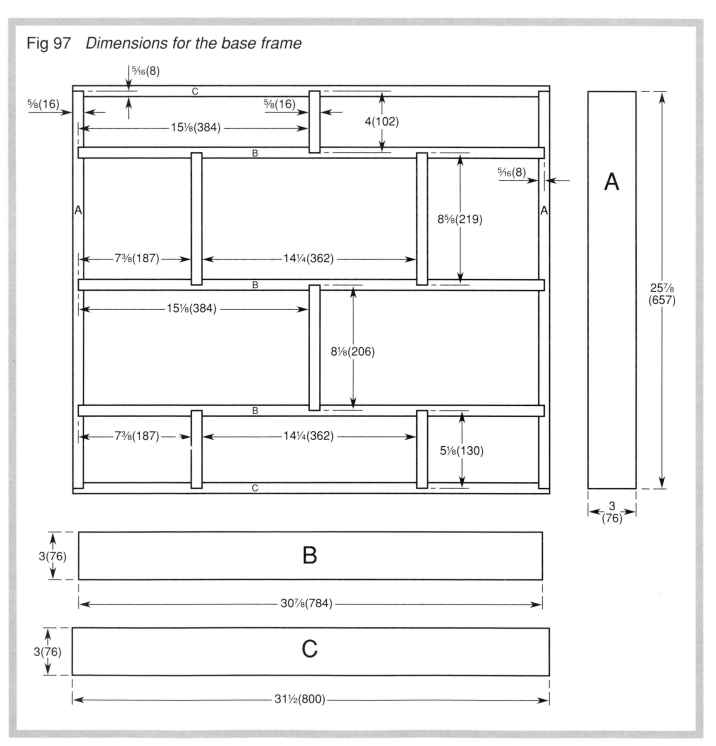

Fig 97 *Dimensions for the base frame*

⁵⁄₁₆(8)
⅝(16)
C
⅝(16)
4(102)
15⅛(384)
B
⁵⁄₁₆(8)
A   A
8⅝(219)
7⅜(187)   14¼(362)
B
15⅛(384)
8⅛(206)
B
7⅜(187)   14¼(362)
5⅛(130)
C

A
25⅞
(657)
3
(76)

3(76)   B
30⅞(784)

3(76)   C
31½(800)

Fig 98 *Plans for the base frame facing*

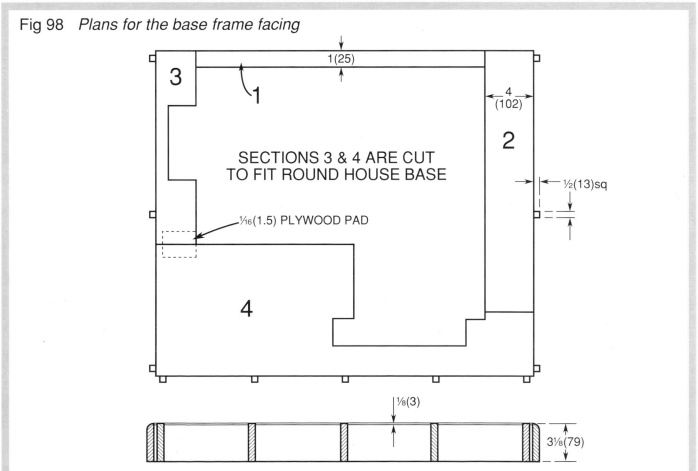

1(25)

3

1

4
(102)

2

SECTIONS 3 & 4 ARE CUT
TO FIT ROUND HOUSE BASE

½(13)sq

1/16(1.5) PLYWOOD PAD

4

1/8(3)

3⅛(79)

Fig 99 *Pattern for the cobbles and paving*

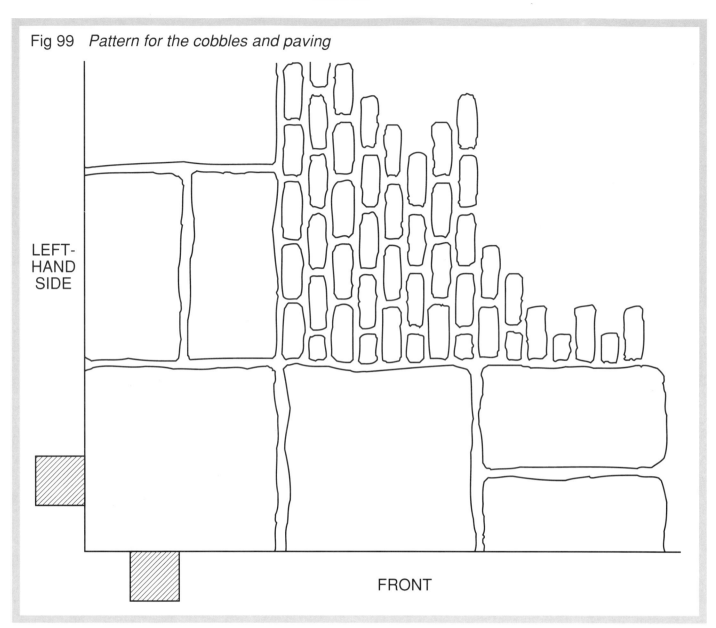

LEFT-
HAND
SIDE

FRONT

FISHERMAN'S COTTAGE – LIST OF SUPPLIERS

The furniture and accessories used in the Fisherman's Cottage are from the following suppliers; see Acknowledgements for addresses.

Rohanna Bryan: Lobster, turbot and plaice.
Bryntor: Sink and draining board.
C & D Crafts: Fish baskets.
Irene Campbell: Cornish pitchers.
Country Treasures: Warming pan.
Terry Curran: Rum flagon.
Dolphin Miniatures: Lobster pots, floats, fish boxes, sack trolley, anchor, barrels, figurehead, sea chest, bed, dresser, table, bench, Windsor chairs, step-

ladder, charts, work bench, wooden blocks, tools and paintpots.
Mainly Men Minis: Fisherman doll.
Leo Pilley: Yard of ale.
Phoenix Model Developments: Range (kit).
Quality Dollshouse Miniatures: Kettle.
The Secret Garden: Potted fern.
Roy Stowe: Ship half model.
Wood 'n' Wool: Lighting.

The bell, diving helmet and ship's lights are from key rings, and the diesel engine, fish-cart, oars, telescope and bargeware are from the author's own collection.

6
THE
TUDOR
HOUSE

*This model is based on 'The House That Moved' in Exeter,
reputed to date from the reign of Henry VII.
The present name was acquired after the building was jacked up and
moved on rollers in 1961 to make way for the new inner by-pass.
Some alterations have been made to the interior of the model
to enhance its scope for miniaturists; for example, the stairs have been
re-positioned, and fireplaces and a chimney added, where none
are in evidence on the original.
Many alterations have been made to the real building over the years,
including a new roof. These additions on the model are speculative, as are
the roof truss and framing, though they do follow the pattern of similar
structures in other timber-framed buildings of the period.*

TIMBER REQUIREMENTS

WOOD	THICKNESS in	THICKNESS mm	WIDTH in	WIDTH mm	LENGTH ft/in	LENGTH m
Lime	1/32	1	3/8	10	3ft	0.92
	5/32	4	3	76	18in	0.46
	1	25	1½	38	2ft	0.61
Lime or Elm	7/8	22	2	51	3ft	0.92
			2¼	57	4ft	1.22
Elm	1/32	1	3/8	10	4ft	1.22
	1/16	1.6	3/8	10	9ft	2.75
			½	13	2ft	0.61
			5/8	16	2ft	0.61
			3/4	19	2ft	0.61
			7/8	22	18in	0.46
	3/32	2	3/16	5	12in	0.31
			7/16	11	5ft	1.53
			½	13	8ft	2.44
			5/8	16	16ft	4.87
	1/8	3	7/16	11	39in	1.0
			½	13	18in	0.46
			7/8	22	4ft	1.22
	3/16	5	3/16	5	6in	0.16
			1/4	6	18in	0.46
			9/32	7	30in	0.76
			5/16	8	4ft	1.22
			7/16	11	17ft	5.18
			9/16	14	13ft	3.96
			5/8	16	2ft	0.61
			11/16	18	2ft	0.61
			3/4	19	3ft	0.92

WOOD	THICKNESS in	THICKNESS mm	WIDTH in	WIDTH mm	LENGTH ft/in	LENGTH m
Elm	1/4	6	1/4	6	4ft	1.22
			5/16	8	20ft	6.09
			3⅛	10	2ft	0.61
			7/16	11	2ft	0.61
			½	13	18in	0.46
			5/8	16	4ft	1.22
			3/4	19	5ft	1.53
			7/8	22	2ft	0.61
			1 3/16	30	3ft	0.92
			1¼	32	18in	0.46
			1½	38	39in	1.0
	5/16	8	5/16	8	9in	0.23
			½	13	4ft	1.22
Elm	3/8	10	½	13	13ft	3.96
	½	13	½	13	5ft	1.53
			5/8	16	9in	0.23
			3/4	19	2ft	0.61
	3/4	19	3/4	19	6in	0.16
	1	25	1½	38	18in	0.46
Pine	1	25	2	51	4ft	1.22

WOOD	THICKNESS in	THICKNESS mm	AREA sq ft	AREA sq m
Birch	3/8	9	20	1.85
Plywood	1/4	6	1	0.09
	1/16	1.5	4	0.37
Microwood Veneer			5	0.5

Construction of the carcase is straightforward — three separate room boxes which are stacked so that the floor of one room forms the ceiling of the room below it. Gaps are left in the ceiling beams on the underside of the middle and upper sections, at the front and right-hand side. Those at the front locate the wall of the section below, while those at the side accommodate a 3/8in (9mm) plywood strip, ½in (13mm) deep, which forms the upper extension of the portable right-hand walls.

Note that the right-hand side of the middle section is angled ¼in (6mm) from the vertical to follow the distortion on the original building.

The timber framing of elm is applied with contact adhesive, and is sanded and scraped for a rough-hewn finish. To preserve the slightly weathered appearance, no surface sealer or varnish is applied.

Exterior of the Tudor House, showing front and right-hand side

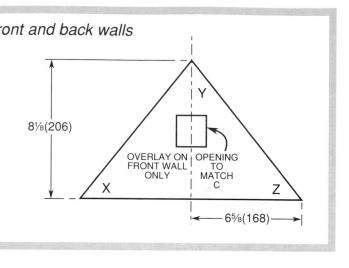

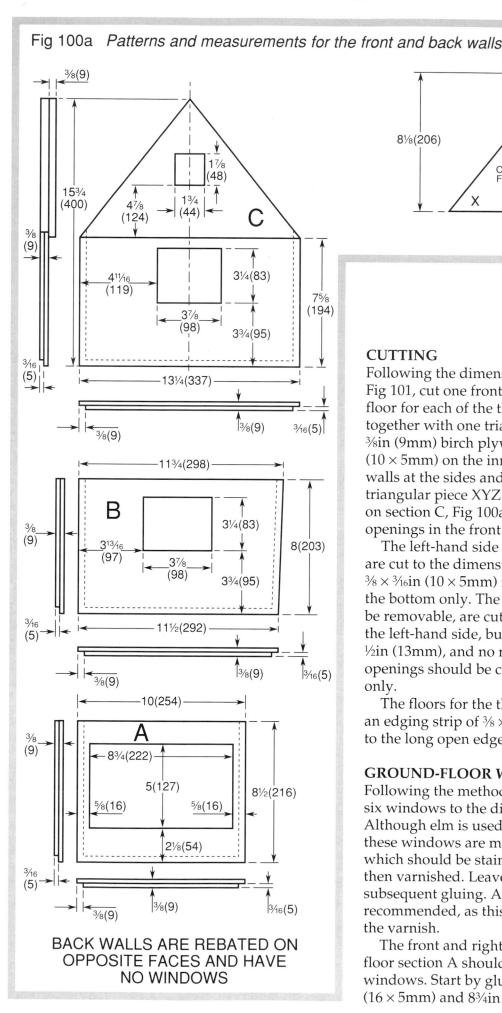

Fig 100a *Patterns and measurements for the front and back walls*

BACK WALLS ARE REBATED ON
OPPOSITE FACES AND HAVE
NO WINDOWS

CUTTING

Following the dimensions in Figs 100a–100c and
Fig 101, cut one front, one back, two sides and one
floor for each of the three sections A, B, and C,
together with one triangular piece XYZ, all from
⅜in (9mm) birch plywood. Cut rebates ⅜ × ³⁄₁₆in
(10 × 5mm) on the inner faces of the front and back
walls at the sides and along the bottom. Glue the
triangular piece XYZ to the outside of the front wall
on section C, Fig 100a; then cut out the window
openings in the front walls only.

The left-hand side walls for sections A, B and C
are cut to the dimensions shown, and have a
⅜ × ³⁄₁₆in (10 × 5mm) rebate on the inside faces at
the bottom only. The right-hand walls, which will
be removable, are cut to the same length as those on
the left-hand side, but their height is reduced by
½in (13mm), and no rebate is needed. The window
openings should be cut out on the right-hand walls
only.

The floors for the three sections should each have
an edging strip of ⅜ × ¹⁄₁₆in (10 × 1·5mm) elm glued
to the long open edge.

GROUND-FLOOR WINDOWS

Following the method described in Chapter 1, make
six windows to the dimensions given in Fig 102.
Although elm is used extensively on this model,
these windows are more easily made from lime,
which should be stained to a medium brown, and
then varnished. Leave the edges bare for
subsequent gluing. A water-based acrylic stain is
recommended, as this will not inhibit the drying of
the varnish.

The front and right-hand panels of the ground-
floor section A should now be lined ready for the
windows. Start by gluing an elm sill ⅝ × ³⁄₁₆in
(16 × 5mm) and 8¾in (222mm) long, into the

Fig 100b *Patterns for the left-hand side walls*

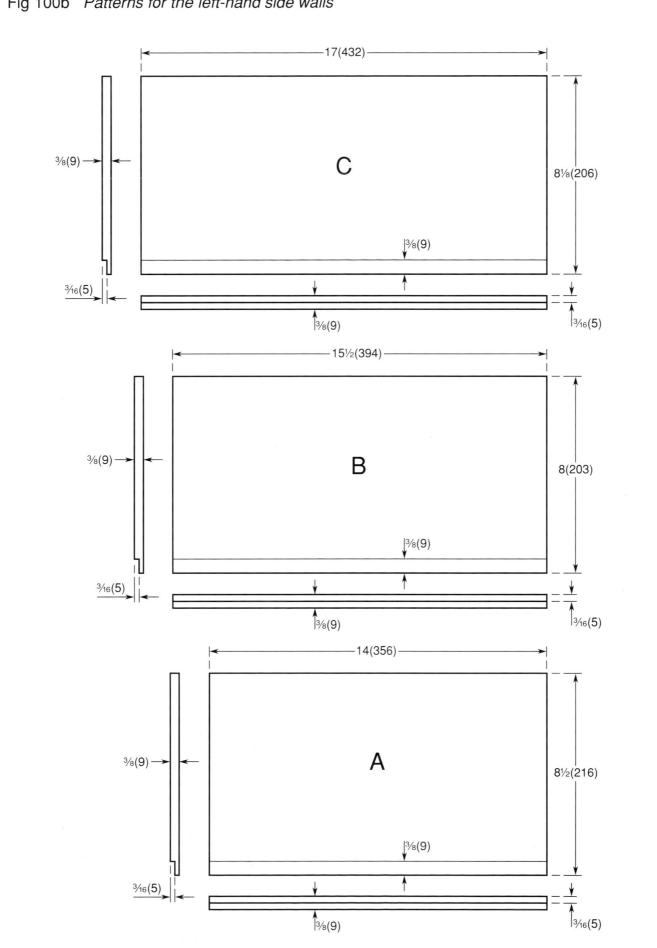

Fig 100c *Plans for the right-hand side portable walls*

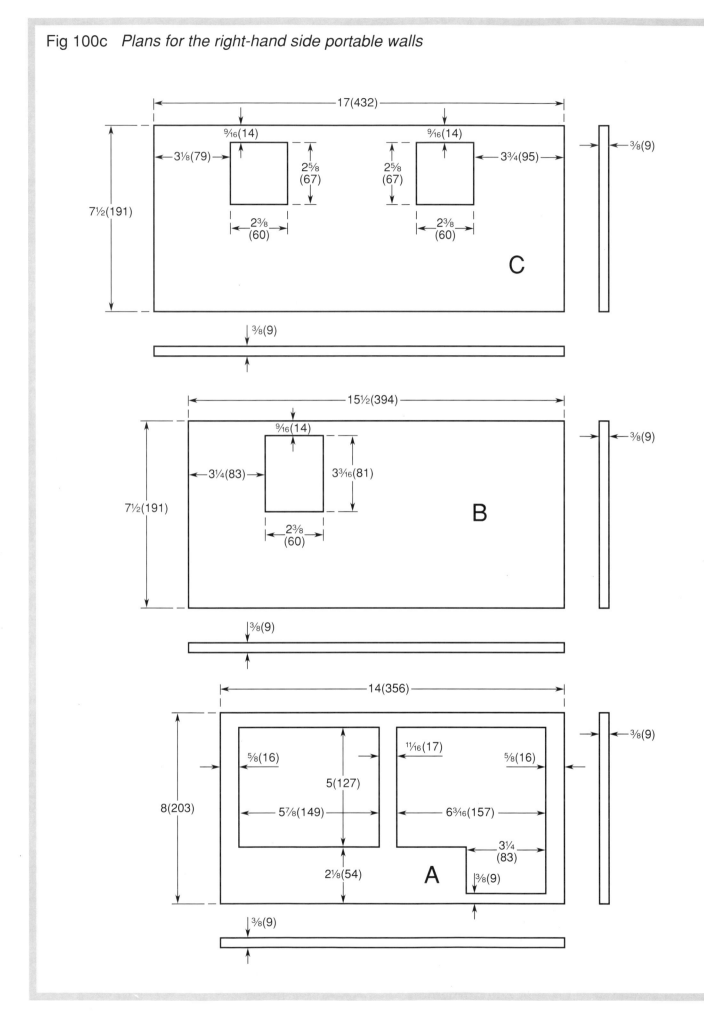

Fig 101   *Cutting out the floors*

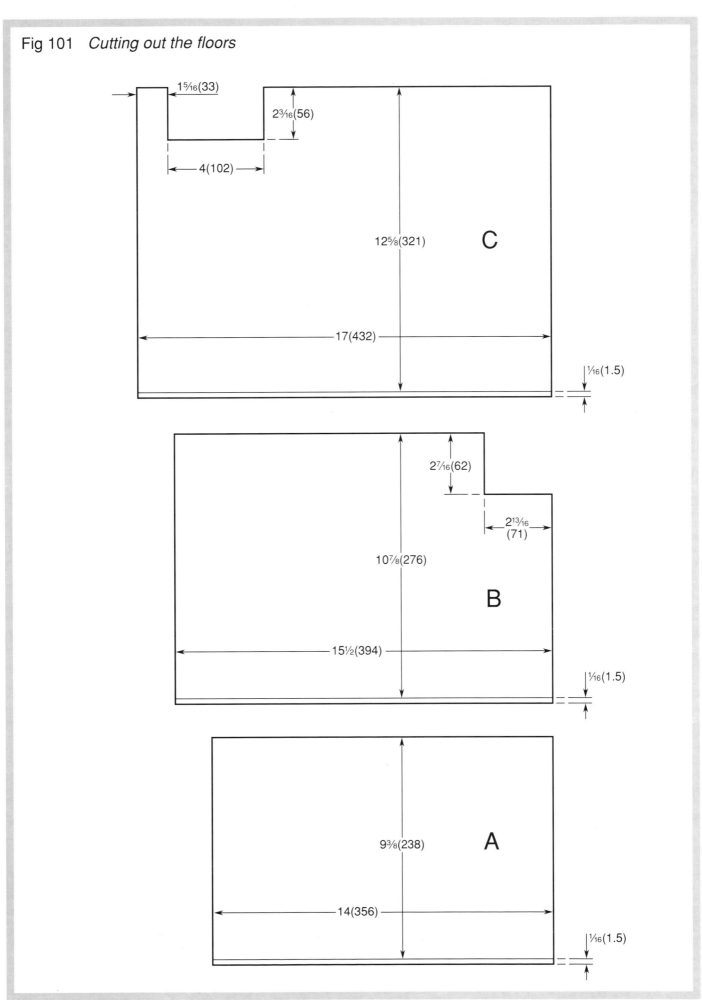

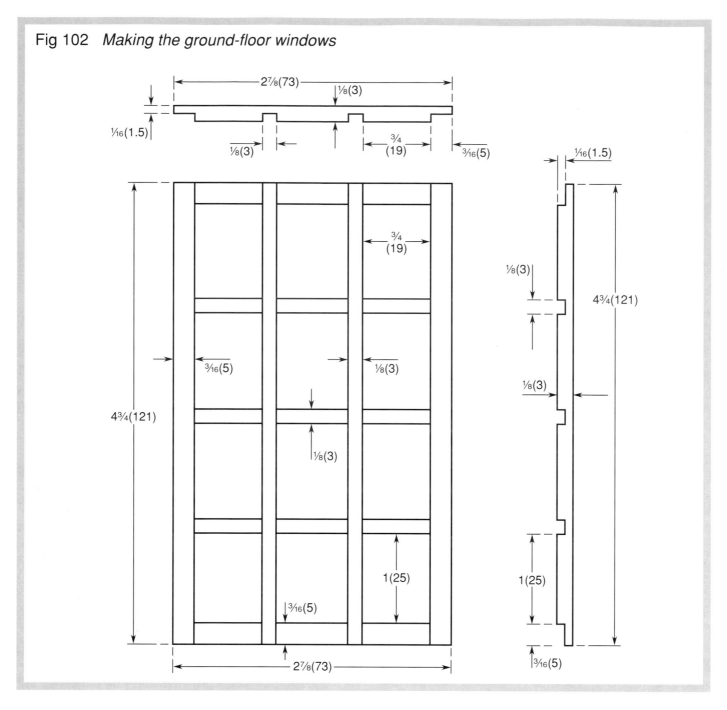

Fig 102 *Making the ground-floor windows*

bottom of the opening in the front panel, flush at the back, and projecting ¼in (6mm) at the front. A similar sill should be glued into each of the two openings in the right-hand panel, 5⅞in (149mm) long in the left-hand opening, and 2¹⁵⁄₁₆in (75mm) in the right-hand opening, reaching only to the extended cutout for the doorway. The top and side edges of these openings should be lined with ⅜ × ¹⁄₁₆in (10 × 1·5mm) elm.

Glue three windows side by side into the opening in the front panel (see Fig 103), making sure they are set ³⁄₃₂in (2·5mm) in from the back, to allow for glazing. The remaining three windows are glued into the side panel, with the right-hand edge of the single window flush with the left-hand side of the door opening (Fig 104).

DOOR

Referring to Fig 105, make the door from ¹⁄₁₆in (1·5mm) plywood, faced with elm planking ¹⁄₃₂in (0·8mm) thick; and the door frames from ⁷⁄₁₆ × ⁵⁄₁₆in (11 × 8mm) elm. The method used for hanging the doors is given in Chapter 1. Glue the door jambs and header into the opening, with the left-hand jamb butting the open edge of the single window. Glue a sill facing of ¹⁄₁₆in (1·5mm) elm across the bottom of the opening between the jambs. After fixing the wooden handle (Fig 105), apply two coats of matt varnish to the door and put it aside.

CARCASE ASSEMBLY

The three carcase sections A, B and C, are now assembled individually with glue and screws,

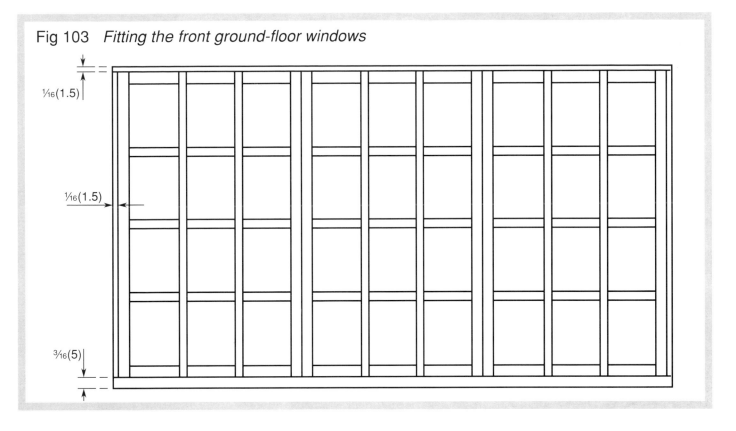

Fig 103 *Fitting the front ground-floor windows*

remembering to keep the elm-faced floor edges on the open side, and the stairwell cutouts at the back, C to the left and B to the right.

EXTERNAL FRAMING

As the dimensions of the timber framing vary considerably between the three sections, it is better to complete the framing on each section and its removable panel in turn, starting with the ground-floor section A and working upwards. Also, glue the framing directly to the plywood panels and paint the walls afterwards, as some loss of adhesion will result if the exterior walls are painted before fixing the framing. Stray paint can be removed with a Skarsten scraper, though any slight penetration of paint into the frame timbers enhances the weathered appearance. On the interior (which is tackled later), the framing is applied over two coats of emulsion, as maximum strength is not so important.

For ease of reference throughout the construction of the framing — both externally and internally — the following terms will be used:

Plate: Horizontal timber at the top of the frame.
Sole plate: Horizontal timber at the foot of the frame.
Rails: Intermediate horizontal timbers.
Posts: Vertical timbers at the frame edge.
Studs: Intermediate vertical timbers.

Only the front and right-hand side of each section are fully framed.

GROUND FLOOR A

Front Following the pattern in Fig 106, apply the framing to the front of A with contact adhesive in the following order:

Start with the top horizontal plate ($\frac{7}{8} \times \frac{1}{4}$in/22 × 6mm); its lower edge should be flush with the underside of the upper window lining, and there should be $\frac{1}{2}$in (13mm) of clear plywood above it. Next apply the $\frac{7}{16} \times \frac{1}{4}$in (11 × 6mm) horizontal sole plate across the bottom edge, followed by the two $\frac{5}{8} \times \frac{1}{4}$in (16 × 6mm) vertical posts.

Plane the outer edges of these two posts flush with the edges of the front panel.

Right-hand Side Still referring to Fig 106, the removable side panel for A should be framed next, noting that both the horizontal plates and the end posts overlap the plywood panel. This overlap should be $\frac{7}{16}$in (11mm) at the left-hand end to cover the remaining $\frac{3}{16}$in (5mm) of the plywood front panel outside the rebate, plus the $\frac{1}{4}$in (6mm) thickness of the front framing. The overlap at the right-hand end is $\frac{3}{16}$in (5mm) to cover the plywood only as there is no framing on the back.

FIRST FLOOR B

Front (Fig 107). Line the front window opening with $\frac{3}{8} \times \frac{1}{16}$in (10 × 1·5mm) elm. Apply the outer border frame of $\frac{9}{16} \times \frac{3}{16}$in (14 × 5mm) elm as for section A. Now fit the two curved braces — these

157

look better if they are cut with the grain following the curve. The two 7/16 × 3/16in (11 × 5mm) vertical studs are applied next, cut to fit above and below the curved braces, and flush with the window lining at their inner edges.

Finally fix the three 5/16 × 3/16in (8 × 5mm) horizontal rails, and the short 1/4 × 3/16in (6 × 5mm) studs below the centre rail.

Right-hand Side (Also Fig 107). Work in the same order as on the front, noting the different dimensions of the end posts and their overlaps.

UPPER FLOOR C

Front (Fig 108). Proceed as for B, but note that the upper plate of 9/16 × 3/16in (14 × 5mm) elm has a further piece 1/2 × 1/8in (13 × 3mm) glued to its top edge to form an angle. This is fitted under the lower edge of the upper wall XYZ (Fig 100A).

A lintel of 1/2 × 1/8in (13 × 3mm) elm is glued above the upper window, with its ends angled to the roof slope, and inset 1/4in (6mm) on each side.

Right-hand Side The dimensions of the end posts, and the overlaps, are the same as section B.

BACKS AND LEFT-HAND SIDES

Elm strips 11/16 × 3/16in (18 × 5mm) should be glued along the backs and left-hand sides of sections B and C, overlapping 1/8in (3mm) at the bottom edges. These will locate the tops of the back and side walls of the sections below them.

Two strips 7/16 × 3/16in (11 × 5mm) are glued one to the left-hand side and the other to the back of section A, flush at the bottom.

A strip of 11/16 × 3/16in (18 × 5mm) elm is glued vertically to the face of each left-hand side panel, to overlap the framing on its corresponding front panel. This strip should extend upwards to 1/8in (3mm) *below* the top of the plywood panel on sections A and B, but level with the top of the angled front beam on section C, where it should be planed to the roof slope.

ORIEL WINDOWS

Referring to Fig 109, make two oriel windows to the dimensions given. The mullions and transoms are made from elm, but the shaped blocks at the top and bottom are more easily made from lime, with the unpainted areas stained.

The shaped lower blocks are notched at either side to fit over the stud framing and rest against the

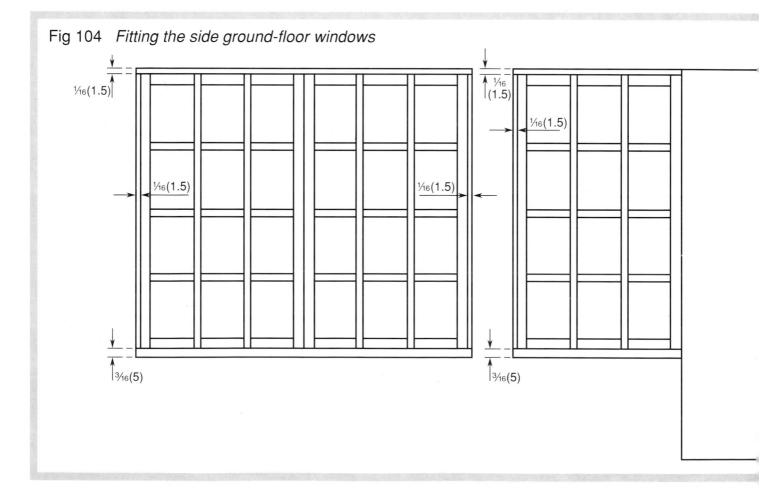

Fig 104 *Fitting the side ground-floor windows*

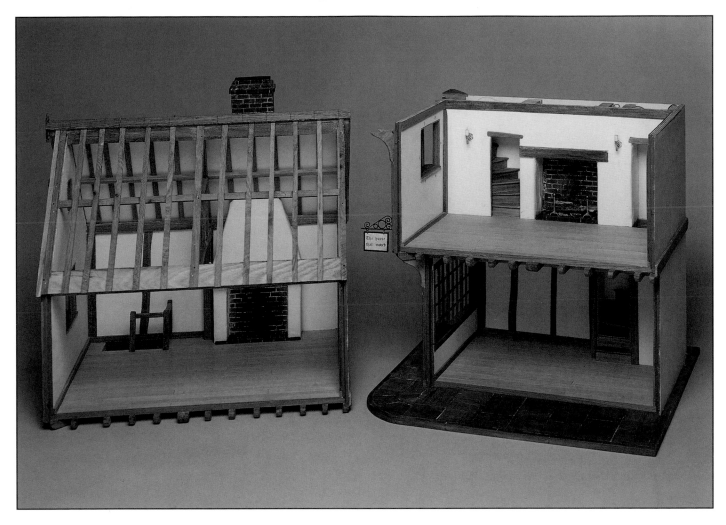

Tudor House with section C and the roof removed, to show the rafters and the internal wall

plywood front panels. The upper blocks fit against the outer face of the ⁹⁄₁₆in (14mm) upper beam. The mullions are pegged to the blocks with ³⁄₃₂in (2mm) diameter bamboo dowels, and a groove ¹⁄₁₆in (1·5mm) wide and ¹⁄₁₆in (1·5mm) deep is cut in both the upper and lower blocks, in line with the mullion grooves to locate the upper and lower edges of the glass. The glass used is 1·2–1·4mm thick and is obtainable from T. and W. Ide and Sons (see Acknowledgements).

The mullions should now be pegged and glued to the lower block, but pegged only at the top to facilitate removal, should a pane get broken. The glass in the side returns reaches to the face of the front panel, where it is held by two angled pieces of elm each 3⅛in (79mm) long, glued to the panel (see Fig 109).

The whole assembly is then screwed to the front panel from the inside. When satisfied that the windows fit correctly, they can be removed and put aside. The ³⁄₁₆ × ³⁄₃₂in (5 × 2·5mm) transoms will be glued in place after final assembly.

Fig 105 *Construction of the external door, and making its handle*

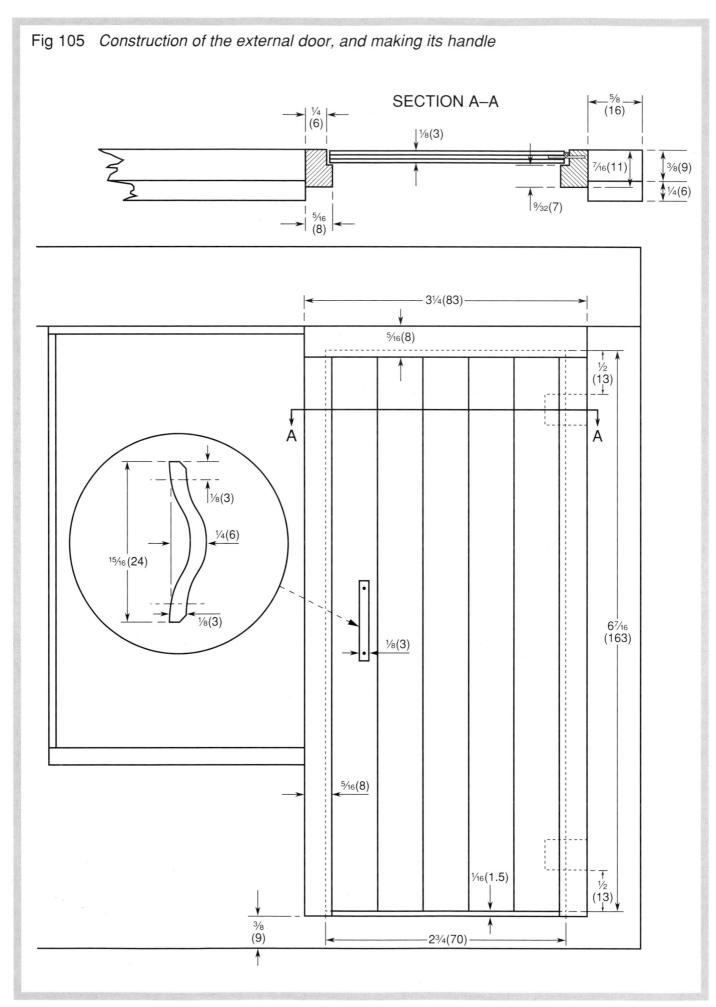

Fig 106 *Making the external timber framing for the ground floor*

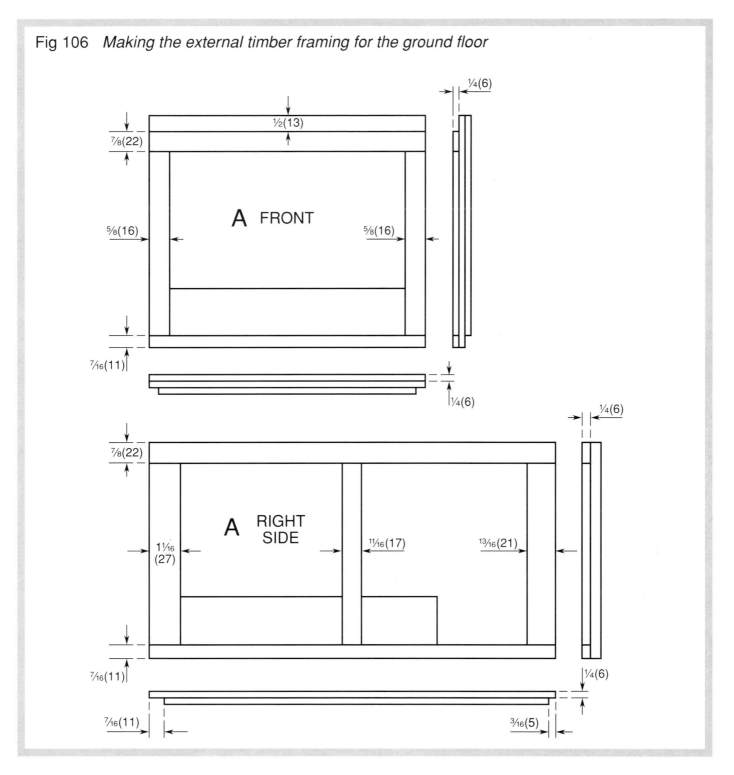

SIDE WINDOWS
Referring to Fig 110, line the window openings in the side panels B and C with a framing of ⁹⁄₃₂ × ³⁄₁₆in (7 × 5mm) elm, inset ³⁄₃₂in (2·5mm) from the back to leave a rebate for glazing. Fit a similar frame to the upper gable window on C. This window will be lined at the back with ³⁄₈ × ¹⁄₁₆in (9 × 1·5mm) elm after glazing.

CEILING BEAMS
Following Fig 111, carefully mark the inner and outer limits of the front and right-hand walls of

section A on to the underside of section B. Now glue and pin the beams and their outer stubs in position, using spacers to maintain an even gap where the front and right-hand walls of section A will locate — a gap of ³⁄₈in (10mm) is required at the right-hand side, and a gap of ¹⁵⁄₃₂in (12mm) is needed at the front to allow for internal framing.

Use fine veneer pins, which should be cut off and filed smooth where they penetrate the upper surface of the floor. Veneer floorboards will later cover this surface. All the beams are ½in (13mm) deep, but there are three different widths: the ¾in

161

Fig 107 *Making the external timber framing for the first floor*

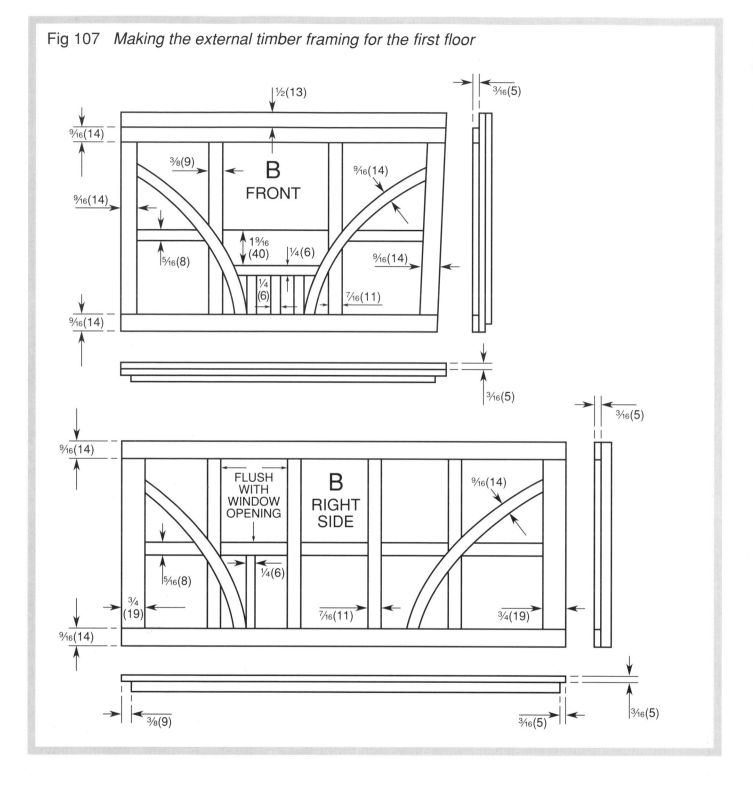

(19mm) wide main beam (number 6) should be fixed first where shown in the drawing, so that it is directly above the centre post on the right-hand wall of section A, followed by the diagonal dragon beam, and then the three ½in (13mm) wide beams in front of the stairwell.

The smaller ⅜in (10mm) beams are spaced at approximately 1⅜in (35mm) centres along the side, and 1⅝in (41mm) centres along the front. In the interests of realism, they should not be positioned too precisely. The outer ends of all the stub beams are radiused (see Fig 112), and inset 1/16in (1·5mm)

from the outer edge of the wall framing. At the right-hand side these stubs support the removable panel, and their projecting upper surfaces must be kept clear of glue. The outer corner between the front and right-hand walls of section A must be chamfered to a depth of ½in (13mm) to fit behind the dragon beam stub.

OPPOSITE *Tudor House, showing the back framing*

The house
that moved

Fig 108   *The timber framing for the top floor*

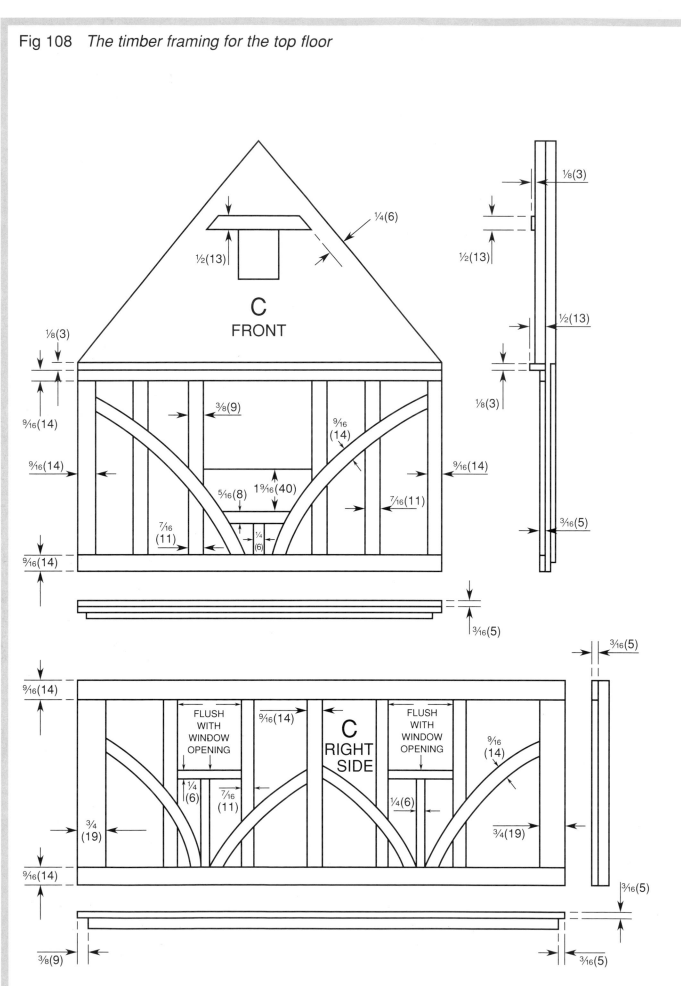

Fig 109 *Detail and measurements for the oriel windows*

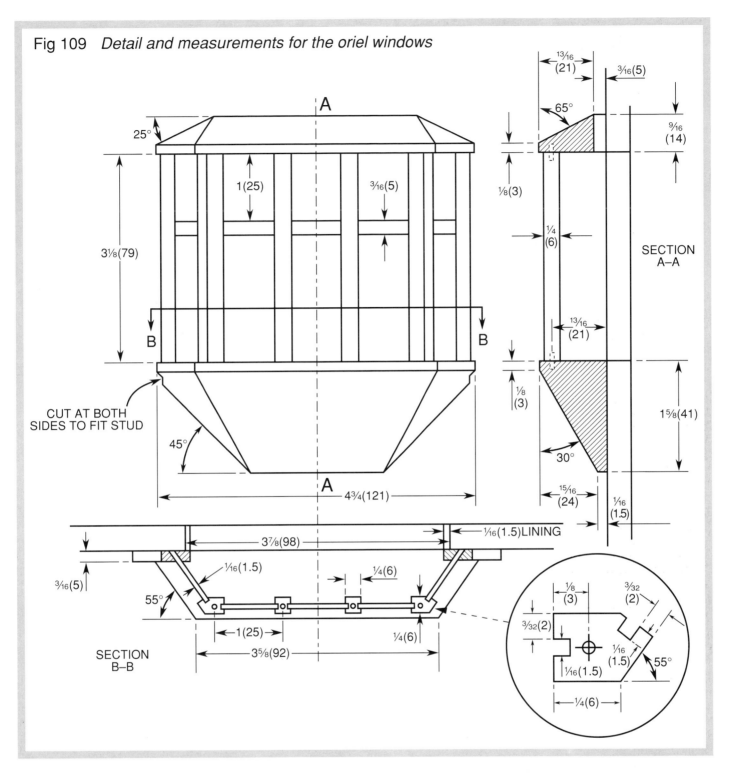

Sections A and B should now fit together, with the front and right-hand walls of A engaging in the space between the beams on B, and the remaining walls of A locating inside the ⅛in (3mm) lip of the elm strips on the back and left-hand side of B.

The pattern for the beams on the underside of section C is given in Fig 113. These should be fixed in the same way as those on B, leaving a 2⅜in (60mm) gap at the back for the internal fireplace wall.

Section C can now be located on top of B. This system of connecting the three sections requires no additional fastenings or glue. The sections can be separated at any time for storage or transport.

INTERNAL WALL AND STAIRS

The internal fireplace wall in section B (against the left-hand side wall) should be made next (see Figs 114 and 115), and the two staircases.

NB When looking at the colour plates, remember that the fireplaces are against the left-hand side walls — not the back walls.

Fig 110 *Plans for the side windows and the upper gable window*

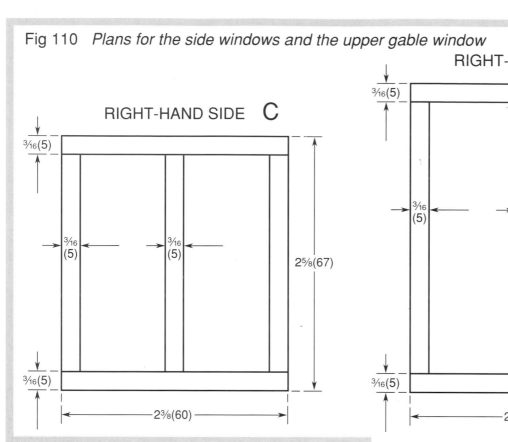

RIGHT-HAND SIDE **C**

3/16(5)

3/16 (5)

3/16 (5)

2⅝(67)

3/16(5)

2⅜(60)

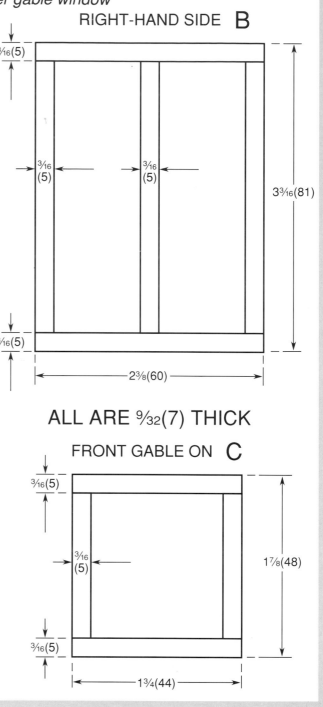

RIGHT-HAND SIDE **B**

3/16(5)

3/16 (5)

3/16 (5)

3³/16(81)

3/16(5)

2⅜(60)

ALL ARE ⁹/₃₂(7) THICK

FRONT GABLE ON **C**

3/16(5)

3/16 (5)

1⅞(48)

3/16(5)

1¾(44)

The wall is made from ¼in (6mm) plywood, mounted on 2 x 1in (51 × 25mm) softwood spacing blocks at either side of the fire opening, and a ⅜in (9mm) plywood spacer, 2in (51mm) deep at the right-hand end (Fig 114). This wall is held in place by ½ × ⅛in (13 × 3mm) elm strips glued to the inside faces of the front and back carcase walls. These strips form part of the internal timber framing to be fitted later, and the wall should be free to slide upwards behind them.

The lintels over the stair openings are made from elm ³/₃₂in (2·5mm) thick, together with the ⅝in (16mm) deep plate at the top of the wall. All are glued to the wall surface. The ⅝ × ½in (16 × 13mm) elm fireplace lintel is recessed into the wall and spacing blocks, leaving a projection of ³/₃₂in (2·5mm) at the front (Fig 115).

Both stairs are made from stacked blocks of elm or lime and the nosings are formed by routing away the front of the step (refer to Figs 116 and 117). The step thickness is ²⁵/₃₂in (20mm) on the lower flight and ²³/₃₂in (18mm) on the upper flight. Loosely stack the stair blocks against the carcase wall and adjust the thickness to bring the top step (no 11) level with the floor. The nosings can then be cut and the steps assembled to each other with glue and pins. The upper staircase (Fig 117) is a sliding fit behind the fireplace wall, with the top step (no 11) cut away to rest over the front wall of section B. The lower staircase (Fig 116) has enclosing panels of ⅜in

(9mm) plywood, fitting between the floors of sections A and B; the top step rises to floor level in the stairwell. Facings of ⅜ × ³/₁₆in (10 × 5mm) elm are glued into the exposed rebates at the back of both stairwells, with a further piece ⁹/₁₆ × ⅜in (14 × 10mm) glued into the rebate at the right-hand side of the stairwell on section B. A slight hollow can be sanded in the exposed treads of both staircases to simulate wear.

OPPOSITE *'Tea break'*

The house that moved

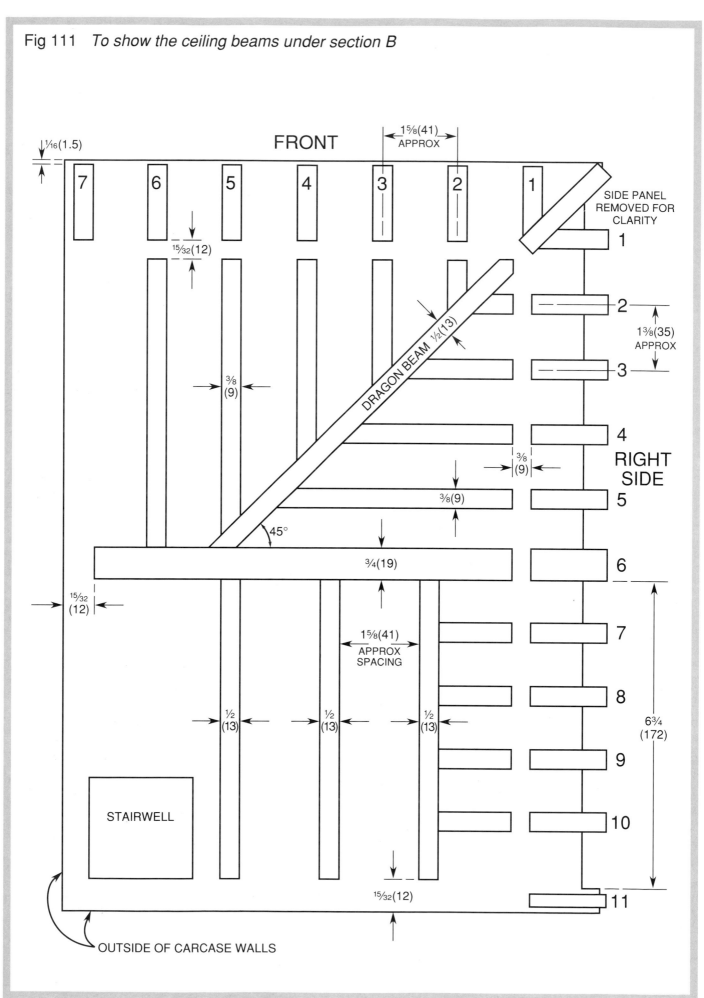

Fig 111 *To show the ceiling beams under section B*

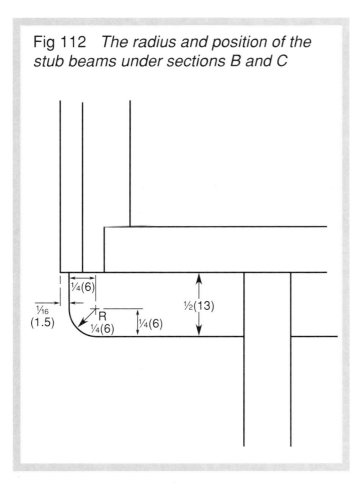

Fig 112 *The radius and position of the stub beams under sections B and C*

INTERNAL TIMBER FRAMING

This is applied after painting the interior walls with two coats of magnolia emulsion. The slight loss of adhesion can be minimised by marking the profile of the frame components *very* lightly on to the wall surfaces, and then scraping the paint from these areas with a small chisel.

The dimensions of the upper plates are critical as they must be deep enough to extend below the ½in (13mm) deep ceiling beams when the three sections A, B and C are fitted together. All other width measurements are nominal, and should not be too uniform. All edges butting against a straight or flat surface should be left straight; other edges, particularly those on the intermediate studs, should be cut with an irregular waney edge. These studs look well if they are not spaced too precisely, and are allowed to lean slightly out of vertical. Reference to the colour plates will give the general idea. The inside faces of the removable panels are not framed.

SECTION A

Plates Starting in section A, with the stair assembly in position, glue plates of ⅝ × ³⁄₃₂in (16 × 2·5mm) elm along the top of each wall. These should butt against the enclosing panels of the staircase, and a further short length should be

added to fill the area above the stairs on the left-hand wall.

Sole plates of ⅜–½ × ³⁄₃₂in (10–13 × 2·5mm) elm are glued to the three walls at the bottom, again butting the stair panels. No further framing is required on the inside of the front wall.

Posts The left-hand and back walls each have two posts ⅝ × ³⁄₃₂in (16 × 2·5mm). On the back wall one is fitted close against the stair panel, and the other inside the rebate for the removable side panel. On the left-hand wall, fit the first post close against the inside of the front wall, and the other against the stair panel.

Studs The left-hand wall has two studs spaced 2–3in (51–76mm) apart, and the back wall has one stud midway between the posts.

SECTION B

Plates Plates and sole plates of similar dimensions to those in section A are glued to the front and back walls extending from the fireplace wall (this already has a plate) to the rebate for the removable side panel.

Posts Posts are glued to both the front and the back wall close against the fireplace wall where they act as retainers. A further post is added to the back wall inside the rebate.

Studs Two only are required on the back wall, spaced 2–2½in (51–64mm) apart.

SECTION C

Roof Truss Following Fig 118, cut the roof truss as one piece from ⅜in (9mm) plywood, and face it with elm. The top and the roof slopes are notched as shown for the ridge beam and the purlins. Note that the outer post is omitted for better access to the room. Cut a ¹⁄₁₆ × ¹⁄₁₆in (1·5 × 1·5mm) groove down the fireplace side of the truss post and drill a ¹⁄₁₆in (1·5mm) hole from the top of this groove to emerge above the tie beam. Drill a further hole through the arched strut, and thread through a 24in (610mm) length of twin wire for lighting. Glue and screw the truss post midway along the left-hand wall, and drill a further hole through the floor beside the groove in the post for the lighting wire.

Plates Glue two sections of plate along the top of the left-hand wall, butted either side of the truss post.

Sole Plates These should be glued to the front and back walls as in the other sections; on the left-hand wall, however, only a short section is needed,

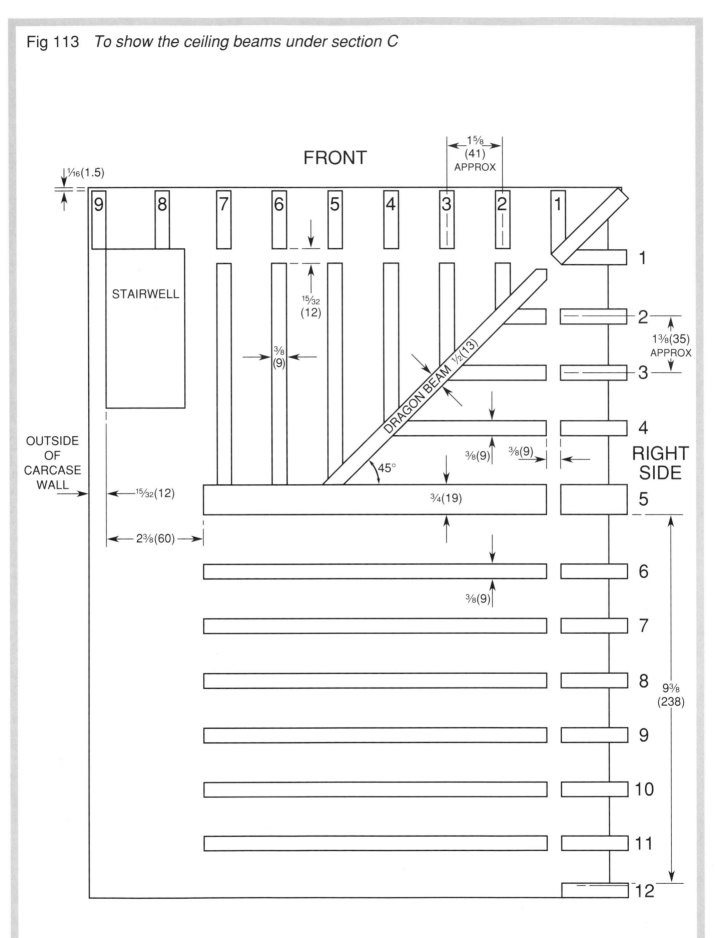

Fig 113   *To show the ceiling beams under section C*

between the front wall and the truss post (see photograph). The upper part of the back wall should be framed following the pattern used for the truss (Fig 118).

Posts and Studs A post is glued to the back wall at the left-hand side, with four studs filling the remaining area. The left-hand wall has a post close against the inside of the front wall and one stud between it and the truss post. Although not shown on the model, similar framing to that on the back walls can be applied to the inside of the front walls on sections B and C.

CHIMNEY AND UPPER FIREPLACE

These are made as two separate assemblies from the patterns in Figs 119 and 120. The external measurements of the stack are critical as they allow for a facing of Houseworks clay bricks.

First, plane a bevel along the left-hand wall of carcase section C, to conform with the slope of the truss and gable ends. Make the chimney from ⅜in (9mm) plywood, noting that the lower edge of its outer wall D must first be bevelled to fit against the top of the carcase wall C. The wedge-shaped formers G are glued and pinned to the middle section of the chimney F, and the smoke-hood panel H is then glued and pinned to the front of them. This panel should be bevelled at the top to fit under E and at the bottom to conform with the horizontal lower edges of the chimney section F and the formers G.

The fire surround is made from two shaped

Detail, showing rafters over smoke-hood

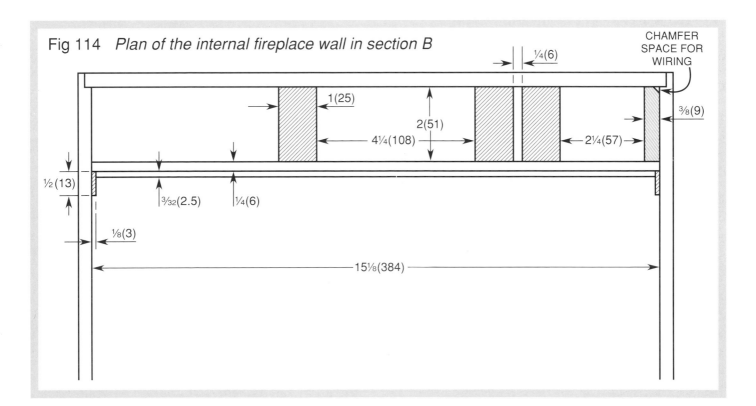

Fig 114 *Plan of the internal fireplace wall in section B*

171

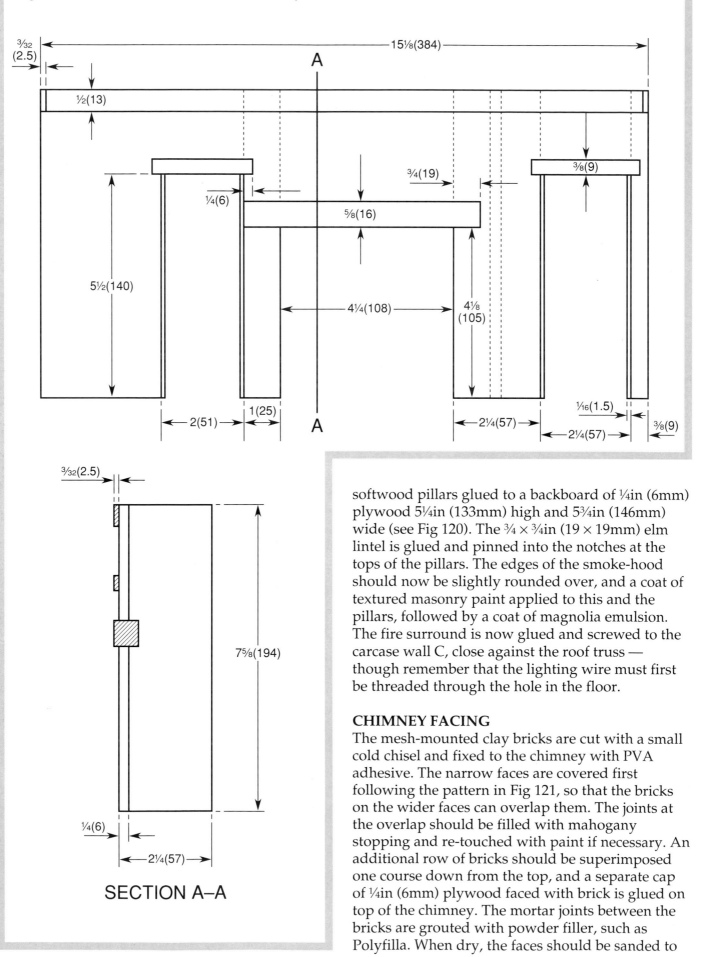

Fig 115 *Front and side elevation of fireplace wall in section B*

SECTION A–A

softwood pillars glued to a backboard of ¼in (6mm) plywood 5¼in (133mm) high and 5¾in (146mm) wide (see Fig 120). The ¾ × ¾in (19 × 19mm) elm lintel is glued and pinned into the notches at the tops of the pillars. The edges of the smoke-hood should now be slightly rounded over, and a coat of textured masonry paint applied to this and the pillars, followed by a coat of magnolia emulsion. The fire surround is now glued and screwed to the carcase wall C, close against the roof truss — though remember that the lighting wire must first be threaded through the hole in the floor.

CHIMNEY FACING
The mesh-mounted clay bricks are cut with a small cold chisel and fixed to the chimney with PVA adhesive. The narrow faces are covered first following the pattern in Fig 121, so that the bricks on the wider faces can overlap them. The joints at the overlap should be filled with mahogany stopping and re-touched with paint if necessary. An additional row of bricks should be superimposed one course down from the top, and a separate cap of ¼in (6mm) plywood faced with brick is glued on top of the chimney. The mortar joints between the bricks are grouted with powder filler, such as Polyfilla. When dry, the faces should be sanded to

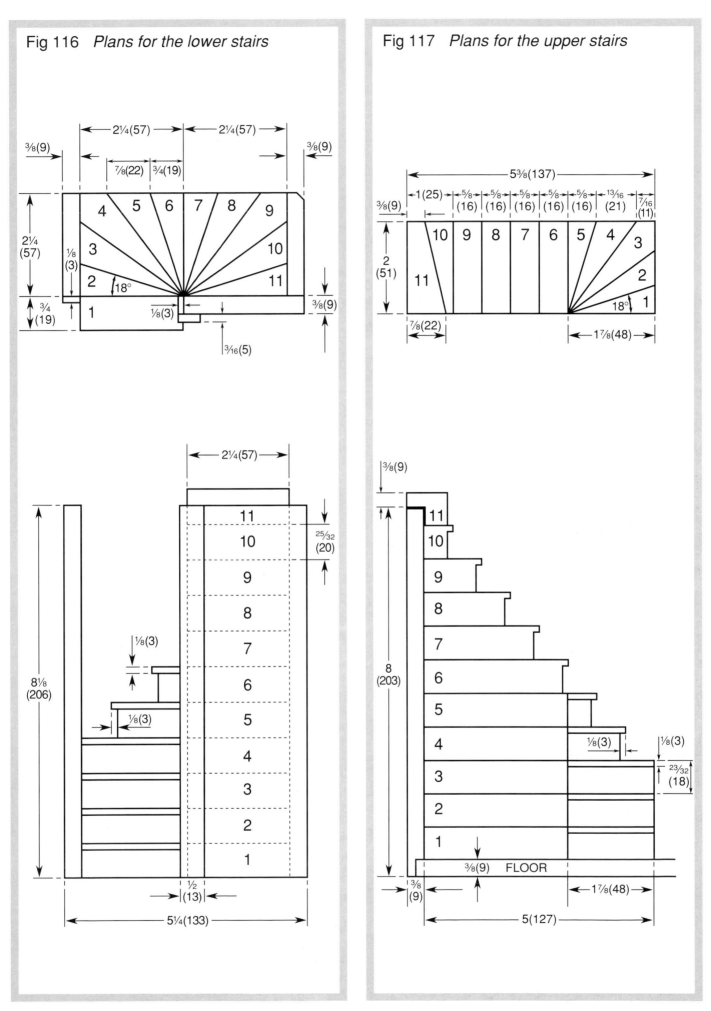

Fig 116 *Plans for the lower stairs*

Fig 117 *Plans for the upper stairs*

Fig 118 *Detailed measurements for the roof truss*

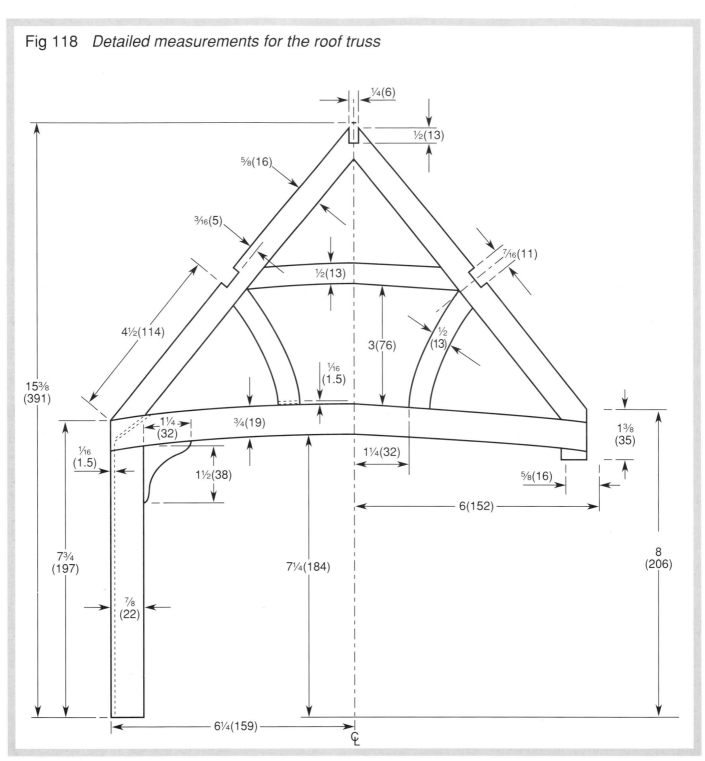

remove the surplus filler and the whole chimney given a wash of diluted black poster paint to simulate soot streaks and weathering.

ASSEMBLY TO CARCASE

Having first removed a section of the wall plate, the chimney can now be glued and screwed to the carcase wall C with the smoke-hood resting on top of the fireplace lintel.

RIDGE BEAM

Following Fig 122, make the beam from three pieces

of elm to the dimensions given. A ⅝in (16mm) gap is left in the side pieces to fit over the truss, and tenons are incorporated, ¾in (19mm) long at the front and ⅜in (10mm) long at the back, to be notched into the gable ends. Ensure that the bevelled sides of the beam conform to the roof slope, and then glue and pin in place.

FRONT EAVES

An elm beam triangular in section, and 17in (432mm) long, is glued and screwed between the front and back walls at the open side of the upper

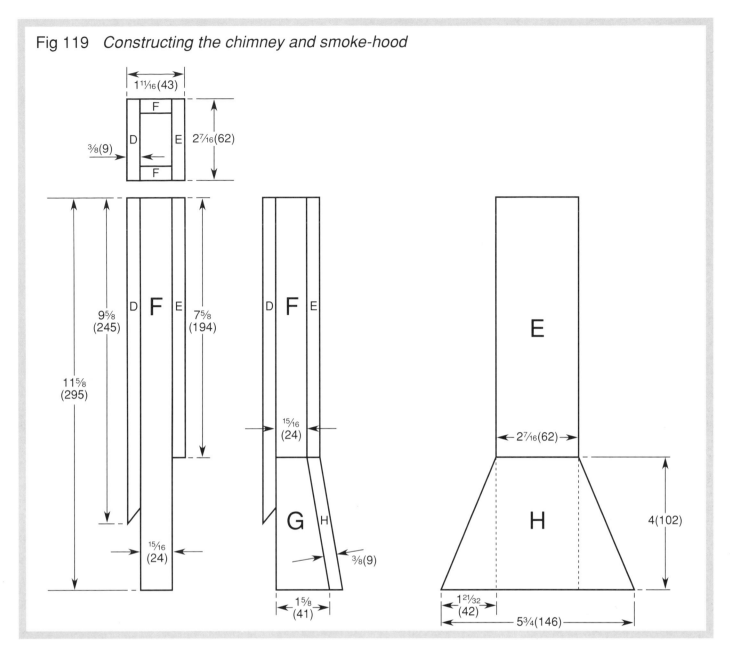

Fig 119 *Constructing the chimney and smoke-hood*

carcase C (Fig 123). It is also glued and screwed at the roof truss. Both ends have tenons ³⁄₁₆in (5mm) long which engage in the wall rebates. The top is bevelled to the roof slope, and a rebate ⁹⁄₁₆ × ⁵⁄₁₆in (14 × 8mm) is cut on the underside to provide a stop for the removable front panel.

PURLINS

Notch the gable ends of the upper carcase ⁷⁄₁₆in (11mm) wide and ³⁄₁₆in (5mm) deep in line with the notches already cut in the roof truss. Cut two purlins to these dimensions with a length of 17¾in (451mm) and then glue and pin them in place. Trim the ends flush with the outside of the front and back walls.

GABLE WINDOW

This should now be glazed, and the inside lining fitted while still accessible.

RAFTERS

These are cut from elm ¼in (6mm) thick and 11¼in (286mm) long. Twenty pieces of ⁵⁄₁₆in (8mm) width, will be needed, together with two each of the following widths: ³⁄₈in (10mm), ⁵⁄₈in (16mm), and ¾in(19mm). Referring to Fig 124, angle the ends so that they fit against the ridge beam at the top, and finish level and flush with the eaves beam at the bottom.

Starting on the chimney side of the roof, cut away the sides of the smoke-hood so that a rafter can be laid against the chimney stack on either side. Glue and pin these in position at the ridge and eaves, followed by a ¾in (19mm) rafter over the front gable, flush with the outer face, a ⁵⁄₈in (16mm) rafter over the truss, and a ³⁄₈in (10mm) rafter over the back gable. Place a narrow rafter between those on either side of the chimney and mark where it meets the inside face of the stack. A length of

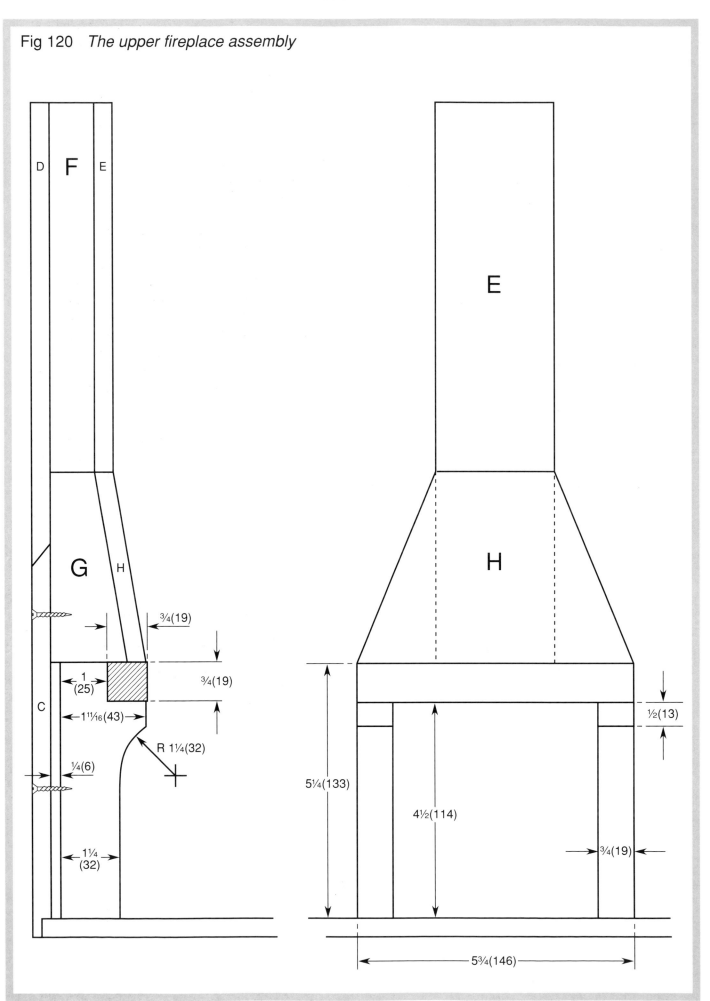

Fig 120 *The upper fireplace assembly*

⁵⁄₁₆ × ¼in (8 × 6mm) elm should be glued to the chimney at this level, as a trimmer for the central rafter, which can now be cut to length and glued between the chimney and the ridge (see colour photograph). Seven further ⁵⁄₁₆in (8mm) rafters should now be spaced approximately 1–1¼in (25–32mm) apart, and fixed at the ridge and eaves.

The rafters on the right-hand side of the roof can now be glued and pinned in the same way.

ROOF PANELS
Cut two roof panels from ¹⁄₁₆in (1·5mm) plywood, each 18⅞in (479mm) long and 11½in (292mm) deep. The top edges of both panels should be bevelled to fit against the ridge beam, and the left-hand panel cut to fit round the chimney.

Prepare two 18⅞in (479mm) lengths of elm as tiltboards: they should be 1½in (38mm) wide, tapering in thickness across the width from ¼in (6mm) to a feather-edge. Glue one length across each roof panel with its feather-edge 1¼in (32mm) above the bottom edge of the panel (see Fig 125). Now plane the bottom edges of both panels and the feather-edged tiltboards so that they are horizontal and level with the underside of the rafters. Glue a soffit of ⁷⁄₁₆ × ⅛in (11 × 3mm) elm along the bevelled lower edge of each panel. These soffits are each 18⅜in (467mm) long, and should be positioned to leave a gap of ¼in (6mm) at each end of the panel.

BARGEBOARDS
Following Fig 126, cut four inner bargeboards from ½ × ⁵⁄₁₆in (13 × 8mm) elm. Glue and screw under the roof panels, inset ¼in (6mm) from the front and

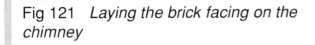

Fig 121 *Laying the brick facing on the chimney*

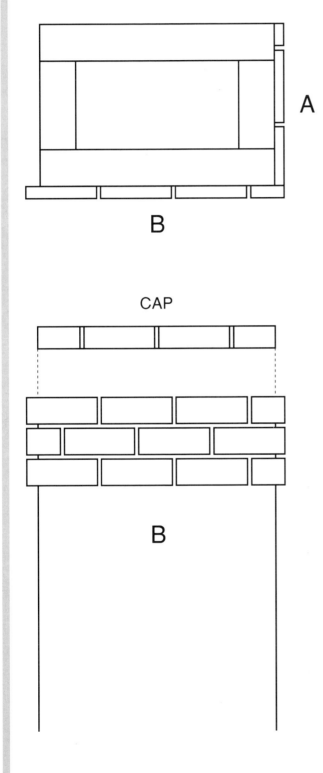

A

B

CAP

B

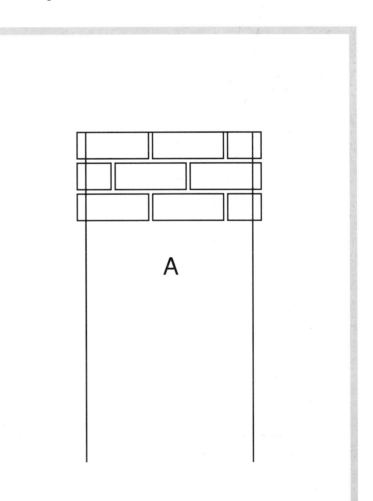

A

Fig 122 *Making the ridge beam*

FRONT

BACK

1(25)

¾ (19)

¼(6)

⅝ (16)

17¾ (451)

TOP

¾ (19)

¼(6)

¼(6)

⅝ (16)

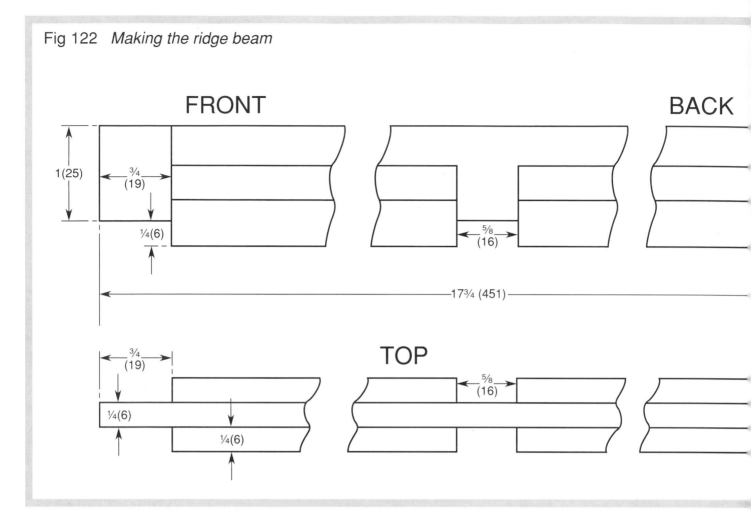

back edges. Note that the bargeboards extend upwards beyond the plywood roof, and are mitred on the centre-line of the gable.

Referring to Fig 127, trim the tiltboards flush with the roof edges. With a sharp chisel cut away the underside of the plywood roof panel, and the tiltboard, reducing the latter to ¹⁄₁₆in (1·5mm) thick outside the bargeboard. This reduction should extend 1¼in (32mm) upwards from the bottom edge, so that the ¹⁄₁₆in (1·5mm) thick projection of the tiltboard becomes a continuation of the ¹⁄₁₆in (1·5mm) plywood roof above it. Now cut four outer bargeboards from ⅞ × ⅛in (22 × 3mm) elm, with their lower ends shaped to fit under the roof overhang and cover the soffit ends. When satisfied that they fit correctly, glue them to the inner bargeboards and to the underside of the roof overhang. A further ⅛in (3mm) of roof overhang should remain outside the bargeboard laminate.

The underside of both roof panels should now be painted with two coats of white emulsion, though leave a border of bare wood on the left-hand panel where it rests on the gables, truss and the bevelled top edge of carcase wall C. This panel can now be glued and pinned in place. The right-hand panel will eventually be portable, but should be

temporarily fastened while the shingles are applied.

Drill a ³⁄₃₂in (2·5mm) diameter hole centrally through the bargeboards at each end of the panel, 1¼in (32mm) from the bottom. These holes should enter the gable walls to a depth of ³⁄₁₆in (5mm). Insert a short length of ³⁄₃₂in (2·5mm) dowel or brass rod to hold the lower part of the roof. The upper part is held by screws into the gables and truss, 1in (25mm) below the ridge. These screws will be removed once the ridge capping has been fixed.

SHINGLES

Greenleaf shingles are fixed with hot-melt glue, as on the Fisherman's Cottage (Chapter 5, Fig 88). Approximately 525 halved shingles are needed for each side of the roof. Starting with an overlap of ¹⁄₁₆in (1·5mm) at the bottom edge, the first fifteen courses are laid with a ³⁄₁₆in (5mm) overlap, leaving ⁹⁄₁₆in (14mm) of exposed shingle. Courses sixteen to twenty are laid with a ¼in (6mm) overlap, leaving ½in (13mm) exposed. The top course is laid with shingles ½in (13mm) deep, to leave a space ⅜ × ⁷⁄₁₆in (10 × 11mm) wide for the ridge tiles.

The ridge tiles are applied as one length of angle moulding, sawn from ⁹⁄₁₆in (14mm) square mahogany to the dimensions in Fig 128. Start

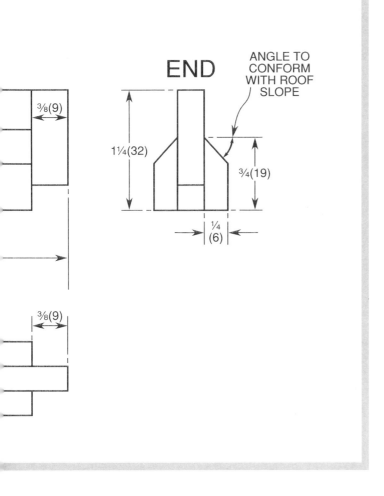

END

ANGLE TO CONFORM WITH ROOF SLOPE

1¼(32)

¾(19)

¼ (6)

⅜(9)

⅜(9)

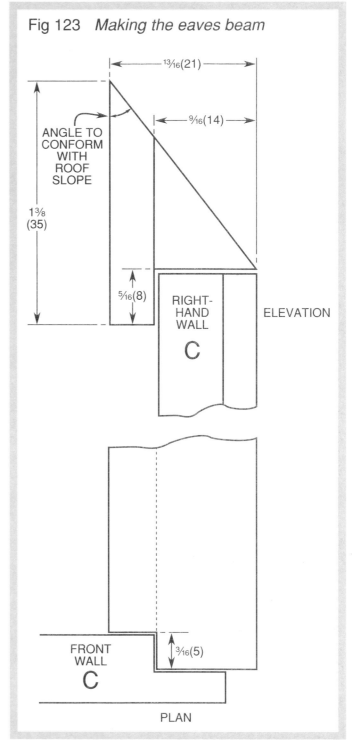

Fig 123 *Making the eaves beam*

¹³⁄₁₆(21)

⁹⁄₁₆(14)

ANGLE TO CONFORM WITH ROOF SLOPE

1⅜ (35)

⁵⁄₁₆(8)

RIGHT-HAND WALL

C

ELEVATION

FRONT WALL

C

³⁄₁₆(5)

PLAN

applying the shingles on the left-hand roof panel (chimney side), and glue the ridge tiles to this side and the sloping top of the ridge-board only. The overlap at the right-hand side of the roof must be kept clear of glue so that the panel can be slipped out from under it.

When fixing the front, remember to remove the screws near the ridge before shingling over them. The joints in the ridge tiles are lightly cut out with a needle file and spaced 1½in (38mm) apart. Clean off any glue that has run out under the shingles, and finish with two coats of Humbrol matt varnish. The right-hand roof can now be removed by extracting the dowels at each end and sliding downwards to clear the ridge tiles.

WIRING
All the wiring connections are made behind the fireplace wall in carcase section B. First screw a connector block to one of the 2 × 1in (51 × 25mm) spacers behind the fireplace wall above the fireplace opening. Drill a ⅛in (3mm) diameter hole through the lower carcase A, just above the floor, in the corner behind the lower stairs. Chamfer the corners of the lower stair assembly and the ⅜in (9mm) plywood spacer at the back of the fireplace

wall, to allow a 36in (915mm) length of twin wire to be led upward in the corner from the hole at ground-floor level, and emerge at the top of the fireplace wall spacer. Grooves are cut in the top edges of the 2 × 1in (51 × 25mm) spacers, to allow this wire to cross over to the connector block in the fireplace opening. The other end of the wire is threaded outwards through the carcase wall at ground-floor level for connection to the transformer.

To simplify separation of the three carcase sections, the wires from the lights in the upper and

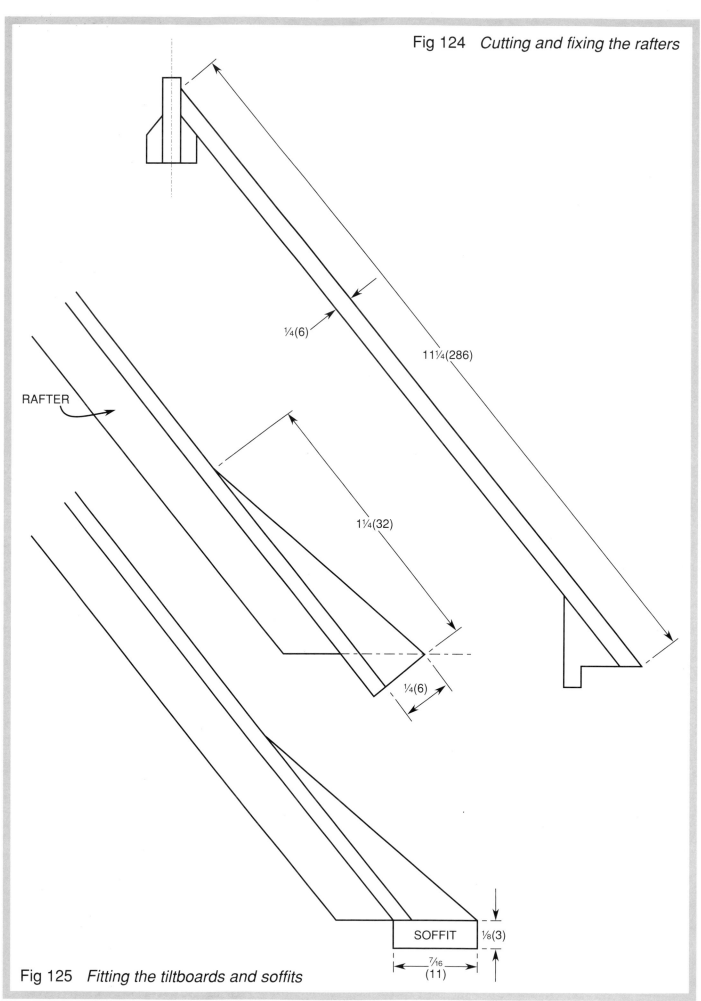

Fig 124   *Cutting and fixing the rafters*

¼(6)

11¼(286)

RAFTER

1¼(32)

¼(6)

SOFFIT

⅛(3)

⁷⁄₁₆
(11)

Fig 125   *Fitting the tiltboards and soffits*

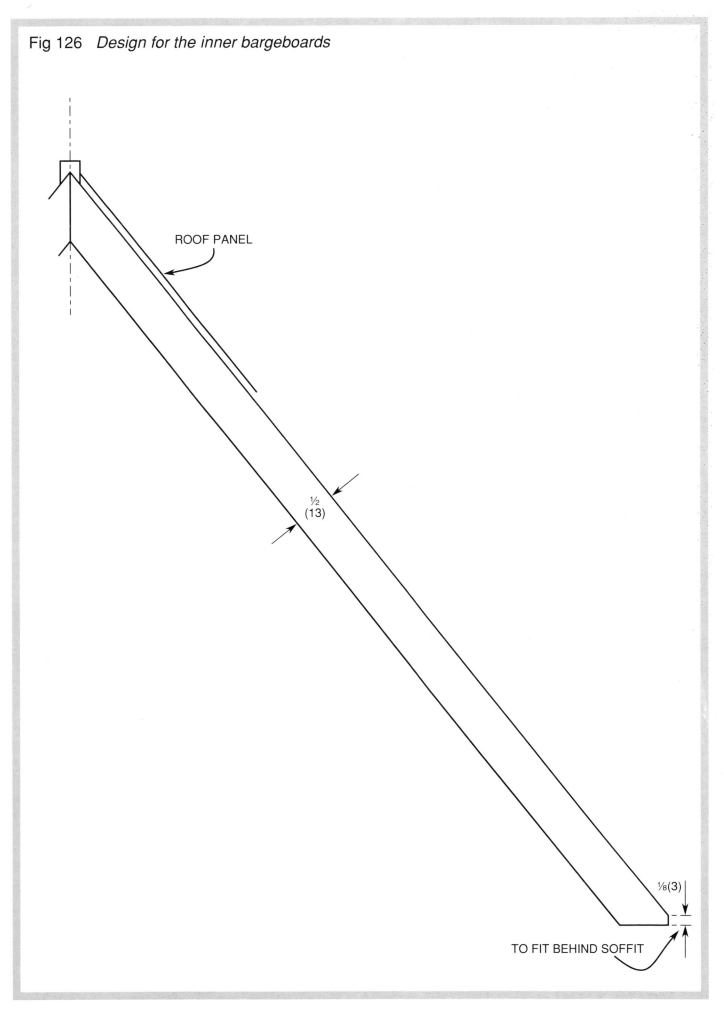

Fig 126   *Design for the inner bargeboards*

ROOF PANEL

½
(13)

⅛(3)

TO FIT BEHIND SOFFIT

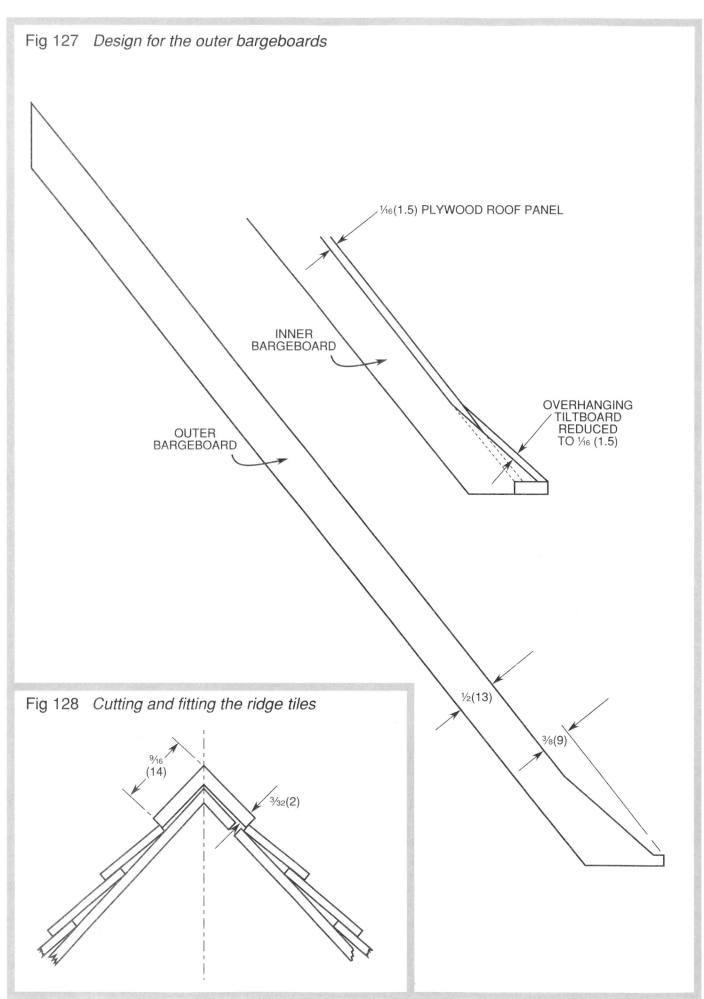

Fig 127 *Design for the outer bargeboards*

¹⁄₁₆(1.5) PLYWOOD ROOF PANEL

INNER
BARGEBOARD

OUTER
BARGEBOARD

OVERHANGING
TILTBOARD
REDUCED
TO ¹⁄₁₆ (1.5)

½(13)

³⁄₈(9)

Fig 128 *Cutting and fitting the ridge tiles*

⁹⁄₁₆
(14)

³⁄₃₂(2)

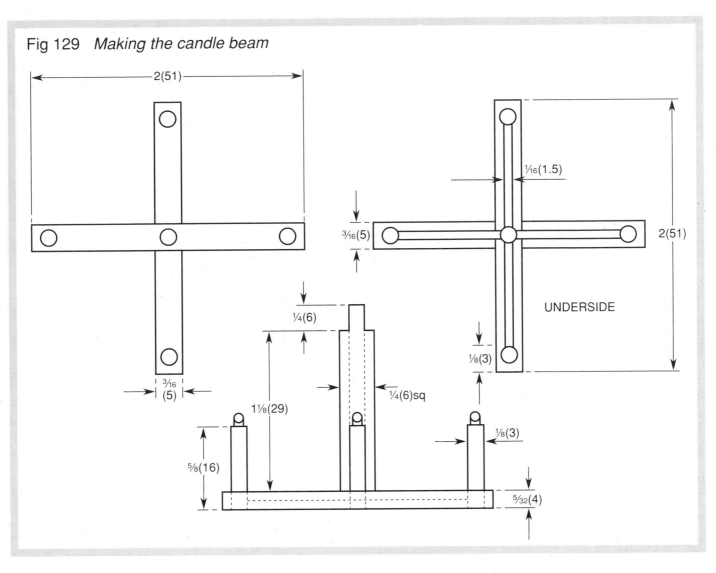

Fig 129 *Making the candle beam*

lower sections A and C are connected to sockets fitted close to the connector block. The wire tails from lights in section B can be taken directly to the connector block.

LIGHTS: SECTION A

A single Cir-Kit candle wall sconce is fitted to a stud on the left-hand wall approximately 5¾in (146mm) from the stairs. It is easier to run the wiring from this light in a groove on the outside of the building which can be plastered over later.

Drill a ¹⁄₁₆in (1·5mm) diameter hole through the stud and the carcase wall behind it, 5½in (140mm) above floor level. Gouge a groove with a depth and width of approximately ³⁄₃₂in (2·5mm) on the outside of carcase wall A, from this hole to the top edge. A further groove is cut in the top edge to reach just inside the fireplace opening on section B. The wire tail from this light should be threaded through the wall and laid in the grooves, finishing with a plug for connection to the socket behind the fireplace wall. A small amount of hot-melt glue will hold the wire in the grooves.

LIGHTS: SECTION B

Two single candle sconces are fitted on the false wall 5½in (140mm) above the floor with their wire tails led directly to the connector block.

LIGHTS: SECTION C

The supply wire was included when fixing the roof truss. Fit a plug at the lower end for connection in section B with the upper end, finishing at a socket on top of the truss tie beam just inside the arched strut at the right-hand side. Following Fig 129, make the candle beam from elm, with four grain-of-wheat bulbs wired in parallel. The four arms are formed by crosshalving two 2in (51mm) lengths of ³⁄₁₆ × ⁵⁄₃₂in (5 × 4mm) elm, with ⅛in (3mm) diameter holes drilled at each end, and through the centre. The candle stems are plastic tube from a ballpoint pen refill, painted white. The vertical post is a ⅛in (3mm) length of elm ¼in (6mm) square with a ⅛in (3mm) diameter hole drilled centrally through it for the plastic tube. On the underside of the cross frame, the holes at the beam ends are linked to the centre with a ¹⁄₁₆in (1·5mm) groove.

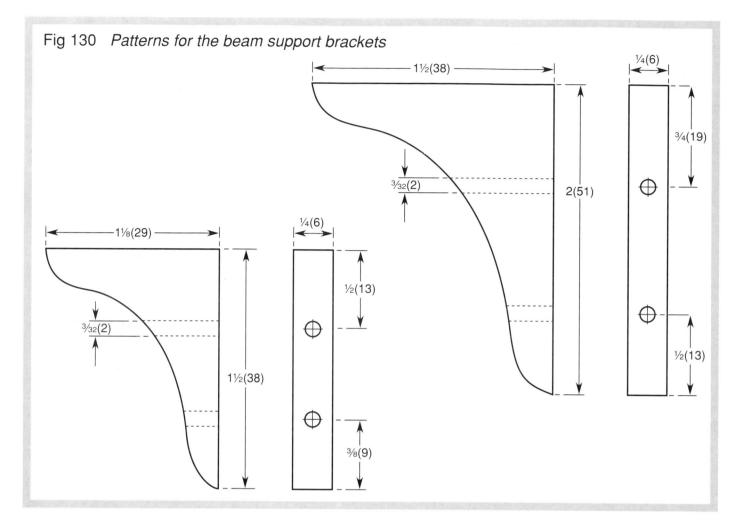

Fig 130 *Patterns for the beam support brackets*

Drill a ⅛in (3mm) diameter hole up through the tie beam. The wire tails from the light are threaded through this, followed by the spigot of tube at the top of the post, which should be a tight push fit.

Twist the wire tails together in a parallel connection and add a plug to suit the socket on the tie beam.

FLOORBOARDS

These are cut from Microwood self-adhesive veneer, available from Hobby's (see List of Stockists). The variety used is Anga. This is cut into strips with random widths between ½in (13mm) and ¾in (19mm), laid lengthways across the floors, and sealed with two coats of matt varnish.

HANDRAIL

The handrail round the stairwell in section C is made from elm, and fitted in the same way as that in the Thatched Cottage (page 100). Two posts of elm ⁵⁄₁₆in (8mm) square and 2½in (64mm) long are pegged to the floor 1⅞in (48mm) apart at the open corner and side of the stairwell. A further post ⁵⁄₁₆in (8mm) wide and ⅛in (3mm) thick, is glued to the left-hand wall of the carcase with its length shortened to fit above the sole plate. A rail of ³⁄₁₆ × ¼in

(5 × 6mm) elm is pegged between the posts (see colour plate on p163).

OPENING SIDE WALLS

The space between the beams and their outer stubs on the underside of sections B and C must now have a strip of ⅜in (9mm) plywood ½in (13mm) deep, glued and screwed into them to form the upper part of the side walls.

The side wall for the upper section C should be planed at the top edge to fit under the eaves beam.

SIDE WALL FASTENINGS

The portable side panels are held in place with brass pins and ball catches. The panels for sections A and B each have one ball catch sunk centrally into the back edge, and two ³⁄₃₂in (2mm) diameter brass pins each ⅝in (16mm) long set into the front edge and projecting ³⁄₁₆in (5mm). These pins are positioned 1in (25mm) from the top and bottom edges of the panels and engage in holes drilled into the lip of the rebate. The striking plates for the ball catches should be discarded, and a ⅛in (3mm) length of ⅛in (3mm) diameter brass tube used instead. This tube is let into the rebate lip at the back, and is lightly countersunk internally to

Fig 131 *To show the pegged joints on the external timber frame*

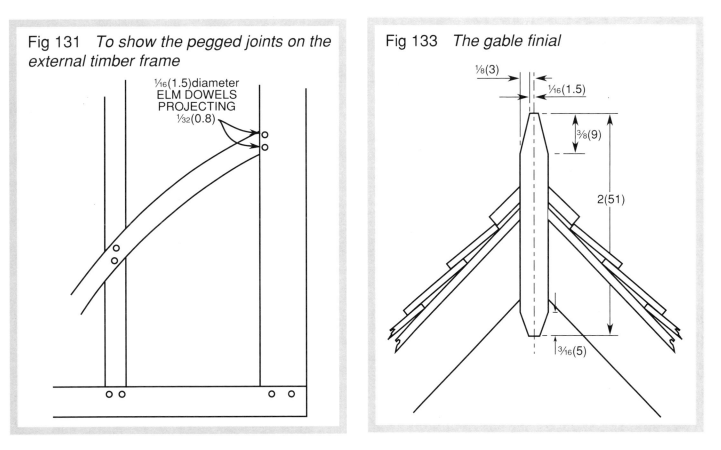

¹⁄₁₆(1.5)diameter
ELM DOWELS
PROJECTING
¹⁄₃₂(0.8)

Fig 133 *The gable finial*

¹⁄₈(3)
¹⁄₁₆(1.5)
³⁄₈(9)
2(51)
³⁄₁₆(5)

Fig 132 *Construction of the base and paving*

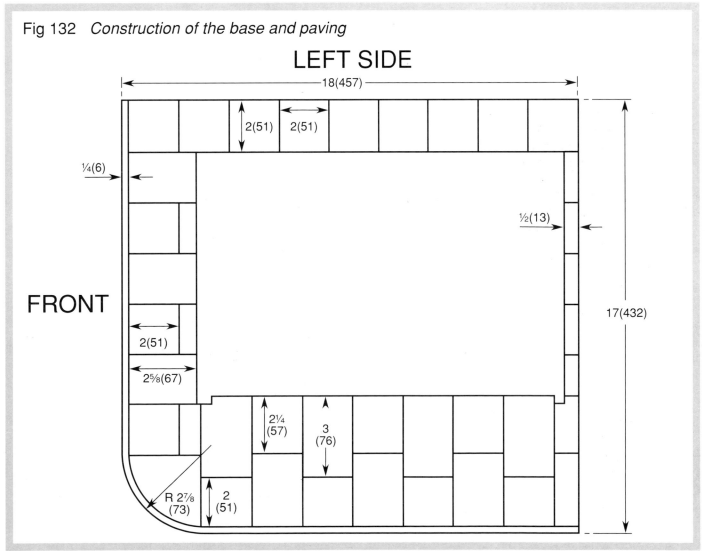

LEFT SIDE

18(457)

2(51) 2(51)

¹⁄₄(6)

½(13)

FRONT

2(51)

2⁵⁄₈(67)

17(432)

2¹⁄₄
(57)

3
(76)

R 2⁷⁄₈
(73)

2
(51)

provide a seat for the ball. It is preferable to use ³⁄₁₆in (5mm) diameter catches, but ¼in (6mm) diameter are acceptable if the flange is skimmed off on a lathe. Care must be taken that the hole bored for the catch is truly central in the plywood edge to avoid splitting. Epoxy resin should be used to secure the barrel of the catch in the hole.

Section C has a ball catch at both the front and back edges, 1in (25mm) above the bottom, and two brass pins in the top edge 1in (25mm) from either end. These engage in holes drilled upwards into the eaves beam.

SUPPORT BRACKETS

Referring to Fig 130, ten small and two large brackets should be cut from elm ¼in (6mm) thick, with the grain running diagonally across them for strength. The large brackets are fitted under the dragon beam projections on sections A and B. The front right-hand corners of these sections should be chamfered for the depth of the brackets to provide a seating. Each bracket is fastened to the wall with glue and two ³⁄₃₂in (2mm) diameter elm pegs. They should *not* be glued to the dragon beams. Referring to Figs 111 and 113, for the beam positions and numbers, the smaller brackets are similarly fastened as follows:

Section A On the front wall under beams 1 and 7. On the right-hand wall under beams 1, 6 and 11.
Section B On the front wall under beams 1 and 9. On the right-hand wall under beams 1, 5 and 12.

The inside front edges of the side panels A and B must be chamfered at the top to fit against the dragon brackets. Following Fig 131, drill two ¹⁄₁₆in (1·5mm) diameter holes ⅛in (3mm) deep at each joint of the external timber frame, and insert ¹⁄₁₆in (1·5mm) diameter elm dowels, leaving a projection of ¹⁄₃₂in (0·8mm).

BASE AND PAVING

Cut the baseboard from ⅜in (9mm) plywood to the dimensions given in Fig 132, and veneer the edges with ⅜ × ¹⁄₃₂in (10 × 0.8mm) lime. Place the lower carcase section A, without its right-hand panel, on top of the base, inset 2in (51mm) at the left-hand side, and ½in (13mm) at the back, and mark round it with a pencil. Paving slabs cut from ¹⁄₁₆in (1·5mm) plywood are glued outside this area, with a kerb ¼in (6mm) wide along the front and right-hand side (Fig 132). The paving should be painted matt grey. The portable side panel will need to have ¹⁄₁₆in (1·5mm) planed off its lower edge to fit over the paving.

COMPLETION

The fireplace openings should each have an internal backing and hearth of Houseworks bricks mounted on card or thin plywood. They are grouted and then given a wash of poster paint to simulate soot blackening. If a glowing fire effect is required, leave space for a small socket at the back of the hearth, and connect this to the wiring system in section B.

The screw holes from the temporary fixing of the right-hand roof panel should now be filled and painted over. Any other areas not yet covered should also now be painted; then re-fit the oriel windows with their transoms added, and glaze the remainder. For this, use 2mm glass or Glodex acrylic sheet, held in place with a mitred border of self-adhesive microwood ⅜in (10mm) wide applied on the inside of the wall.

A finial cut from elm ¼ × ⅛ × 2in (6 × 3 × 51mm) is fitted to the front end of the roof; it is recessed into the projecting ridge tiles and glued and pinned to the ridge and left-hand bargeboard only (Fig 133).

Hang the door, using quick-setting epoxy resin to secure the hinges.

THE TUDOR HOUSE – LIST OF SUPPLIERS

The accessories used in the Tudor House are from the following suppliers; see Acknowledgements for addresses.

Blackwells: Houseworks clay bricks.
Cir-Kit Concepts (Dijon): Lighting.
Dolphin Miniatures: Step-ladder, tool chest and tools, trestles, paint pots and brushes, beer crates, cement bags and extending ladder.
Dorking Dollshouse Gallery: Tea chest.

Hobby's: Apprentice painter.
Isobel Hockey: Sweater kit for painter.
Mainly Men Minis: Builders' foreman and the 'Guv'nor'.
Miniature Model Imports: Radio, Pepsi bottle.
Quality Dollshouse Miniatures: Spade, sign bracket.
Thames Valley Crafts: Beer bottle.

The handcart is from the author's own collection.

Acknowledgements

Firstly my thanks must go to Barbara Davies for her help and encouragement when I first started making dolls' houses and miniatures.

Thanks are also due to the late Fred Eaton for his assistance with the drawings, and to June Stowe of International Dolls' House News. Finally, may I thank Jonathon Bosley for the superb photography.

FEATURED MAKERS AND RETAILERS

The furniture and accessories featured in this book are from a selection of craftspeople with widely differing marketing policies. Some have small showrooms and can be visited by prior appointment, some sell only at fairs or by mail order, and others are wholesale suppliers whose products are only available from miniatures shops. Most have a catalogue for which a charge is made, but *please remember,* when writing for details, to enclose a stamped, addressed envelope or international reply coupons, otherwise you are unlikely to receive a reply.

Acorn Crafts: Vectis Cottage, 250 Botley Road, Burridge, Southampton, Hants S03 7BL. Tel: 0489 575797.

Lucy Askew: 5 Sibella Road, London SW4 6JA. Tel: 071 720 5812.

Avon Miniatures: 20 Brandize Park, Okehampton, Devon EX20 1EQ. Tel: 0837 53237.

Peggy Birrell: 5 Norwich Road, Exwick, Exeter, Devon EX4 2DN. Tel: 0392 438511.

Gordon Blacklock: 18 Countisbury Road, Norton, Stockton-on-Tees, Cleveland TS20 1PZ. Tel: 0642 554851.

Blockhouse Models: 16 Quantock Road, Worthing, Sussex BN13 2HG. Tel: 0903 64549.

Patricia Borwick: Lihou Island, Guernsey, Channel Islands. Tel: 0481 65656.

Rohanna Bryan: 1 Alexandra Street, Blandford Forum, Dorset DT11 7EY. Tel: 0258 52578.

Bryntor Miniatures: 60 Shirburn Road, Torquay, Devon TQ1 4HR. Tel: 0803 323393.

Irene Campbell: Littlefields Studio, Bishopswood, Chard, Somerset. Tel: 0460 34236.

C and D Crafts: 133 Lower Hillmorton Road, Rugby, Warwickshire CV21 3TN. Tel: 0788 74540.

Malcolm Chandler: 47 Station Road, Thurnby, Leicester LE7 9PW. Tel. 0533 417927.

Véronique Cornish: Rose Cottage, The Street, Dilham, North Walsham, Norfolk NR28 9PX. Tel: 069260 6164.

Country Treasures: Rose Cottage, Dapple Heath, Admaston, Rugeley, Staffs WS15 3PG. Tel: 0889 500652.

Terry Curran: 27 Chapel Street, Mosborough, Sheffield, Yorks S19 5BT. Tel: 0742 484369.

Dolphin Miniatures: Myrtle Cottage, Greendown, Membury, Axminster, Devon EX13 7TB. Tel: 040488 459.

Marie Theresa Endean: Station House, Station Road, Elburton, Plymouth, Devon. Tel: 0752 401784.

Escutcheon: 28 Queslett Road East, Streetly, Sutton Coldfield, W Midlands B74 2EX. Tel: 021 353 5596.

Isobel Hockey: 34 Cranmere Road, Higher Compton, Plymouth, Devon PL3 5JY. Tel: 0752 708546.

Tony Hooper: 3 Bunting Close, Ogwell, Newton Abbot, Devon TQ12 6BU. Tel: 0626 60628.

Peter Kennedy: 50 Crownhill Park, Torquay, Devon TQ2 5LP. Tel: 0803 295503.

Lesley Anne Dolls: 22 The Birchwoods, Tilehurst, Reading, Berks RG3 5UH. Tel: 0734 429137.

Carol Lodder: Brooks Cottage, Belchalwell, Blandford Forum, Dorset DT11 0EG. Tel: 0258 860222.

Stuart McCabe: 119 Springfield Road, Elburton, Plymouth, Devon. Tel: 0752 406289.

Mainly Men Minis: # 1602, 180 Bold Street, Hamilton, Ontario, Canada L8P 453.

Marions Miniature Millinery: Salmaur, Gipsy Lane, Weymouth, Dorset DT4 0BZ. Tel: 0305 786141.

John and Pauline Meredith: Badgers' Mead, Hawthorn Hill, Bracknell, Berks RG12 6HG.

Anita Oliver: 24 Nelson Road, Harrow-on-the-Hill, Middx HA1 3ET. Tel: 081 864 2868.

Petite Porcelain Miniatures: 9 Kingswood, Marchwood, Southampton, Hants SO4 4YQ. Tel: 0703 871365.

Leo Pilley: Chy An Chy Glass Studio, St Ives, Cornwall. Tel: 0736 797659.

Smallholdings: 55 De Montfort Road, Lewes, E Sussex BN17 1SS. Tel: 0273 479080.

June and Roy Stowe: 147 Wilton Road, Shirley, Southampton, Hants SO1 5JU. Tel: 0703 771995.

Bernardo Traettino: 33 Hertford Avenue, London SW14 8EF. Tel: 081 878 9055.

Featured Mail Order Suppliers
Blackwells of Hawkwell (UK distributors for Houseworks): 733/5 London Road, Westcliff-on-Sea, Essex SS0 9ST. Tel: 0702 72248.
Borcraft Miniatures: Fairfax View, Scotland Lane, Horsforth, Leeds, Yorks LS18 5SZ. Tel: 0532 585739.
W. Hobby Ltd: Knights Hill Square, London SE27 0HH. Tel: 081 761 4244.
Phoenix Model Developments Ltd: The Square, Earls Barton, Northampton NN6 0NA. Tel: 0604 810612.
Sunday Dolls: 7 Park Drive, East Sheen, London SW14 8RB. Tel: 081 876 5634.
Sussex Crafts: Hassocks House, Comptons Brow Lane, Horsham, W Sussex RH13 6BX. Tel: 0403 54355.
Thames Valley Crafts: Mere House, Dedmere Road, Marlow, Bucks SL7 1PD. Tel: 0628 890988.
Wood 'n' Wool Miniatures: Yew Tree House, 3 Stankelt Road, Silverdale, Carnforth, Lancs LA5 0RB. Tel: 0524 701532.

Featured Wholesale Suppliers
Dijon Ltd (UK distributors for Cir-Kit): Ash Grove, Cross in Hand, Heathfield, Sussex TN21 0QG. Tel: 04352 4155.
Miniature Model Imports: 11 Mizen Way, Cobham, Surrey KT11 2RG. Tel: 0932 67938.
Quality Dolls' House Miniatures: 55 Celandine Avenue, Priory Park, Locksheath, Southampton, Hants SO3 6WZ. Tel: 04895 78420.

Warwick Miniatures: Bramley Cottage, Weston-under-Wetherley, Leamington Spa, Warks CV33 9BW. Tel: 0926 632330.
Wentways Miniatures: Wentways, West End, Marden, Kent TN12 9JA. Tel: 0622 831765.

GLASS
T. & W. Ide and Sons: Glasshouse Fields, Stepney, London E1. Tel: 071 790 2333.

Featured Shops
Blackwells': 733 London Road, Westcliff-on-Sea, Essex SS0 9ST. Tel: 0702 72248.
Dolls and Miniatures: 54 Southside Street, Barbican, Plymouth, Devon. Tel: 0752 663676.
The Dolls' House Toys: 29 The Market, Covent Garden, London WC2E 8RE. Tel: 071 379 7243.
Dorking Dolls' House Gallery: 23 West Street, Dorking, Surrey RH14 1BY. Tel: 0306 885785.
From Kitchen to Garret: Fishers' Bridge Mill, Topsham, Exeter, Devon EX3 0QQ. Tel: 0392 877600.
Miniature Curios: 59 High Street, Honiton, Devon EX14 8PW. Tel: 0404 46499.
The Mulberry Bush: 9 George Street, Brighton, Sussex BN2 1RH. Tel: 0273 493781.
Royal Mile Miniatures (Stockists for David Edwards): 154 Canongate, Royal Mile, Edinburgh EH8 8DD. Tel: 031 557 2293.
The Secret Garden: 109 Camden Road, Tunbridge Wells, Kent TN1 2QY. Tel: 0892 541332.
The Singing Tree: 69 New Kings Road, London SW6. Tel: 071 736 4527.

Magazines & Further Information

There are currently three specialist dolls' house and miniatures magazines in the UK. Each magazine has a diary section giving dates of fairs and exhibitions.

International Dolls' House News: PO Box 79, Southhampton, Hants SO9 7EZ; tel: 0703 771995; published quarterly, annual subscription £12, sample copy £3.

The Home Miniaturist: 2 Croft Courtyard, The Croft, Haddenham, Bucks HP17 8AS; tel: 0844 291419; published bi-monthly, annual subscription £11·50, sample copy £2.

Dolls' House World: Ashdown Publishing Limited, Shelley House, 104 High Street, Steyning, W Sussex; tel: 0903 815622; published bi-monthly, annual subscription £18.

The British Dollshouse Hobby Directory: Published by LDF Publications, 25 Priory Road, Kew, Richmond, Surrey TW9 3DQ; cost £2·50 including postage (1990). This has a listing of makers and retailers both alphabetically and geographically, and a product index.

Dollshouse Information Service: offered by Dijon Ltd, Cross in Hand, Heathfield, Sussex TN21 0QG. Enquiries should be accompanied by a stamped, addressed envelope.

US SUPPLIERS AND MAGAZINES

Due to the enormous following for the hobby in the US, it is impractical to give a full listing. Reference should be made to one or other of the specialist publications. Two suppliers have been listed because their products have been used extensively in this book:

Cir-Kit Concepts Inc: 407, 14th St NW, Rochester MN 55901; suppliers of dolls' house lighting.
Houseworks Ltd: 2388 Pleasantdale Road, Atlanta, GA 30340; suppliers of hardware and building components.

The main publications in the US are the *Nutshell News, Miniatures Showcase* and *The Miniatures Catalog*: these are published by Kalmbach Miniatures Inc., 21027 Crossroads Circle, PO Box 1612, Waukesha, Wisconsin 53187.

Also *The Miniature Collector*, PO Box 631, Boiling Springs, PA 17007.

AUSTRALIA

The Australian Miniaturist magazine, 40 Cusack St, Wangaratta, Vic 3677, is also an excellent source of suppliers.

INDEX